Understanding Chi
Adolescent Grief

Understanding Child and Adolescent Grief incorporates theory, clinical applications, case studies, and current research on contemporary models of grief pertaining to children and adolescents. The integration of developmental perspectives, attachment theory, and neurobiological implications provides a thorough summary of the many factors that can affect a child's growth and development and the subsequent influence on grief expression. Chapters explore relevant social topics rarely addressed in other texts, such as the death of African American men, suicide among Aboriginal youth in Canada, death/suicide among LGBTQ youth, and social media's influence. Also included are practical tips for helping professionals who want to better understand how grief and loss affect children and teens, as well as a meditation guide that provides concrete opportunities for growth and healing.

Carrie Arnold, MEd, has been an adjunct faculty in thanatology and psychology at King's University College, Western University since 2005. She is a Canadian Certified Counsellor with the Canadian Counselling and Psychotherapy Association and is registered with the Ontario College of Social Workers and Social Service Workers. She has provided psychotherapy and counseling to children, adolescents, and adults since 1999.

The Series in Death, Dying, and Bereavement
Robert A. Neimeyer and Darcy L. Harris, Series Editors

For a complete list of all books in this series, please visit the series page at:
https://www.routledge.com/series/SE0620

Understanding Child and Adolescent Grief

Supporting Loss and
Facilitating Growth

Edited by Carrie Arnold

NEW YORK AND LONDON

First edition published 2018
by Routledge
711 Third Avenue, New York, NY 10017

and by Routledge
2 Park Square, Milton Park, Abingdon, Oxon, OX14 4RN

Routledge is an imprint of the Taylor & Francis Group, an informa business

Library of Congress Cataloging-in-Publication Data
Names: Arnold, Carrie, 1980- editor.
Title: Understanding child and adolescent grief : supporting loss and
facilitating growth / edited by Carrie Arnold.
Description: New York, NY : Routledge, 2017. | Series: Death, dying,
and bereavement | Includes bibliographical references and index.
Identifiers: LCCN 2017023704 | ISBN 9781138740877
(hardcover : alk. paper) | ISBN 9781138740884 (pbk. : alk. paper) |
ISBN 9781315164250 (e-book : alk. paper)
Subjects: LCSH: Grief in children. | Grief in adolescence.
Classification: LCC BF723.G75 U53 2017 | DDC 155.9/
37083—dc23
LC record available at https://lccn.loc.gov/2017023704

ISBN: 978-1-138-74087-7 (hbk)
ISBN: 978-1-138-74088-4 (pbk)
ISBN: 978-1-315-16425-0 (ebk)

Typeset in Bembo
by Keystroke, Neville Lodge, Tettenhall, Wolverhampton

This book is dedicated to Dr. Darcy Harris for her unconditional support, boundless generosity, and unwavering belief in my abilities.

Also, to the students and clients who have provided such inspiration over many years, thank you for all the ways in which you have openly and willingly shared your losses, and your selves.

And lastly, to my children, Olivia and Ethan, for being incredibly gifted teachers. I offer you deep gratitude and much love.

Table of Contents

List of Illustrations

Figures

Tables

Boxes

Series Editor's Foreword

Not long ago, children were treated as "little adults," and their unique ways of seeing and being in the world were viewed through the lens of adult perspectives and experiences. Obviously, much has changed, both in the understanding of loss and bereavement in general, and of children's navigation through events involving loss and grief specifically.

Understanding Child and Adolescent Grief provides us with a multifaceted view of some of the losses that young people may encounter, exploring these experiences from various developmental, neurobiological, psychological, and sociological perspectives. Common childhood losses, such as the loss of a parent, a sibling, a friend, and the loss of self through a life-threatening health condition, are discussed from the perspective of the child/youth, with an emphasis on specific approaches that provide the supportive care and assistance that may be the most helpful and effective for young people. Case studies are woven throughout the chapters and keep us focused, always, on the voices and unique needs of the children who experience various types of life-changing loss events.

Unique to this particular book is the undercurrent of compassion, both for children and those who care for them in their personal lives and in the professional spheres in which they present. Carrie Arnold and her contributors invite us to enter the world of grieving children, not to have pity or to be overwhelmed by the trauma, loss, and pain that these children endure; rather, we see the reframing of such events in ways that highlight children's resiliency, caregivers' creativity, and the formative (and normative) role of loss and grief in everyday life.

When given appropriate care and support, we are reminded that children can rise from the pain and suffering that they have endured, perhaps even becoming wounded healers themselves as they mature, moving forward in the world with a desire to relieve the suffering of others who have had similar experiences. The approach of the book is one that carefully avoids pathologizing language and negative assumptions about the outcomes for children who experience losses—even those that are traumatic in nature. Instead, we are made aware of children's potential for growth and understanding about the world when there are adults who walk alongside and support them sensitively when they are hurting.

The inclusion of a chapter on the topic of ethically competent caregiving and a meditation guide that is designed specifically for use with youth underscore the holistic perspective of the editor and contributors from the field. We care for children and we care for ourselves. We respect the children in our care, even as we respect the professional values and ethics of our practice. And finally, the inclusion of meditation practices reminds us that something as simple as our breath and focused attention can provide us with the ability to fully engage with ourselves and those children among us who face losses of many different types. The overarching theme hints at the interconnectedness of us all—younger, older, family members, friends, and professionals—enabling us to open to an expansive perspective that embraces human experiences across all developmental stages in life.

Darcy Harris, PhD, FT
Thanatology Coordinator,
King's University College
Series Co-Editor,
Routledge Series in Death, Dying, & Bereavement

Acknowledgments

This project arose out of many conversations with students and colleagues regarding the diverse and nuanced experiences that children and adolescents encounter in a complex and multidimensional world. The desire to have a book that captured the theoretical foundations of loss and transformation, and the lived realities of bereaved children and adolescents was a shared vision. I am profoundly grateful to my many collaborators for our collective effort in compiling this volume.

I am so very thankful to Dr. Darcy Harris for her mentorship, support, encouragement, and guidance throughout this process, and within my life. I would also like to thank Dr. Robert Neimeyer for his insightful comments and assistance at a transitional time in this project. This book underwent various transformations and their expert guidance carried this book to its completion. A special thank you to Jenifer Freedy and Adam Koenig, not only for their contributions, but for being good sounding boards, providing assistance with research, and for their editorial feedback.

Within my roles as a therapist, educator, and student, I am fortunate to have incredible mentors who embody skill, intelligence, and compassion. I wish to offer my gratitude to Doris Heinrichs, Dr. Alan Leschied, Dr. Abbe Blum, Dr. Robert Flax, and Dr. Terri Goslin-Jones for their instruction, patience, guidance, and ongoing invitation to live fully.

Lastly, I wish to offer love and gratitude to my incredible circle of family and friends, who have been extraordinarily gracious with their love, time, and encouragement. This book project has journeyed alongside my doctoral studies, and the steadfast support of this amazing group of people has made it possible to embrace the lessons that have unfolded amidst these life-changing opportunities.

About the Editor

Carrie Arnold obtained a Bachelor of Arts (Honors) in psychology and a Master of Education (Counseling), both from the University of Western Ontario. She is currently a doctoral student at Saybrook University in California, in the Psychology of Interdisciplinary Inquiry program, in the Consciousness, Spirituality and Integrative Health specialization. Carrie has been offering psychotherapy and counseling since 1999 and areas of clinical interest include trauma, attachment, grief, loss, anxiety, and parenting. She is a Canadian Certified Counsellor with the Canadian Counselling and Psychotherapy Association, is registered with the Ontario College of Social Workers and Social Service Workers, and is an approved service provider with the First Nations and Inuit Health Branch of Health Canada. She has coauthored articles on issues related to the experiences of adolescent girls and on attachment and loss. Carrie first began teaching at King's University College, Western University in 2005 and is currently adjunct faculty in the thanatology and psychology programs.

About the Contributors

Carrie Arnold, MEd, CCC, RSW, is adjunct faculty in the thanatology and psychology programs at King's University College, Western University. She has provided psychotherapy and counseling to children, adolescents, and adults since 1999. She is currently pursuing a PhD in psychology at Saybrook University.

Carine Blin, BA, MBA, has worked as a grief support volunteer and group facilitator with Bereaved Families of Ontario and the Scarborough Centre for Healthy Communities since 2001. She is a freelance writer and bereaved mother enrolled in the loss, grief, and bereavement studies program at King's University College, Western University.

Tashel C. Bordere, PhD, FT, is an assistant professor of human development and family science and state extension specialist in youth development at the University of Missouri-Columbia. Her research focuses on African American youth grief, homicide loss, coping, and socially just practice. Dr. Bordere also developed S.H.E.D. Grief Tools for schools and organizations.

Jenifer Freedy, MEd, RSW, has provided psychotherapy to children, adolescents, and adults since 1998, and has been adjunct faculty in thanatology at King's University College, Western University since 2014. Jenifer has special interest and extensive training in the area of trauma treatment.

Linda Goldman, MS, FT, LCPC, NBCC, has been adjunct faculty at John's Hopkins Graduate School of Education and King's University College at Western University, teaching classes on children's grief and trauma. She works as a grief therapist with children and adults. Her books include *Life and Loss: A Guide to Help Grieving Children, 3rd Edition* and *Raising Our Children to Be Resilient.*

Eunice Gorman, RN, PhD, RSW, is a registered nurse and social worker with a long history of working in oncology, palliative care, and bereavement. Eunice is currently an associate professor at King's University College, Western University where she has been employed since 2004.

Brad Hunter, BA, has practiced meditation for over 40 years and now teaches mindfulness and courses in grief and trauma, as well as facilitates conscious living/conscious dying retreats and several grief support groups. He also works in end-of-life chaplaincy in a variety of roles.

Christine Jonas-Simpson, PhD, is an associate professor of nursing at York University. She is an arts-based researcher and teacher who has produced and directed several research-based short films on living and transforming with loss.

Adam Koenig, MA, RP, has been providing psychotherapy within the Ontario College and University systems since 2013 and is adjunct faculty in thanatology at King's University College, Western University.

James A. Larsen is currently a doctoral student at The University of Missouri in the department of human development and family science. He is particularly interested in issues of social justice, equality, and inclusivity, especially as they relate to child development and education.

Rebecca T. Machado, MEd, RP, is a psychotherapist with a clinical focus on trauma and traumatic bereavement. She has been adjunct faculty at King's University College, Western University since 2012 where she teaches in the thanatology program. At present, she serves as executive director of Daya Counselling Centre in London, Ontario.

Sheila O'Donovan, BA Psych, Dip AT, OATR, CTS, RP, is a registered art therapist and clinical trauma specialist. She has been in private practice for over 20 years working with children, adolescents, and their families. She is passionate about her work and believes that positive relationships are the foundation for healing.

Lisa Pearlman, RN(EC), BA MN NP-Paediatrics, is a nurse practitioner and clinical lead of Paediatric Symptom Management & Supportive Care (PSMSC) at the Children's Hospital London Health Sciences Centre. PSMSC specializes in caring and advocating for the best quality of life possible for children with serious life-limiting illnesses.

Stephanie Rabenstein, MFT, is a child and family therapist at the Children's Hospital, London Health Sciences Centre. She is also an assistant professor at the Schulich School of Medicine and Dentistry at Western University and has been a lecturer in the thanatology program at King's University College, Western University.

Carla Sofka, PhD, is a professor of social work at Siena College in Loudonville, New York, and teaches a range of courses in the BSW program, including an elective course on death and grief in the digital age. She is a past president of the Association for Death Education and Counseling.

Kip G. Williams, MFT, is a community activist and psychotherapist in the San Francisco Bay Area, where he works with sexual minority men in private practice. He codirected the 2009 National Equality March on Washington and is currently pursuing his PhD at Saybrook University.

1   Introduction

Carrie Arnold

Several years ago, a colleague told me a story about a 10-year-old boy, named Sam[1], who had experienced the death of his best friend. At this young boy's wintry funeral, Sam was making a snowman. This activity was deemed "inappropriate" and "disrespectful" by many at the funeral and Sam was admonished for "playing" at such a sombre time. Some time later, within the context of grief counseling, the therapist asked him why he was making a snowman at his best friend's funeral. Sam replied that one of the favorite activities for him and his friend was to make snowmen, and he wanted to leave a really good one at his friend's grave.

This story highlights several key aspects of how children make sense of death, process their grief, and the importance of adults understanding and appreciating the different ways that children make meaning of such events. While it is understandable that the adults in Sam's life were overcome with their own anguish at the death of a child, their inability to understand Sam's actions likely turned what could have been a beautiful tribute to his best friend into something where Sam was made to feel ashamed. Had the adults in Sam's life been curious enough to ask, or to recognize that 10-year-olds tend to be quite concrete in their thoughts and actions, there may have been the opportunity for others to join with Sam and support him in his tribute to his best friend.

The goal of this volume is to highlight the fundamental need for adults to understand and support bereaved children and adolescents in their unique ways of grieving. There are many insightful and accomplished books written from various perspectives on the topic of children's experiences with death, grief, and loss. This particular book has arisen from the contributors' collective work as clinicians, educators, researchers, and consultants in the field. Our hope is to contribute to the ongoing conversation about bereaved children and youth and offer suggestions for facilitating growth and transformation amidst the pain of loss. We emphasize that the way children grieve is naturally embedded in the ways that they live. While various theoretical perspectives and clinical applications advance our capacity to offer support and assistance, the writings in this book add to these perspectives a holistic and multidimensional framework, exploring contemporary perspectives on grief and loss in addition to developmental considerations; interpersonal neurobiology; the political, social, and cultural realities in Canada and the United States; the influence of social media; and the potential benefits of attending to the mind–body connection for children who are bereaved, as well as for those who care for these children. Our collective effort is one that we hope contributes a unique and meaningful dialogue within the field.

Overview of Chapters

Beginning with an overview of developmental considerations, Chapter 2 provides the foundation for central concepts that will be noted throughout the book. The significance of attachment, its influence in the expression of loss, current perspectives on development stages, and the role of caregivers are presented. A potentially unique feature of this chapter is the integration of contemporary thinking from the field of interpersonal neurobiology, where the significance of somatic regulation and the implications for bereaved youth are discussed. The importance and applicability of developmental information is then explored further in Chapter 3, which includes an overview of typical grief responses for each age group based on developmental stages. There is an emphasis on holistic assessment processes including medical, physical, and spiritual dimensions, as well as family and social support, within the context of the child's relationship with the deceased.

One of the more influential perspectives within thanatology is Doka's (1989, 2002) conceptualization of disenfranchised grief. Chapter 4 begins with an explanation of this framework and its implications for young grievers. The chapter includes ways that children's grief can be acknowledged and supported through open communication, modeling, and engagement in ritual. The significance of acknowledging children's grief is central in Chapter 5, as it provides an overview of the relational bonds that exist between children and parents, along with typical responses of children and adolescents to the death of a parent. Additionally, there is an insightful commentary on the losses that can occur within the context of divorce, adoption, or placement in foster care.

Chapter 6 reviews the characteristics of sibling bonds and current research regarding the prevalence of childhood deaths and the subsequent responses of bereaved siblings. Typical reactions, types of support, and developmental considerations are included, as well as possible negative outcomes and the potential for growth. The benefits of therapeutic support are presented in Chapter 7, which focuses on the use of art and play therapy with bereaved children and adolescents. By highlighting grief that occurs after the death of a friend, this chapter describes the use of various creative modalities to facilitate the grief process due to their intrinsic alignment with development stages of children. This chapter provides information about the research behind, and the use of, expressive arts therapies for bereaved youth in clinical practice.

While the majority of this book explicates research and praxis related to bereaved youth, Chapter 8 offers an overview of palliative care and the children who benefit from this type of support. Related factors, such as symptom burden, maintaining quality of life, open communication, and decision making, are also featured. A poignant case study in this chapter highlights the central role of a palliative care team in providing compassionate care and support to an ill child and his or her family.

One emerging area of thanatology is the intersection between trauma and grief. Schuurman (2017) explained that the use of appropriate language is imperative when discussing these overlapping phenomena. Stating that "Death is a life-altering event but grief is not a pathological condition," (personal communication, April 6, 2017), Schuurman cautioned against being overly diagnostic with respect to the natural distress that accompanies loss. Within this context, Chapter 9 presents contemporary conceptualizations and clinical implications for grief and trauma. This chapter also integrates Porges' (2011) polyvagal theory of trauma within the framework of bereavement. This interdisciplinary approach helps to address these overlapping phenomena while transcending the various conceptualizations and terminologies that may not be helpful within a clinical setting.

Understanding the significance of both trauma and grief is essential within the context of suicide. Whether bereaved by suicide, or experiencing suicidal ideation, it is necessary for those working in the field to be adept at recognizing a young person's distress and to provide effective interventions. An overview of the prevalence of suicide amongst youth in Canada and the United States is the focus of Chapter 10, along with research findings and clinical implications when working with children and adolescents.

The realities of suicide or homicide cannot be divorced from the sociopolitical realities of contemporary culture. In an effort to address issues of social justice and to highlight the political and societal realities that affect bereaved youth, Chapter 11 skillfully draws parallels between the types of traumatic and disenfranchised losses that are experienced by First Nations youth (Canada) and African American youth (United States). By including information about the current suicide crisis in Attawapiskat in Northern Ontario and the high-profile deaths of Trayvon Martin, Tamir Rice, and Michael Brown in the United States, the authors depict the emotional, social, and cultural losses that are embedded within the historical oppression and dehumanization of First Nations and African American communities. The chapter includes implications for future research and an outline of how to engage youth in culturally conscientious practice.

Continuing with the theme of social and political change, Chapter 12 presents information regarding the ways in which gender and sexual minority (GSM) youth are at increased risk for mental-health issues and suicide, and how they often experience numerous losses that are nonfinite and often disenfranchised. Typically referred to as LGBTQ, the term *gender and sexual minority* (GSM) helps to convey a more inclusive way of acknowledging how both gender and sexual orientation exist along continuums. This topic has received greater attention in both Canada and the United States due to the increased visibility of transgender youth, public advocacy for political and legal changes for those in the GSM community, and the need to have greater inclusivity and representation in grief-and-loss literature.

An additional contemporary societal phenomena related to grief and loss is the ubiquitous use of social media, particularly among youth. Chapter 13 contains current findings with respect to social media usage and the ways it may influence grieving teens. The chapter offers current statistics and skillfully illustrates the ways in which social media use can have profound effects on the transmission of emotional support and information among teens when someone dies. With examples of public tragedies and their representation on Facebook, Twitter, and text communication, the chapter explores the ways that social media can assist with the formation of continuing bonds, helpful memorialization, and survivor advocacy.

Chapter 14 includes current conceptualizations, research, and practice regarding resilience and the potential that exists for growth and transformation within the context of grief. Citing poignant examples from children's art work, this chapter outlines the characteristics of resilient children, as well as ways that caring adults can promote this aspect of development within an increasingly complex and global society.

Being immersed as helping professionals in the complex and multifaceted communities in which bereaved children reside requires solid theoretical knowledge, strong clinical skills, self-awareness, and the responsible and ethical use of self. Chapter 15 contains an overview of key ethical principles and decision-making models that guide service sector care in Canada and the United States. Research and practical applications will be featured in this chapter, along with an exploration of the ethical practice implications that accompany self-care and attention to one's well-being in this area of practice.

Lastly, this volume includes a brief meditation guide for children. There are several breathing exercises designed for youth to assist them in recognizing how the mind–body connection can help in times of sadness, fear, or worry. The inclusion of a meditation guide for children was done thoughtfully. While perhaps not the norm in many texts, there is a growing awareness of the benefits of acknowledging the mind–body connection and its relationship to overall health and well-being. While this book does not advocate that one *ought* to actively engage in this type of practice, it does offer an invitation for children and families who may wish to embrace the benefits of some form of contemplative practice, particularly when living in the midst of loss.

Intended Audience and Purpose

This book is intended for educators, clinicians, and students, as well as for caregivers of bereaved children. One goal of this volume is to offer an integrated conceptualization of childhood grief and bereavement, as well as ways of facilitating growth and transformation. For many adults, it can be unbearably painful to accept the reality that it is not possible to shield children from pain, and, as such, witnessing this anguish can be utterly devastating. That said, the grief process can also be an opportunity for growth, connection, and resilience if there is a willingness to *lean into it*, despite the natural inclination to avoid grief's accompanying thoughts and feelings. Healing can unfold within a context that is guided by developmental awareness, understanding the unique needs of each child, the willingness of adults to be sensitively attuned, and the ability to be compassionately present towards oneself and others.

It may also be useful to remember that interactions with children and adolescents can involve elements of play, lightheartedness, and fun. Many years ago, in a conversation with a mentor, I was expressing concern about the devastating realities that some children experience and was looking for guidance. This mentor replied, "Remember that they are children *first*." This simple message has remained with me and beautifully highlights that our focus on *who this child is* remains the priority, alongside his or her story of loss. While the pain and sadness that accompanies grief is reflected in these chapters, we also provide guidance regarding potential ways to foster growth and transformation. Each one of us could share stories of anguish that we have witnessed during our experience in the field, yet we could also share countless stories of healing, hope, and strength.

Lastly, it may also be wise to remember that healing can happen in moments of levity, particularly with respect to children and adolescents. A story that demonstrates this type of spontaneous humor occurred when I was teaching a class regarding the ways in which children's age and stage of development affects their ability to make sense of death. One student shared a story of how, at the age of 7, she learned about her grandmother's impending death. Growing up on a farm, it was the norm to take sick animals out behind the barn and euthanize them. When her mother told her that Grandma was ill and would die, she replied, "So, do we need to take Grandma out behind the barn and shoot her?" While some might find this to be a shocking response from a child, it is quite accurate when we apply the fundamental principles of how 7-year-olds make sense of death. Because the students in this class had developmental insight into how children understand such issues, they responded with uproarious laughter.

Although the focus of this book is to share knowledge regarding grief and loss among children and adolescents, there is also an opportunity for all of us, as adults, to perhaps think critically about the diverse types of losses (i.e., both death and non-death) that are all too often present in the lives of our youth. Alongside contemporary grief theory and our collective ability to respond in sensitive, informed, and attuned ways are the social, political, and cultural realities that directly shape how our young people make meaning of their experiences. It seems necessary to equip ourselves more fully in order to foster healing, resilience, and growth in children who have experienced significant losses.

Thus, we invite you to read these pages as we share an integrated perspective of children's development and the ways in which these multidimensional processes influence their understanding, expressions of grief, and growth. We also invite you to be mindful of the need to ask a child or teen about his or her experiences, be patient enough to listen, and be willing to honor the ways in which a child makes sense of his or her losses, as well as recognize that adult discomfort with grief and loss will directly influence how youth are able to understand and live within their own experience of grief and loss.

Note

1. Name has been changed to protect privacy.

References

Doka, K. (Ed.). (1989). *Disenfranchised grief: Recognizing hidden sorrow.* New York, NY: Free Press.

Doka, K. J. (Ed.). (2002). *Disenfranchised grief: New directions, challenges, and strategies for practice.* Champaign, IL: Research Press.

Porges, S. W. (2011). *The polyvagal theory: Neurophysiological foundations of emotions, attachment, communication, and self regulation.* New York, NY: W.W. Norton & Co.

Schuurman, D. (2017, April). *An uneasy alliance? The integration of trauma and bereavement.* Presentation at the Association for Death Education and Counselling 39th Annual Conference, Portland, Oregon.

2 Developmental Considerations for Grieving Youth

Carrie Arnold

The ability to support a grieving child or adolescent is informed not only by one's knowledge of bereavement but also by an understanding of his or her unique grief expression along with an awareness of *who that young person is*. The way in which grief manifests in the life of a child or teen is of great significance, yet what is important is adults' ability to be sensitively attuned to their distinctive needs, while simultaneously acknowledging the developmental imperatives that accompany their various life stages. Children and adolescents develop and grow within interrelated networks (e.g., family, peers, school, cultural- or faith-based communities); thus, loss can bring about significant changes within many aspect of their lives.

Grief, Bereavement, and Mourning

Within the literature on childhood grief and bereavement are discussions with respect to whether children can actually grieve or mourn, and conclusions are often determined by the way in which each concept is defined (Webb, 2010). In the absence of universally agreed-upon definitions for these constructs, perhaps what is more of a priority within this debate is the reality that children and teens inarguably feel the absence of those to whom they are connected. Their multifaceted response will be influenced by personality, temperament, family dynamics, health, peer relationships, experiences with loss, relationship to the deceased, concurrent events, and their developmental stage. To better understand how loss is conceptualized in this volume, grief, bereavement, and mourning will be defined.

Grief is the adaptive response to loss that involves all aspects of the human experience, including social, emotional, cognitive, behavioral, and spiritual dimensions (Harris & Winokuer, 2016). *Bereavement* is the, "objective situation of having lost someone significant through death" (Stroebe, Hansson, Schut, & Stroebe, 2008, p. 4). *Mourning* constitutes the public displays, social expressions, or acts of expressing grief that are socially and culturally determined (Stroebe, et al., 2008). Mourning is also characterized as the overall process of readjusting to life without the deceased. These terms are most commonly associated with death-related losses, however there is increasing recognition that non-death (i.e., nonfinite) losses can also elicit a grief response (Harris & Gorman, 2011). Children can change schools, have a best friend move away, or encounter significant health concerns, all of which can result in grief. Additionally, various developmental factors will shape how the child or adolescent responds to death or non-death losses.

Developmental Considerations: An Overview of Central Concepts

Cognitive Development

The influential work of Piaget (1955, 1972) is often cited with respect to children's cognitive development. His theoretical paradigm was not specifically done within the context of grief and loss, yet his perspective on children's cognitive progression provides a helpful outline for appreciating children's capacity to understand death.

Piaget's *sensorimotor stage* (ages 0–2) is a time when infants learn object permanence and begin to understand cause-and-effect relationships. Bowlby's (1953, 1969, 1973, 1980) and Ainsworth's (Ainsworth & Wittig, 1969, 1971; Ainsworth, 1989) substantial work in the field of infant attachment demonstrated that infants do feel distress at the separation from their caregiver. Piaget's *preoperative stage* (ages 2–7) is characterized by magical thinking, use of fantasy, and egocentricity. Typically, at this stage, children do not yet grasp that death is permanent and irreversible. The next stage in Piaget's progression is *concrete operational* (ages 7–11), where egocentricity diminishes and children have greater capacity to use reasoning skills and organize information sequentially. Subsequently, it is during this stage that children begin to more fully understand the permanence of death, yet believe that it is more likely to occur to the elderly or weak (Webb, 2010). The final stage in Piaget's framework is *formal operations* (ages 11 and up). At this stage, children become more logical, are capable of abstract thought, and can hold many variables in their awareness at one time. As a result, children at this stage typically understand that death is permanent and irreversible.

Piaget's (1972) cognitive stages help to highlight the efficiency of Speece and Brent's (1996) concepts regarding how children acquire knowledge of death:

Universality—all living things must die; death is inevitable, unpredictable, and inclusive;
Irreversibility—death is final and permanent;
Non-functionality—all life functions cease (e.g., breathing, eating, talking);
Causality—understanding that something has to happen for death to occur (e.g., accident, injury, illness); and
Non-corporeal continuation—a connection to the deceased continues after death.

Speece and Brent (1996) explained that the first four bioscientific concepts are typically understood by age 7 (i.e., the transition between preoperative and concrete operational stages). Non-corporeal continuation is more abstract, thus children typically grasp this by age 10 (i.e., the end of concrete operations and the transition into formal operations). The integration of such concepts can be helpful in knowing how to offer explanations and address children's needs in age-appropriate ways.

Another notable concept within children's development is magical thinking, whereby very young children (approximately 2–7 years of age) frequently believe that their thoughts have influence over what happens around them. Magical thinking, while developmentally normative, can result in a child reaching inaccurate conclusions about many aspect of their life, as well as details related to death (e.g., "If I eat all my vegetables, daddy will not die"). Children with magical thought may also believe that they can eliminate grief for themselves or others. If not addressed, it can result in a child thinking that he or she is responsible for the loss; moreover, acceptance of this kind of destructive thinking could potentially lead to ongoing concerns in a child's emotional and psychological development (e.g., if a child argued with a sibling on the day of his or her death, that child may grow up believing that the death was his or her fault).

Understanding basic concepts related to a child's cognitive development can be a tremendous asset in the midst of a family's loss experience. For example, explaining causality is one way in which to address magical think-ing. If a child is too young at the time of a death to fully comprehend this concept (i.e., under the age of 7), it is recommended that conversations and explanations occur over time so that the child can integrate accurate infor-mation. For example, if Grandma died when a child was 5 years old, the ongoing family stories about Grandma can include meaningful memories along with a factual statement, such as, "Grandma died because her heart stopped working." This type of recollection helps to promote understanding and memory integration (Siegel & Bryson, 2011) and can allow the child to acquire knowledge of death that is sensitive to his or her developmental stage.

Given the significance of such concepts, it is necessary to highlight the need for correct terminology when talking to children. Words such as *death*, *dead*, *died*, and *dying* ought to be used instead of euphemisms. Using phrases such as "gone away," "Grandpa has gone to heaven," or stating that a pet has "been put to sleep" do not convey the bioscientific concepts of death. Moreover, these explanations may create feelings of confusion, as children may worry about what has actually happened, or there may be an increased likelihood for distorted magical thinking.

While the above frameworks are useful for gaining insight into children's acquisition of death-related knowledge, it is helpful to remember that within the field of developmental psychology, there are an infinite number of theo-retical orientations that explain the myriad ways children and adolescents grow and develop. These interpretations provide useful guidelines in understanding relevant cognitive, emotional, social, and psychological aspects of children's growth; however, such formulations are guidelines only, rather than prescriptive dictums. Attending to the unique needs of each child is strongly encouraged. Additionally, children's growth and development is influenced by the quality of their relational networks.

Attachment, Attunement, and Regulation

Bowlby (1953, 1969, 1973, 1980) and Ainsworth and colleagues (Ainsworth & Wittig, 1969, 1971; Ainsworth, 1989), pioneers in contemporary attachment research, have demonstrated that children can be deeply affected by separation from their parent(s), and require consistent, sensitive, and attuned caregiving. While it was previously believed that children attached to parents primarily for food and survival (Cassidy, 2008), interdisciplinary frameworks throughout the twentieth century demonstrated that children seek comfort, love, and protection within the safety of the parental bond (Cassidy & Shaver, 2008; Siegel, 2012; Neufeld & Maté, 2004).

Through her well-known Strange Situation experiment, Ainsworth and colleagues (Ainsworth & Wittig, 1969, 1971; Ainsworth, 1989) established three attachment styles: secure, fearful-avoidant, and anxious-ambivalent. A fourth attachment style, disorganized/disoriented, was later recognized by Main and colleagues (Main & Solomon, 1990). Attachment researchers continue to investigate the nature of these bonds and the implications for the parent–child relationship. What is central within attachment is the child's need to maintain proximity to a caregiver who is viewed as being better able to cope, and who can provide security and comfort (Bowlby, 1988). As children become adolescents, there is less need for *proximity*, yet an ongoing need for *availability* (e.g., if a teen needs help, he or she can count on a caregiver to be available and sensitive to his or her needs; Strauss, 2007). The consistent presence of sensitive caregivers promotes a deeper sense of object permanence, both in childhood and in later life, forming a template for relationships and adaptive responses to difficulties such as significant losses.

These attachment styles are foundational in the Dual Process Model of grief (Stroebe & Schut, 1999), whereby the bereaved oscillate between *loss orientation* (e.g., sadness, grief work, intrusion of grief, continuing bonds) and *restoration orientation* (e.g., attending to life changes, new roles, distraction from grief). Due to children's short sadness spans, they tend to naturally move in and out of their grief, where sadness or anger can quickly be followed by play (Webb, 2010). The ability to oscillate between loss and restoration is also determined by attachment style. Securely attached individuals tend to be the most capable of this oscillation pattern without being likely to remain "stuck" in either restoration orientation (e.g., fearful-avoidant style) or loss orientation (e.g., anxious-ambivalent style), or experiencing trauma-like symptoms following a loss (disorganized/disoriented style; Stroebe, Schut, & Stroebe, 2005).

Neufeld (2004) explained that attachment is created through six features: senses, sameness, belonging and loyalty, significance and specialness, emotional intimacy, and psychological intimacy. This developmental progression first involves connecting through sight, hearing, touch, or smell, and the goal is to maintain proximity with an attachment figure. Secondly, when attaching to someone, there is a need to look for similar expressions, features, or behaviors. Thirdly, to feel a connection with someone, we seek a sense of belonging or loyalty (e.g., in young children, this can be seen in the often-used phrase "mine," which is about belonging, not ownership). The fourth way involves feeling special or significant, which allows for closeness and connection (e.g., young children enjoy hearing endearing stories of their infancy). The fifth way of seeking closeness is through warm feelings of love, which involves a deep sense of vulnerability. "To give one's heart away is to risk it being broken" (Neufeld, 2004, p. 5). The final means of attaching is psychological intimacy, or being known by another. Sharing secrets and revealing oneself to another is a form of closeness and is the most vulnerable way of attaching.

Neufeld (2004) also explained that when caregivers actively cultivate a secure attachment with their child(ren), the parent–child bond is preserved and protected. He emphasized that it is the parent's responsibility to set the tone for the relationship with the child, and to recognize that attachment is arranged hierarchically. Children are to be embedded within the safety and security of adults (e.g., caregivers, extended family, teachers, coaches), and he cautioned against parent–child dynamics where the child is "in charge," controlling the relationship, resistant to guidance or direction, or lacks the capacity to be vulnerable. Rather than promoting *independence*, Neufeld (personal communication, December 9, 2013) emphasized *interdependence*, stating that children achieve maturation through deepening attachments, rather than through separation.

A related concept of attachment is *attunement*, which is conceptualized as the process where one person focuses attention on the internal experience of another whereby that person "feels felt" (Siegel, 2007, p. xiv). In a neuro-biological sense, attunement specifically allows the different structures of the brain to properly separate into their rightful jobs, while still allowing those areas to be integrated properly. This neural integration allows for proper information intake, processing, and responding, both in day-to-day life and in crises or times of loss (Siegel, 2007; Siegel & Bryson, 2011). Research into the role of mirror neurons has provided insight into the influence of neuronal circuitry on empathy, attunement, and emotional sharing after researchers discovered that, in macaque monkeys, the same neuronal groups are activated in the observing monkey's brain as in the brain of the monkey performing an action (e.g., picking up a peanut; Gallese, 2006). The significance of mirror neurons is tied to the sharing of feelings, thoughts, imitation, and communication (Davies, 2011).

Constancy and attunement also support the development of emotional regulation. Utilizing MacLean's (1985) triune model of the brain—composed of the brainstem (i.e., instinctive responses, heart rate, breathing), the limbic system (i.e., nonverbal, emotional, and relational experiences, gut feelings), and the frontal lobes (i.e., reasoning, problem solving, memory, facts)—the process of regulation can be better understood. Ogden, Minton, and Pain (2006) described the three core concepts in regulation: hyperarousal (e.g., emotional overwhelm, panic, impulsivity, anger), hypoarousal (e.g., numb, passive, no feelings, no energy, disconnected, shut down), and the *window of tolerance,* which is between the two arousal states (e.g., the adaptive ability to think and feel in ways that fit the current situation).

It is through this neurobiological process of regulation and dysregulation that life difficulties and losses, may be experienced and processed. Consistent attunement from adults allows children the ability to maintain, or reestablish, a sense of regulation (e.g., window of tolerance) as opposed to more primitive responses involving fight or flight (e.g., hyperarousal) or freeze/shutdown (e.g., hypoarousal) defenses.

Additionally, more contemporary perspectives are emerging within such fields as traumatology, interpersonal neurobiology, and somatic-based therapies (e.g., sensorimotor psychotherapy and somatic experiencing). Clinicians, authors, and/or researchers such as van der Kolk (2015); Siegel (2007, 2013); Levine (2010); Minton, Ogden, and Pain (2006); and Ogden and Fisher (2015) continue to advance our understanding regarding the centrality of the nervous system in our emotional and psychological health, and within our interpersonal relationships. Psychological theories and research have typically investigated the interrelatedness of thoughts, feelings, and behaviors; however, our current understanding is expanding to include more holistic perspectives that include the mind/brain, heart (see HeartMath Institute, www.heartmath.org) and nervous system in an integrated process of regulation (see Porges, 2011).

A Focus on Child Development

Siegel and Bryson (2011) explained that childhood is a time to attain a balance between *chaos* and *rigidity* by navigating between impulsivity and lack of control and the ability to flexibly adhere to rules. The prefrontal cortex is the region in the brain that allows children to gradually develop their ability to control impulses and make sound decisions (Siegel, 2007). In order to promote ongoing development and integration, children benefit from adult guidance in naming and processing their emotions, developing empathy, and adapting to various circumstances that allow children the ability to become increasingly capable of attending to their own well-being (McCoyd & Walter, 2016). Siegel and Bryson (2011) characterized this balance, or developing ability to achieve integration, as the *river of well-being.* They encouraged adults to conceptualize experiences of chaos (e.g., aggressive behavior) or rigidity (e.g., believing that all grades must be A's) as bumping up against the banks of the "river," with the aim of moving back into the middle. They instruct adults how to guide children to integrate their "downstairs brain" (i.e., strong emotion) with their "upstairs brain" (i.e., good decisions; Siegel & Bryson, 2011, p. 62) through empathy, sound decision-making, and bodily regulation. This process is predicated on adults being in a state of regulation themselves.

With respect to grief, (Webb, 2010) highlighted six ways in which children's grief differs from adults:

1. Children's immature cognitive development interferes with their under-standing of irreversibility, universality, and inevitability;
2. Children have a limited capacity to tolerate emotional pain (i.e., a "short sadness span");
3. Children's acute feelings of loss may occur in bursts over several years;
4. Children are limited in their ability to express their feelings verbally;
5. Children are sensitive about "being different" from their peers; and
6. Children express various feelings through their play.

Given these notable differences for grieving children, the applicability of Siegel and Bryson's (2011) model can assist adults in facilitating a child's grief process in developmentally sensitive ways.

After experiencing a significant loss, upon return to school, Massat, Moses, and Ornstein (2008) emphasized the role of school social workers or counselors in their ability to attend to children's grief. Referencing the Dual Process Model (Stroebe & Schut, 1999), these authors acknowledged that a child's natural oscillation between restoration orientation and loss orientation is potentially disrupted because children often return to school soon after a death, which can disrupt their natural inclination towards oscillation. Given that 10–15% of students in the average Canadian classroom are grieving or in the process of losing someone close to them (Tremonti, 2017), teachers and other school staff can play a vital role in supporting bereaved youth.

A Focus on Adolescent Development

Neufeld (2004) has characterized adolescence as *the womb of adulthood* in which teens need to *grow their adult self.* A bereaved teen's developing identity will be influenced by their loss and corresponding grief. Although we often associate adolescence with a maturational "letting go," Neufeld and Maté (2004) maintained that a secure bond with a caregiver must still be the priority over peers as the main source of emotional and psychological connection. For adolescents to adapt and move through their grief, Neufeld (2004) stated that their ability to do so is shaped by their capacity to "hold on sufficiently enough to not be alarmed" (p. 29). The capacity to feel, to recognize that "being with" is no longer possible, and the ability to experience one's tears all allow for potential transformation.

Additionally, Neufeld (2004) explained that if sensitive and attuned adults can work at the attachment relationship and provide more than what is required by the teen (i.e., allowing the teen to feel special, significant, known, and understood) he or she can experience adaptation and individuation within this transitional stage of development. Applying this perspective may be of benefit for bereaved teens who tend to feel caught between an obligation to act like an adult, amidst feeling vulnerable or in need of caregiving as they did when they were younger.

Establishing Rapport

The ability to connect with children and adolescents is shaped by *who we are* more than *what we do*. In our various roles as adults, maintaining an open, warm, and nonjudgemental attitude conveys safety and a sense of acceptance, which is particularly important to bereaved youth. If adults are routinely overwhelmed, dealing with many stressors, or are unable to tend to their own needs and sense of well-being, the quality of their interactions with the children and adolescents in their lives will be directly affected in a negative way (Kabat-Zinn & Kabat-Zinn, 1997). Therefore, one of the first steps in building successful rapport is for adults to be mindful and attentive to their own well-being. Adequate rest; proper nutrition; meaningful relationships; finding ways to experience joy; and tending to physical, social, and emotional needs are some of the ways in which adults can ensure their ability to be sensitive, present, and attuned to others.

When supporting bereaved youth, it is also the responsibility of adults to be self-aware and demonstrate a willingness to examine their own experiences with loss. Helping professionals who work in bereavement should seek ways to gain insight into the losses in their own lives. Counseling may be helpful to process these loss experiences so that they do not interfere with the professional's ability to be fully present to those who are bereaved and vulnerable. If this loss exploration is not done with intention or genuine self-reflection, adults can inadvertently communicate their discomfort with pain, anger, sadness, or grief when in the presence of grieving individuals. If the relational need is for adults to assist in the emotional and somatic regulation of children and teens (Neufeld & Maté, 2004; Siegel, 2013; Siegel & Bryson, 2011), it makes sense for adults to be as *present, congruent,* and *integrated* as possible. Such terms are often used within mindfulness practice (Kabat-Zinn, 1997; Siegel, 2007) and the literature on therapeutic presence (Geller & Greenberg, 2002, 2012).

One way in which to conceptualize this idea of congruence or integration within a helping context is to consider how one's heart, body, and mind are aligned. For example, if a grief counselor working with teens has not addressed the death of her own mother when she was 15 years old, she may feel the pain and anguish of this extraordinary loss as well as the somatic distress (e.g., increased heart rate, feelings of anxiety) that can accompany such feelings. Such re-experiencing has the potential to significantly affect her ability to be fully present, and she may inadvertently increase the pain of her grieving clients by her inability to be fully present to them and their experiences. Based on the current findings from the field of interpersonal neurobiology (e.g., Fosha, Seigel, & Solomon, 2009; Seigel & Solomon, 2013), it is likely that she will not be attuned, despite good personal and professional intentions, and therefore may not be capable of accurately engaging in what Siegel (2007) described as *attending to the narrative of the other* (NOTO) or being able to align herself with the *internal state of the other* (ISO).

Subsequently, this counselor will be diminished in her capacity to establish empathy and rapport with bereaved youth. Inevitably, our own healing may inadvertently double onto that of our clients at times, particularly if there are similar losses. However, our own healing cannot come at the expense of the young people that we are supporting, and we are thus required to be attentive and responsible for our own needs. Tending to our own losses and sense of wellness is an ongoing aspect of working with bereaved youth so that we create environments that are conducive to growth, healing, and transformation.

Lastly, on a more pragmatic level, rapport is built through such features as inviting, warm locations. For therapeutic spaces, furniture, lighting, art, and other décor elements ought to be designed according to the needs of children and/or adolescents. With respect to adults (which can include helping professionals, teachers, coaches, etc.), tone of voice, facial expression, and open demeanour help bereaved youth to enter into the relationship feeling that they, and their grief, will be accepted. Siegel (2007) characterized this type of relational stance using the acronym COAL: curiosity, openness, acceptance, and love.[1]

Conclusion

In our collective effort to support bereaved youth, it is necessary to possess knowledge and understanding of significant developmental concepts that inform a young person's ability to comprehend death and grief. Ongoing inquiry into fields such as attachment or interpersonal neurobiology continues to create opportunities to acquire a more integrated and holistic body of knowledge with respect to children's growth and development. This type of multidimensional approach results in a greater capacity to acknowledge and appropriately respond to the myriad ways that grief presents in the life of a child or adolescent in order to optimally support the interrelated processes of growth, regulation, and resilience amidst loss.

Discussion Questions

1. Discuss the importance of somatic regulation for children. How might caring adults help to promote this process?
2. Given that magical thinking is a developmentally normative concept, how might you support a young child in his or her grief when that child is too young to understand the permanence of death?

3.   Discuss the benefits of having a holistic and integrated understanding of child development.

Note

1.   Some professionals may feel uncomfortable with the use of the word *love*. The author notes that there are many variations of love, which include friendship, romantic bonds, and familial love. Writers from Freud on have cited that healing occurs within the context of loving relationships. Martin Luther King and many others wrote about *agape* which is a type of universal love for all, based on a sense of goodwill and benevolence for others. It is this author's understanding that Seigel (2007) is referring to this type of universal love.

References

Ainsworth, M. D. S., & Wittig, B. A. (1969). Attachment and exploratory behaviour of one-year-olds in a strange situation. In B.M. Foss (Ed.), *Determinants of infant behaviour* (Vol. 4). New York, NY: Barnes & Noble.

Ainsworth, M. D. S. & Wittig, B. A. (1971). Individual differences in strange situation behaviour of one-year olds. In H.R. Shaffer (Ed.), *The origins of human social relations* (pp. 17–57). London, UK: Academic Press.

Ainsworth, M. D. S. (1989). Attachments beyond infancy. *American Psychologist, 44*, 709–716.

Bowlby, J. (1953). *Child care and the growth of love.* Harmondsworth, UK: Penguin.

Bowlby, J. (1969). *Attachment and loss: Attachment* (Vol. 1). London, England: Hogarth.

Bowlby, J. (1973). *Attachment and loss: Separation* (Vol. 2). New York, NY: Basic Books.

Bowlby, J. (1980). *Attachment and loss: Sadness and depression* (Vol. 3). New York, NY: Basic Books.

Bowlby, J. (1988). *A secure base.* New York, NY: Routledge.

Cassidy, J. (2008). The nature of the child's ties. In J. Cassidy & P. R. Shaver (Eds.), *Handbook of attachment: Theory, research and clinical applications* (2nd ed,). New York, NY: The Guilford Press.

Cassidy, J. & P. R. Shaver (Eds.), Handbook of attachment: Theory, research and clinical applications, (2nd ed). New York, NY: The Guilford Press.

Davies, D. (2011). *Child development: A practitioner's guide* (3rd ed.). New York, NY: The Guilford Press.

Fosha, D., Siegel, D. J., & Solomon, M. F. (Eds.), (2009). *The healing power of emotion: Affective neuroscience, development and clinical practice.* New York, NY: W.W. Norton & Co.

Geller, S. M., & Greenberg, L. S. (2002). Therapeutic presence: Therapist's experience of presence in the psychotherapy encounter. *Person-Centred and Experiential Psychotherapies, 1*(1–2), 71–86.

Geller, S. M., & Greenberg, L. S. (2012). *Therapeutic presence: A mindful approach to effective therapy.* Washington, DC: American Psychological Association.

Gallese, V. (2006). Intentional attunement: A neurophysiological perspective on social cognition and its disruption in autism. *Brain Research, 1079*(1), 15–24.

Harris, D. L., & Gorman, E. (2011). Grief from a broader perspective: Nonfinite loss, ambiguous loss, and chronic sorrow. In D. L. Harris (Ed.), *Counting our losses: Reflecting on change, loss, and transition in everyday life* (pp. 1–13). New York, NY: Routledge.

Harris, D. L., & Winokuer, H. R. (2016). *Principles and practices of grief counselling* (2nd ed.), New York, NY: Springer.

Kabat-Zinn, M., & Kabat-Zinn, J. (1997). *Everyday blessings: The inner work of mindful parenting.* New York, NY: Hyperion.

Levine, P. (2010). *In an unspoken voice: How the body releases trauma and restores goodness.* Berkeley, CA: North Atlantic Books.

MacLean, P. D. (1985). Brain evolution relating to family, play, and the separation call. *Archives of General Psychiatry, 42*(4): 405–417. doi:10.1001/archpsyc. 1985.01790270095011.

Main, M., & Solomon, J. (1990). Procedures for identifying infants as disorganized/disoriented during the Ainsworth strange situation. In M. T. Greenberg, D. Cicchetti, & E. M. Cummings (Eds.), *Attachment in the preschool years: Theory, research, and intervention* (pp. 121–160). Chicago: University of Chicago Press.

Massat, C. R., Moses, H., & Ornstein, E. (2008). Grief and loss in schools: A perspective for school social workers. *School Social Work Journal, 33*(1), 80–96.

McCoyd, J. L. M., & Walter, C. A. (2016). *Grief and loss across the lifespan: A biopsychosocial perspective.* New York, NY: Springer.

Minton, K., Ogden, P., & Pain, C. (2006). *Trauma and the body: A sensorimotor approach to psychotherapy.* New York, NY: W. W. Norton.

Neufeld, G. (2004). *Making sense of adolescence.* [PowerPoint slides]. London, Canada.

Neufeld, G., & Maté, G. (2004). *Hold onto your kids: Why parents need to matter more than peers.* Toronto, ON: Vintage Canada.

Ogden, P., Minton, K., & Pain, C. (2006). *Trauma and the body: A sensorimotor approach to psychotherapy.* New York, NY: W. W. Norton & Co.

Ogden, P., & Fisher, J. (2015). *Sensorimotor psychotherapy: Interventions for trauma and attachment.* New York, NY: W. W. Norton.

Piaget, J. (1955). *The child's construction of reality.* New York, NY: Basic Books.

Piaget, J. (1972). Intellectual evolution from adolescence to childhood. *Human Development, 15,* 1–12.

Porges, S. W. (2011). *The polyvagal theory: Neurophysiological foundations of emotions, attachment, communication, and self-regulation.* New York, NY: W. W. Norton & Co.

Siegel, D. J. (2007). *The mindful brain: Reflection and attunement in the cultivation of well-being.* New York, NY: W. W. Norton & Co.

Siegel, D. J. (2012). *The developing mind: How relationships and the brain interact to shape who we are* (2nd ed,). New York, NY: The Guilford Press.

Siegel, D. J. (2013). *Brainstorm: The power and purpose of the teenage brain.* New York, NY: Penguin.

Siegel, D. J., & Bryson, T. P. (2011). *The whole-brain child: 12 revolutionary strategies to nurture your child's developing mind.* New York, NY: Bantam.

Siegel, D. J., & Solomon, M. (Eds.) (2013). *Healing moments in psychotherapy.* New York, NY: W. W. Norton & Co.

Speece, M. W., & Brent, S. B. (1996). The development of children's understanding of death. In C. A. Corr & D. M. Corr (Eds.), *Handbook of childhood death and bereavement.* New York, NY: Springer.

Strauss, M. (2007). *Adolescent girls in crisis: Intervention and hope.* New York, NY: W. W. Norton & Co.

Stroebe, M., & Schut, H. (1999). The dual process model of coping with bereavement: Rationale and description. *Death Studies, 23*(3), 197–224. http://dx.doi.org/10.1080/074811899201046

Stroebe, M. S., Hansson, R. O., Schut, H., & Stroebe, W. (2008). Bereavement research: Contemporary perspectives. In M. S. Stroebe, R. O. Hansson, H. Schut, & W. Stroebe (Eds.), *Handbook of bereavement research and practice: Advances in Theory and intervention* (pp. 3–25). Washington, DC: American Psychological Association.

Stroebe, M. S., Schut, H., & Stroebe, W. (2005). Attaching in coping with bereavement: A theoretical integration. *Review of General Psychology, 9*(1), 48–66.

Tremonti, A. (Producer). (2017, April 11). *Why an ICU doctor says death ed is as essential as sex ed in high school* [Audio podcast]. Retrieved from http://www.cbc.ca/radio/thecurrent/the-current-for-april-11-2017-1.4064410/april-11-2017-full-episode-transcript-1.4066634

van der Kolk, B. (2015). *The body keeps the score: Brain, mind, and body in the healing of trauma.* New York, NY: Penguin Books.

Webb, N. B. (2010). The child and death. In N.B. Webb (Ed.), *Helping bereaved children* (3rd ed., pp. 3–21). New York, NY: The Guilford Press.

3 Assessing Grief and Loss in Children and Adolescents

Stephanie Rabenstein

Bereaved youth come to the attention of clinicians for many reasons. They are brought by concerned caregivers who share their experience of loss and want to know how to be supportive. They can also be referred by other caring adults who are concerned about the course a child's grief is taking, and the potential effects on health and well-being. Others are sent because of their observable struggles with depression, suicidality, anxiety, or self-injury. Although a death-related loss or the experience of multiple losses may not be mentioned in the referral, what may eventually unfold is the grief that lies beneath the presenting concern, which then plays a significant role in the child's ability to adapt to ongoing changes. A thorough assessment is the essential first step to gathering the information necessary to better understand the effects of grief, provide recommendations, and when necessary, move ahead with appropriate support. This chapter expands Webb's tripartite model for assessing grief and loss in children, adolescents, and, their families (Webb, 2010) and provides resources that can assist in the assessment process.

Conceptualizing Typical Grief

Loss and death are part of the human condition. Every day, children and teens will experience the death of family, friends, or pets. They will also undergo myriad nonfinite losses, such as saying good-bye to friends, a school, or neighborhood when a family relocates; temporary or chronic loss of health when sick or injured; loss of family structure as they have known it when parents divorce; or loss of safety when abused or bullied. Most children and adolescents adapt and even thrive amidst the pain and sadness of everyday life. Although these losses may shape how the child or youth sees him- or herself, relationships, and the world, it is possible to live without significant and enduring impairment. Even after the unexpected death of a parent, researchers have found that over 50% of bereaved children experienced significant resolution of their grief symptoms in a year or less; a little over 30% have a more gradual easing of their grief symptoms, while approximately 10% of children maintained high levels of prolonged grief symptoms for almost 3 years following the death of their parent (Melhem, Porta, Shamsddeen,

Walker Payne, & Brent, 2011). Most children, like their adult counterparts, can and do recover from the death of a close family member over time—some more quickly than others. For roughly 10% of children whose bereavement is characterized by significant levels of grief-related distress lasting for 3 or more years, assessment is the key to early and appropriate intervention.

Assessment begins with the understanding of what distinguishes normative grieving for infants, young children, school-age children, and teenagers from atypical grieving. Normative grief refers to the child's developmentally appropriate ability to:

- accept the reality of the death,
- cope with its emotional ramifications,
- adjust to the resulting changes in his or her life,
- move through current and subsequent normal developmental stages, and
- remain functional in school and other contexts (Dyregrov, 2013).

In this discussion, *developmentally appropriate* refers to the maturity of a child's thinking, including the ability to reason, process information, and respond emotionally compared to other children at the same chronological age (University of Rochester, 2016). The following lists provide a general guide to how children think about and experience death at each of the developmental stages of childhood, from infancy to adolescence.

Infants (approximately birth to 1 year):

- Have no concept of death.
- React to separation from their parents and caregivers and to the emotions of those who remain following the death of a close family member; how the death took place is irrelevant (Cohen, Mannarino, Greenberg, Padlo, & Shipley, 2002).
- Are sensitive to changes in the structure and routines of their lives.
- Cry and are irritable; crying is their primary means of expressing pain, confusion, and anxiety.
- In the midst of grief, are also able to express joy and engage in play with pleasant affect.

Toddlers (approximately 2 to 3 years):

- Do not understand the permanence of death when a close family member dies.
- Are vulnerable and responsive to the sadness, fear, confusion, and/or anger of caregivers and also to separation from them.
- Often respond to the caregiver's strong negative emotions with anxiety and irritability.

- May temporarily regress in previously achieved abilities to separate easily, fall asleep alone, and/or maintain toileting milestones.
- Are susceptible to changes in routine and structure.
- Able to be happy and wholly immersed in periods of fun activities with peers and family members, laughing and focused on play.
- Express emotions through crying, irritability, and newly acquired language (e.g. "Where's daddy?").

Preschoolers (4 and 5 years):

- View death as temporary and reversible, not permanent and universal.
- Begin to perceive death as an event to which grown-ups have strong negative reactions (American Academy of Child and Adolescent Psychiatry, 2013; University of Rochester, 2016).
- Do not understand that when people or things are dead they do not eat, sleep, or breathe (Speece & Brent, 1996).
- Express sadness, anxiety, confusion, and irritability.
- Are able to be happy and wholly immersed in periods of fun activities with peers and family members, laughing and focused on play.
- May persist in the belief that the family member is still alive (American Academy of Child and Adolescent Psychiatry, 2013).
- May temporarily regress to previous developmental stages and have separation anxiety, problems settling at bedtime, and issues with soiling or urinating clothing.
- From an egocentric worldview, may attribute the death of someone they know to their own thoughts or actions.
- Are sensitive to changes in routine and structure.
- Persistently question many aspects of death and dying that they do not understand (e.g., "Where did Nana go?" "Why isn't she moving?" "Why is everyone sad?").

School-Age Children (6 to 12 years):

- By the age of 7, cognitive abilities enable the child to struggle with the four bioscientific concepts that are part of death: its universality, irreversibility, nonfunctionality (that the biological, sensational, emotional, and cognitive functions of life cease), causality (death is caused), and non-corporeal continuation (some form of personal continuation exists following the death; Speece & Brent, 1996), yet still struggle with its relevance to them and its finality.
- Express sadness, anger, anxiety, confusion, and irritability.
- May articulate worry for the safety of family and friends.
- Are able to be happy and wholly immersed in periods of fun activities with peers at school and after school, laughing and focused on play.
- May struggle at bedtime with getting to and staying sleep.
- May find it difficult to focus following the loss.

- May experience decreased energy.
- May lose their appetite for a short time.
- May lose interest in school, hobbies, or sports temporarily.
- Can verbalize thoughts and feelings related to the deceased and questions related to death and what happens afterwards.

Adolescents (13 to 19 years):

- Understand the bioscientific aspects of death.
- Have thoughts and feelings about the deceased that are similar to those of adults.
- Explore existential questions of life's purpose and what happens after death, seeking an integration or clarification of family and personal values (e.g., "Why am I living?" "What would happen if I died?"). This can sound like suicidal ideation, and requires closer investigation.
- Are influenced by the presence or absence of past experiences of losses, death, dying, and bereavement.
- May want to have religious or cultural rituals observed (University of Rochester Medical Center, 2016).
- Are guided by the developmental tasks of establishing own identity and independence in terms of what thoughts and feelings are shared and with whom. Peers may be an important source of support.
- May experience that the strong emotions associated with grief and loss may intensify the "turbo-charged feelings" of adolescence coupled with "relatively unskilled set of cognitive abilities" (Dahl, 2004, p. 17), making it more difficult to modulate strong feelings and impulsive actions.
- May resort to substance use as a means to cope with intense grief.
- May encounter a temporary decrease in concentration.
- Often have disruptions in sleep, appetite, and energy.

A unique feature of childhood and adolescent grief that distinguishes it from adult grief is that as the young person matures, he or she will revisit the grief and loss in a new way at subsequent developmental stages. Wolfelt (1996) suggested that clinicians working with "bereaved children must stay available to help them for years after the event of the death. Mourning is a process, not an event" (p. 42).

Conceptualizing Atypical Grief

There is lively discourse among researchers and clinicians about what constitutes "maladaptive," or atypical, grief in children. Current conceptualizations regarding atypical grief are presented within this chapter, with the caveat that these are socially constructed definitions that require ongoing exploration and research. The fields of thanatology and traumatology have not been adequately integrated in the literature, particularly related to the pediatric population (Schuurman, 2017). Thus, it behooves us to be discerning within the assessment process, and mindful of our use of terminology, so that grief is not viewed as a pathological condition or a "mental disorder."

One school of thought with regard to atypical grief is held by Shear and colleagues (Shear et al., 2007; Shear et al., 2011) who used the term *complicated grief* (CG) to describe qualitative aspects of the problematic grieving process that distinguish it from adaptive grieving. These aspects include yearning for the deceased; having intrusive, preoccupying thoughts; and experiencing emotional numbness. Given the lack of clarity regarding CG in children and teens, Melhem et al. (2007) conducted a study exploring the correlates of complicated grief among youth. Using a modified version of the adult *Inventory of Complicated Grief–Revised* (ICG-R), they demonstrated early evidence that the ICG-R is a sound measure for children and teens, and the correlated symptoms were shown to be partially independent from depression, anxiety, and PTSD.

Another school of thought represented in the research and writing of Prigerson and colleagues (2009) is about prolonged grief. *Prolonged grief* focuses on normative grief symptoms that persist over long periods of time, impairing an individual's ability to function at home, school, in the community, or with others. This constellation of grief symptoms has typically been applied to adult grief, therefore in the absence of substantial research with the pediatric population, one must be cautious about extrapolating a potentially adult framework onto this age group. A third group (Cohen, Mannarino, & Deblinger, 2006) examined the overlap of posttraumatic symptoms with grief symptoms when the death of someone close to the child dies under sudden, violent circumstances. They refer to this as *childhood traumatic grief* (Kaplow, Layne, Pynoos, Cohen, & Lieberman, 2012).

The fourth group, Kaplow, Layne, and Pynoos (2014), argued for a unified approach to research and clinical intervention based on persistent complex bereavement disorder (PCBD), a "condition for further study," identified in the *Diagnostic and Statistical Manual* (American Psychiatric Association, 2013). PCBD identifies common grief constructs such as: separation distress, reactive distress, existential/identity related distress, and distress over circumstances of the death *and* the intensity and duration of these symptoms (Layne, Kaplow, & Pynoos, 2015). PCBD also has a traumatic death specifier that identifies when the death is sudden and violent. Layne et al. (2015) developed a 39-item Persistent Complex Bereavement Disorder Checklist–Youth Version that was written to correspond to the DSM-5 diagnostic criteria.

Separation distress is defined "as yearning or longing for the deceased." Toddlers may stand by a door waiting for the deceased to return, while older children may linger at the place where they last saw the deceased or become anxious when separated from an item closely associated with the deceased. It also includes intense sorrow or emotional pain that persists for 6 months or more (Kaplow, Layne, Pynoos, Cohen, & Lieberman, 2012, p. 233).

Reactive distress to the death encompasses the youth's difficulty accepting that the death has occurred due to cognitive immaturity or ineffective communication about death and inadequate support of the child by surviving caregivers (Kaplow et al., 2014). It may include the young person's struggles to remember positive aspects of the deceased and their relationship, anger that is acted out through disruptive behaviors, or "maladaptive appraisals about self relative to the loved one" (Kaplow et al., 2014, p. 254), such as, "It was my fault that my friend was so sad, he killed himself."

Existential/identity related distress identifies a cluster of symptoms that includes a desire to die in order to join the deceased. A 7-year-old client preferred to curl up under the headstone of his 2-year-old brother who he saw drown. Older survivors may engage in high-risk behaviors and substance use, viewing these behaviors fatalistically (e.g., "If I live, I live. If I die, I'll see my family member/friend"). It may also include difficulties trusting others, feeling isolated, and a sense that life lacks meaning (Kaplow et al., 2014).

Distress over circumstances of the death or *"traumatic death specifier"* refers to the characteristics extensively studied in the childhood traumatic grief literature including the overlapping of trauma and grief, the possible effects when the death has occurred under traumatic circumstances, and how traumatic grief is unique from PTSD (Kaplow et al., 2014).

Kaplow, Layne, and Pynoos (2014) exhorted researchers and clinicians to use a common language and share constructs in research and clinical work to refine our understanding of how typical grief and atypical grief may affect children and adolescents at different developmental stages. For the assessing clinician, this integrated paradigm would allow for identification of empirically supported symptoms that suggest a bereaved child or teen is in need of more intensive clinical attention. It would also streamline communication so that colleagues across disciplines and schools of thought can communicate quickly and effectively about the bereaved child who is in need of support.

The Clinician's Use of Self

Assessors meeting bereaved youth should consider their therapeutic use of self, means of assessing the client and his or her family, and use of language. Youth who have experienced loss are vulnerable; therefore, developing rapport consists of being warm, open, and curious, and this therapeutic imperative holds across contexts, modalities, and presenting concerns. The degree to which the clinician uses warmth and friendliness should match the goal of the relationship with the grieving child, who is likely to be more sensitive to loss in a relationship, even when the contact is brief. Therefore, if the relationship will only last as long as the assessment, the therapeutic stance might be warm but somewhat less engaged, as the assessor may be acting as a bridge to other services. If the assessor will also be providing treatment, he or she may choose to be more engaging and spend time building trust and rapport. These initial interactions are also guided by a practice of cultural humility, in which the assessor is open and inviting to important aspects of the family's cultural milieu.

The assessment begins when the therapist meets the client and family for the first time with a warm greeting and simple orientation to the clinical space, the interview process, and the goals of the meeting. When considering the length of an initial session, "briefer may be better," particularly with young children. It is more productive to have 45 minutes of positive inter-action and information gathering than 90 minutes in which exhaustion and irritability occur.

Lastly, terms such as *death, dying*, and *died* should be used instead of *passed away, passed on*, or *lost*, even when this may not be the language of the family, as these terms are clear and unambiguous (Goldman, 2014). The clinician's language and comfort level when asking about the family's experience signals that he or she can tolerate painful stories and high levels of strong emotion.

The Tripartite Model for Assessing Bereaved Children and Adolescents

Webb's (2010) work with children and families in crisis (including those who have experienced loss) spans more than 20 years and has had substantial influence on clinicians and researchers. Her three-part, transactional assessment of the bereaved child covers three domains: (a) individual factors, (b) death-related factors, and (c) family/social/religious/cultural factors.

Individual Factors

Individual factors include developmental age, temperament, spirituality, coping styles, and mental and physical health ascertained through a medical history.

Temperament

Temperament generally refers to the biological predisposition to be more or less sensitive, reactivity to stimulus and stress, and the time required to return to a calm state. Webb (2010) identified temperament utilizing the classic Thomas and Chess (1977) typology of the difficult, easy, and slow-to-warm up temperament. This is ascertained by questioning a caregiver about the child or adolescent's infancy and early childhood. Children with a difficult temperament do not sleep or eat on a schedule, are sensitive to change, and struggle with separation from caregivers throughout early childhood. Other children will have what is described as an easy temperament, and, prior to the loss or death, are described as happy babies and toddlers who slept and ate regularly and were able to manage change in their routine. Older children and teens as well as caregivers may be questioned directly about emotional reactivity (e.g., before the deceased died, did you tend to have intense emotional reactions? Do you find that you are frequently overwhelmed by strong emotions? When you are experiencing a strong feeling, does it take you longer than other people your age to calm down? Do you pick up easily on the emotions or stress of others?).

Spirituality

Emerging research suggests that an adolescent's personal connection to the creator, nature, or the universe, referred to as *personal devotion*, is "the most robust protective factor" identified in adolescent physical and mental health (Miller, 2006). Although shaped by the religious and cultural beliefs of the family and community, personal devotion is a discrete personal trait that is more protective than social support or frequently identified features of religiosity, such as denomination or attendance at religious services. It is closely associated with spiritual coping and daily spiritual experience (Miller, 2006; Miller & Gur, 2002).

Mental Health

Mental health is important to assess for commonly occurring mental health issues, both past and current. This includes asking about worries; fears; obsessive thoughts; compulsive behaviors; anxiety associated with social situations; longstanding struggles with concentration, attention, and following rules; and asking about historical or ongoing traumatic events in the client's life, both past and current. If there is a traumatic aspect to the death, the assessor should ask about symptoms related to the major three domains of traumatic stress: (a) reexperiencing (Do memories of what happened pop into your head unexpectedly?), (b) hyperarousal (Do little things bother you more now than they did before? Do you have more trouble paying attention since this event took place?), and (c) avoidance (Do you stay away from people, places, things or emotions that are connected to the bad thing that happened?).

Clinicians in mental health care settings triaging youth referred for mood and anxiety issues must also expand their assessment lens to explore losses, grief, and trauma. For example, a 9-year-old girl presented to a mental health clinic generalized worries, including failure at school, fears of the future, and concerns about the safety of her family. She struggled to settle at night and had not slept in her own bed for a year. With a focus on anxiety symptoms only, she was evaluated and referred to a program for school-age kids with anxiety. Another clinician who worked with her sibling recognized the girl as part of a family who had several close family deaths over a 2-year period, including the sudden death of the child's mother. The reassessment included a look at the family's grief-and-loss history. The clinician confirmed that her preoccupation and worry about health and the future were well-founded. Although she met criteria for generalized anxiety disorder, her lived experiences contraindicated her participation in an anxiety group with peers who had not had an immediate family member die. The revised treatment plan focused on family therapy with the little girl and her surviving caregiver to understand her worries and fears from a bereavement-informed perspective.

Depression can occur alongside bereavement in a child or adolescent, but is not typical (Dillen & Fontaine, 2009; Melhem et al., 2011) When both depression and grief are present, the child or teen's ability to function day to day can be significantly impaired; the path to recovery is not as positive (APA, 2013) and may require the involvement of a physician. Indicators to watch for in children and adolescents include depressed and/or irritable mood most of the day, every day for a 2-week period or longer; low energy and fatigue; not sleeping or sleeping too much; weight loss (more than 5% of body weight in a month); or, with young children, failing to gain expected weight; struggles staying focused; and loss of interest in previously engaging activities, such as dance, sports, or hobbies.

Medical History

Webb's (2010) medical history–taking includes asking about illness, injury, and hospitalizations because they can constitute experiences that may compromise the child's ability to adapt to a current loss. Chronic medical conditions are stressors that may tax a grieving child's personal resources. Expanding the medical history to include medically intrusive procedures is important because painful or frightening treatments can themselves traumatize, and may complicate a child's traumatic grief (Children's Hospital of Philadelphia, 2016; Kazak, Schneider, & Kassam-Adams, 2009). Additionally, it is important to keep in mind that what a child might consider intrusive may not be seen as such to adults or health-care providers (e.g., an injection may seem like a mundane procedure, but may be a significant incident to a child, especially if the child was held down for the procedure).

In the course of investigating individual characteristics, Webb utilized the *Global Assessment of Functioning*, a subjective measure of functioning that has been used in adult mental health for several years (Webb, 2010). The *Child Global Assessment Scale* (C-GAS) is a comparable measure adapted for use with children under the age of 18 (Shaffer et al., 1983). The C-GAS requires the clinician to rate the child's current levels of functioning at home, school, and with peers on a scale of 1 through 100. It can be a helpful triaging tool, and can measure change in the child or adolescent's symptoms and levels of impairment over time.

Coping Skills and Adjustment

The tripartite model also looks at the child or adolescent's adjustment to home, school, and within his or her peer relationships, and extracurricular activities. This can be a challenging line of questioning because it requires the child, adolescent, and caregivers to reflect on preloss coping skills. Similar to the use of the C-GAS, alternatives to verbal questions, such as clinician-completed rating scales, paper-and-pencil self-reports, and art-based activities, are methods of evaluation that yield important information and keep the young client engaged in early stages of the therapeutic relationship.

Death-Related Factors

Evaluating factors related to the deceased is central to determining the risk of grief complications. Understanding the interaction of these individual, family, and community factors allows for identification of potential targets for intervention.

"The Death Surround": How Death Is Communicated to the Child

Rando's term *the death surround* is a helpful concept for assessing event characteristics. It refers to details of where and when the death took place, how and why it occurred, and how much time survivors had to prepare (Rando, 1991). *How* the surviving adults respond to the death and *what* they tell or do not tell the child can also have a profound impact. For example, one 15-year-old boy is haunted by the memory of his mother collapsing on the floor, overwhelmed by grief when police notified the family of his father's death in a car collision. The boy was 12 at the time. "I lost both parents that night," he said.

Well-intentioned adults may use language that intensifies the child's distress. For example, a school principal told a group of grieving students that a classmate who died from a suicidal overdose "went to sleep and never woke up." A week later, the sleep-deprived parents of a second grader at that school reported to their family doctor that their son was too terrified to sleep because he thought he would die. Evenings had become unbearable for him, and the family was urgently referred for treatment. Goldman (2014) emphasized how a cliché like this can inadvertently impede the grief process and that accurate language is essential.

Depending on the age of the child or adolescent, specific aspects of the death can affect how the young survivor experiences it. These characteristics include:

- Whether the death was sudden; expected; viewed by adults as appropriate, such as the long-anticipated death from cancer (Webb, 2010); or prolonged and accompanied by physical or emotional suffering (Walsh, 2007).
- The extent to which death might have been prevented.
- The presence of pain, violence, and/or trauma.
- Stigma related to the circumstances and/or cause of death (Webb, 2010; Walsh, 2007), such as the death of the deceased deemed a "homegrown terrorist" while committing a crime against his or her country of origin or on foreign soil.

- Whether death is unconfirmed and the loss is considered ambiguous because the deceased is missing (Walsh, 2007), as is the case with the many children and families of missing Aboriginal women in Canada who are assumed to have died but their bodies have not been recovered.
- Pile-up effects: children and families who sustain multiple deaths, traumas, losses, and transitions, including immigration, war, and natural disasters (Walsh, 2007).

Contact With the Deceased

Webb identifies "four points of contact" when children and adolescents are in the presence of the deceased. These are (a) when the person is dying, (b) viewing the body, (c) attending ceremonies, and (d) being at the grave or mausoleum (Webb, 2010). The decision to include children is often strongly influenced by culture, the age of the child, and the child's temperament.

Expression of Good-Bye

The literalness of a child's thinking makes the finality of death difficult to comprehend (Webb, 2010). In Western/European cultures, youth are often provided opportunities to have physical contact with the deceased, and this provides the child with a degree of control and self-efficacy in a life event that is characterized by powerlessness (Webb, 2010). At a viewing that preceded the funeral service, the sibling of a 12-year-old killed in a bike accident repeatedly touched the lining of his brother's casket, his brother's hands, face, and hair, remarking, "He feels so cold and hard." Later, he unobtrusively tucked a note in next to his brother but would not talk about its content. For this child, physically interacting with his brother's body made his sibling's sudden and unexpected death more real, giving him the opportunity to say good-bye in a deeply personal way. Other children overtly avoid the casket or stand nearby, but do not want to touch it and do not seem to require the reassuring presence of an adult or close friend. Adults should keep in mind that children and adolescents should never to be forced to do more than what is comfortable for them.

It is important to consider that the need to "say good-bye" by seeing and touching the body is informed by the child's developmental stage, the perceptions of family members, the family's culture, and spiritual beliefs. In some Aboriginal cultures, the dead are understood to always be present with the living. For example, two sisters, 4 and 6, who were members of the Anishinaabe or Ojibway First Nations, were referred by their non-Aboriginal child welfare worker. The professional was worried that the little girls were experiencing "hallucinations," demonstrating early signs of severe mental illness because they incorporated their 2-year-old brother, who died 9 months previously, into their play. The sisters attended the second play-therapy session with their maternal grandmother. She had no concerns about how her granddaughters were coping with their brother's death. "In our culture, the dead are always with us," she explained. "Of course they play with him. This is how we understand death."

Grief Reactions

Assessing the grief responses of the bereaved child includes exploring his or her beliefs, feelings, behaviors, and the nature of his or her relationship with the deceased at the time of, and following, the death. Goldman (2014) and Lowenstein (2006) provided a variety of creative language-based, expressive art- and play-based assessment techniques to facilitate this process.

Gathering the parents/caregiver's perceptions and collateral data is critical, often done through separate interviews. Alternatively, a family meeting with parents and children together can yield even more valuable information, especially when members are grieving the death of someone in, or close to, the family. The family interview allows the clinician to observe the interaction of the family members, the communication styles in the family, and the nonverbal responses of family members to the stories and descriptions being shared. However, the implementation of a family session with children intimidates many family therapists who may be concerned about losing control of the therapy or exposing young children to topics or emotions that would be harmful. Children often act out the stresses of the family system. If the child who is reacting to family stress is treated in isolation, little headway can occur in the child's therapy unless the underlying family dynamics are also addressed (Rabenstein & Harris, 2017). Children's reactions can be closely related to those of their parents and other family members, and most children rely upon their parents for a sense of safety and security when there is uncertainty or stress (Webb, 2010).

Family/Social/Religious/Cultural Factors

Grief "reverberates among the clan" (Kissane, 2014, p. 6). For this reason, Webb (2010) includes the family's religion and cultural beliefs as a critical context in which to understand the bereaved child. Recently, psychiatry has come to acknowledge this as well. Almost everywhere that bereavement is discussed in the *Diagnostic and Statistical Manual for Mental Disorders* (DSM-5), clinicians are directed to evaluate whether the "intensity, quality, and persistence of grief reactions exceeds what normally might be expected, when cultural, religious, or age appropriate norms are taken into account" (APA, 2013, p. 287). Religious and cultural beliefs permeate the intergenerational family system, shaping how family members express strong emotion and reach out to one another. The transmission of "either compassionate support or avoidant silence" can be traced across generations (Kissane, 2014, p. 6).

The functioning of the bereaved family—particularly the child or adolescent's primary attachment figures—contributes to the child's likelihood of being at risk (Cohen et al., 2006; Kaplow et al., 2014; Worden, 1999; Webb, 2010) and is one of the better-established indicators in the field of child bereavement.

Conclusion

A thorough assessment of the grieving child, adolescent, his or her family, and the culture and community of which they are members, is a clinician's critical first step towards understanding the child. This assessment provides essential information that identifies the minority of particularly vulnerable bereaved young people who are at risk for experiencing significant distress related to their grief and who are in need of professional support. A comprehensive evaluation determines whether treatment is necessary, and, if so, where subsequent interventions should be focused. Finally, these early moments of contact provide the clinician with the chance to create a supportive relationship with the young client and family that either establishes a basis for their future therapeutic work, or provides a positive counseling experience from which a future clinician and child can build.

Discussion Questions

1. Most children and adolescents who have had a family member die experience normative grief. Chose an age group and list the characteristics of typical versus atypical grief and choose a course of action for each.
2. Define Rando's concept of *the death surround*. Why is assessing the death surround important when working with a grieving child or teen?
3. How can a family's cultural beliefs affect the bereaved children in the family?

References

American Academy of Child and Adolescent Psychiatry. (2013). *Facts for families: Children and grief, No. 8*. Retrieved from www.aacap.org/AACAP/Families_and_Youth/Facts_for_Families/FFF-Guide/Children-And-Grief-008.aspx

American Psychiatric Association. (2013). *Diagnostic and statistical manual of mental disorders* (5th ed.). Arlington, VA: American Psychiatric Association.

Children's Hospital of Philadelphia, Pediatric Traumatic Stress Website. (2016). www.chop.edu/centers-programs/center-pediatric-traumatic-stress

Cohen, J. A., Mannarino, A. P., & Deblinger, E. (2006). *Treating trauma and traumatic grief in children and adolescents*. New York, NY: The Guilford Press.

Cohen, J. A., Mannarino, A. P., Greenberg, T., Padlo, S., & Shipley, C. (2002). Childhood traumatic grief: concepts and controversies. *Trauma, Violence and Abuse, 3*, 307–327.

Dahl, R. A. (2004). Adolescent brain development: A period of vulnerabilities and opportunities. *Annals of New York Academy of Science, 1021*, 1–22. doi:10.1196/annals.1308.001

Dillen, L., & Fontaine, J. R. R. (2009). Confirming the distinctiveness of complicated grief from depression and anxiety among adolescents. *Death Studies, 33,* 437–461.

Dyregrov, A. (2013). *Normal and complicated grief in children and adolescents.* Presentation in Tampere Finland, April 12, 2013.

Goldman, L. (2014). *Life & loss: A guide to help grieving children* (3rd ed.). New York, NY: Routledge.

Kaplow, J. B., Layne, C. M., & Pynoos, R. S. (2014). Persistent complex bereavement disorder as a call to action. *Stresspoints,* International Society of Traumatic Stress Studies. Retrieved from www.istss.org/education-research/traumatic-stresspoints/2014-january/persistent-complex-bereavement-disorder-as-a-call.aspx

Kaplow, J. B., Layne, C. M., Pynoos, R. S., Cohen, J., & Lieberman, A. (2012). DSM-V diagnostic criteria for bereavement-related disorders in children and adolescents: Developmental considerations. *Psychiatry, 75,* 243–265.

Kazak, A., Schneider, S., Kassam-Adams, N. (2009). Pediatric medical traumatic stress. In M. Roberts & R. Steele (Eds.), *Handbook of pediatric psychology* (4th ed., pp. 205–215). New York, NY: The Guilford Press.

Kissane, D. W. (2014). Family grief. In D. W. Kissane & F. Parnes (Eds.), *Bereavement care for families.* New York, NY: Routledge.

Layne, C. M., Kaplow, J. B., & Pynoos, R. S. (2015, January). Persistent complex grief disorder (PCGD) checklist–Youth Version. ResearchGate. Retrieved from www.researchgate.net/publication/273460715_Persistent_Complex_Bereavement_Disorder_PCBD_Checklist_-_Youth_Version

Lowenstein, L. (2006). *Creative interventions for bereaved children.* Toronto, ON: Champion Press.

Melhem, N., Porta, G., Shamseddeen, W., Walker Payne, M., & Brent, D. (2011). Grief in children and adolescents bereaved by sudden parental death. *Archives of General Psychiatry, 68,* 911–919. doi:10.1001/archgenpsychiatry.2011.101

Melhem, N. M., Moritz, G., Walker, M., Shear, K., & Brent, D. (2007). Phenomenology and correlates of complicated grief in children and adolescents. *Journal of the American Academy of Child and Adolescent Psychiatry, 46*(4), 493–499.

Miller, L. (2006). Spirituality, health and medical care of children and adolescents. *Southern Medical Journal, 99,* 1164.

Miller, L., & Gur, M. (2002). Religiosity, physical maturation and depression in girls. *Journal of the American Academy of Child and Adolescent Psychiatry, 41,* 206–214.

Prigerson, H. G., Horowitz, M. J., Jacobs, S. C., Parkes, C. M., Asian, M., Goodkin, K., & Maciejewski, P. K. (2009). Consensus criteria for traumatic grief: A preliminary empirical test. *British Journal of Psychiatry, 174,* 67–73.

Rabenstein, S., & Harris, D. (2017). Family therapy and traumatic losses. In N. Thompson, G. R. Cox, & R. G. Stevenson (Eds.), *Handbook of traumatic loss: A guide to theory and practice.* New York, NY: Routledge.

Rando, T. (1991). *How to go on living when someone you love dies.* New York, NY: Bantam Books.

Schuurman, D. (2017, April). *An uneasy alliance? The integration of trauma and bereavement.* Presentation at the Association for Death Education and Counseling 39th Annual Conference, Portland, Oregon.

Shaffer, D., Gould, M. S., Brasic, J., Aluwahlia, R., Rothman, D., Sorrells, J., & Heldman, P. (1983). Children's global assessment scale (CGAS). *Archives of General Psychiatry, 40,* 1228–1231.

Shear, M. K., Monk, T., Houck, P., Melhem, N., Frank, E., Reynolds, C., & Sillowash, R. (2007). An attachment-based model of complicated grief including the role of avoidance. *European Archives of Psychiatry and Clinical Neuroscience, 257*, 453–461.

Shear, M. K., Simon, N., Wall, M., Zisook, S., Neimeyer, R., Duan, N., & Keshaviah, A. (2011). Complicated grief and related bereavement issues for DSM-5. *Depression and Anxiety, 28,* 103–117.

Speece, M., & Brent, S. (1996). The development of children's understanding of death. In C. A. Corr & D. M. Corr (Eds.), *Handbook of childhood death and bereavement.* New York, NY: Springer.

Thomas, A., & Chess, S. (1977). *Temperament and development.* New York, NY: Brunner/ Mazel.

University of Rochester, Medical Center, Health Encyclopedia. (2016). *A child's concept of death.* Retrieved from www.urmc.rochester.edu/Encyclopedia/Content. aspx?ContentTypeID=90&ContentID=P03044

Walsh, F. R., (2007). Traumatic loss and major disasters: Strengthening family and community resilience. *Family Process, 46*, 207–227.

Webb, N. (Ed.) (2010). *Helping bereaved children* (3rd ed.). New York, NY: The Guilford Press.

Wolfelt, A. (1996). *Healing the bereaved child: Grief gardening, growth through grief and other touchstones for caregivers.* Fort Collins, CO: Companion Press.

Worden, J. W. (1999). Comparing parent loss with sibling loss. *Death Studies, 23*(1), 1–15.

4 Disenfranchised Grief Among Bereaved Youth

Carine Blin and Christine Jonas-Simpson

Notable thanatologist Kenneth Doka coined the phrase *disenfranchised grief* to describe grief that is not openly acknowledged, socially sanctioned, or publicly mourned (Doka, 1989). Although much of the literature focuses on adult disenfranchised grief, bereaved children also experience the effects of disenfranchisement. In the same way adults seek validation when they grieve, children also need to find acceptance in their expressions of grief; otherwise, normal responses to grief, such as feelings of anger, sadness, loneliness, and guilt, can become intensified (Doka, 1989).

Remaining attuned to children's grief over time is particularly important since children revisit loss at different stages of development (Baker, Sedney, & Gross, 1992), often maintaining an attachment with the deceased that provides a space for transforming loss and integrating the experience through continuing bonds (Klass, Silverman, & Nickman, 1996). When they experience disenfranchised loss, children can be resilient and creative in navigating the pain, particularly when they are supported in their search to make sense of the loss (Jonas-Simpson, Steele, Granek, Davies, & O'Leary, 2015). When caring adults are present to model grief, acknowledge it, and legitimize their individual responses, the experience of loss in childhood can lead to greater capacity for empathy, growth, and understanding (Jonas-Simpson et al., 2015).

Without the spoken or unspoken approval of others, it is difficult to normalize grief, to express strong reactions, or to feel validated in exploring creative and meaningful ways to adapt. Permission to grieve helps us come to terms with the difficult and sometimes overwhelming emotions we encounter amidst significant loss. Whether disenfranchised grief happens as a result of omission or from a conscious act of renunciation, it impedes an individual's effort to process grief. When social systems act out of indifference or misunderstanding, causing some aspect of a person's grief to be ignored, disenfranchised grief is a result of an empathic failure (Neimeyer & Jordan, 2002). Disenfranchised grief can also be a more intentional process of disavowal whereby society determines who has a right to grieve, as well as when and how it should be expressed (Corr, 2002). Attig (2004) stated that "disenfranchising messages actively discount, dismiss, disapprove, discourage, invalidate, and delegitimate the experiences and efforts of grieving. And disenfranchising behaviors interfere with the exercise of the right to grieve by withholding permission, disallowing, constraining, hindering, and even prohibiting it" (p. 198).

Factors Causing Disenfranchised Grief

In his original volume, Doka (1989) outlined three factors that caused grief to be disenfranchised: (a) the exclusion of the griever (e.g., children, the elderly); (b) lack of recognition of the type of relationship (e.g., ex-spouse, extramarital affair); and (c) lack of acknowledgement of the type of loss (e.g., miscarriage, pet). Doka (2002a) later expanded on these factors to include: (a) the type of death (e.g., a stigmatized death, such as suicide or homicide) and (b) ways in which individuals grieve (e.g., too much or too little emotion).

The Nature of the Griever

Children, especially young children or those with disabilities, are frequently excluded as grievers. There is a common misconception that children are not capable of grief because of their limited understanding of death (Crenshaw & Lee, 2010); however, children understand death in varying ways from a very young age. Bowlby's (1960) research revealed that even very young children with a strong attachment to their mothers would become frantic when they were separated, just as a bereaved adult would react with strong emotions facing the death of a loved one (Bowlby, 1960). Through cognitive development and lived experience, children gain a mature understanding of death as irreversible, universal, and inevitable.

Piaget's seminal work (1954) outlined cognitive stages of development in children, which provide an instructive framework for explaining how they perceive death as they mature (Goldman, 2005; Webb, 2010). Young children (ages 2–7) expect the deceased to return because they often believe death is temporary. Their egocentric worldview places them at the center of everything that happens; consequently, they are prone to *magical thinking*, believing their own thoughts or words may have caused the death (Goldman, 2005; Webb, 2010).

With a burgeoning curiosity and an increased desire for realistic information, school-age children (ages 7–12) form a deeper understanding about the finality, and even the universality, of death, often displaying more logical thoughts as well as increased fears and anxieties related to death (Goldman, 2005; Webb, 2010). By the time they become teenagers, children learn to view death as a natural process, but they continue to have difficulty imagining the possibility of their own deaths (Goldman, 2005; Webb, 2010).

While the developmental stages are important to understand, it is also helpful to recognize the dynamic concept of continuing bonds by which children, even young children, form a relationship with the deceased.

Jonas-Simpson et al. (2015) found that while the evolving nature of the bond with the deceased baby sibling reflected the child's normal development, it was more than that; the relationship was uniquely crafted, emergent, and changing over time. These researchers noted that this important nuance— that is, the unique relationship each child has with the deceased that evolves over time—is important to acknowledge and make space for beyond the time that is dedicated for family rituals and traditions (Jonas-Simpson et al., 2015, p. 246).

Adults may discount children's grief because of their limited verbal capacity and differences in how children react to loss. Children may find it difficult to communicate feelings or thoughts about death; consequently, their reluctance to talk may be misconstrued as an absence of strong emotions or understandings related to the loss. Language and euphemisms around the topic of death may also add to a child's confusion when explanations are not presented in a clear and age-appropriate manner. Webb (2010) provided the example of a 4-year-old girl who heard the adults in her midst refer to the *loss* of her father; she understandably came to the conclusion that her father was simply lost and looking for the way home.

When children's behaviors differ from adults' typical reactions to loss, their responses can also be misconstrued. For example, children's inability to tolerate the pain of grief for long periods of time (Webb, 2010) may look like avoidance, or acting out aggressively may simply appear as rebellion, rather than an expression of the deep underlying pain of grief (Crenshaw & Lee, 2010). A limited understanding of death, undeveloped communication skills, and differences in how children express their grief do not mean that young people are not experiencing intense reactions to a loss.

The Nature of the Relationship

A child's grief may be minimized when strong relationships forged by the child are not considered significant (Crenshaw, 2002). In Western society, rules regarding appropriate grieving and mourning customs are generally limited to the death of a close family member, regardless of the attachment. In reality, the bond between the bereaved and the deceased is a primary factor in determining the intensity of the grief, whether or not the loss involves next of kin. In the case of children, disenfranchised grief may not directly result from the sanctioning of a particular relationship as it often does with adults (as in the case of gay partners, extramarital affairs, ex-spouses), but, rather, from a lack of awareness of the importance of the relationship in the child's life (Crenshaw, 2002). In the case of divorce, for example, strong attachments may exist between the child and the absent parent or the new partner of one of the parents (Crenshaw & Lee, 2010). Childhood friendships, adolescent romances, and bonds with teachers or foster parents may also represent deep attachments that can be minimized when adults fail to recognize the significance of these relationships and thus, the child's experience of grief (Crenshaw, 2002; Crenshaw & Lee, 2010). Adults may also overlook childhood fixations with rock stars or other famous people who signify strong connections and whose deaths can evoke painful responses in children and teens.

The Nature of the Loss

Children are also vulnerable when faced with disenfranchised losses that are not considered significant. The most common example in a child's life is the loss of a pet, which is often the first encounter with death and the rupture of a cherished relationship. Adults can unwittingly discount the magnitude of such a loss, justifying their response by reasoning that it is "only an animal," or that the pet is easily replaceable. By doing so, they risk disrespecting the strong emotional response that children experience when they bond with a family pet (Crenshaw & Lee, 2010).

An underdeveloped area of research is the disenfranchised grief experienced by children following the loss of a baby sibling as a result of perinatal death during pregnancy, at birth, or within 1 year after birth. When parents experience the death of an infant, disenfranchisement occurs as a result of the "juxtaposition of personal feelings of extreme grief with society's dismissal of such a short-lived or even 'unborn' life" (Lang et al., 2011, p. 184). Likewise, when children experience the death of a baby sibling, "because the children have very little or no physical contact with the infant sibling, some people may consider the loss after perinatal death as minimal" (Jonas-Simpson et al., 2015, p. 243). Like parents, siblings anticipate the birth of a new baby and look forward to welcoming him or her into the family. When a baby dies, feelings of loss are intense; disappointment, sadness, and longing are compounded by the need to navigate social forces that do not validate those reactions.

Other disenfranchised losses include non-death related losses that affect children and youth, such as placement in foster care, divorce, moving to a new neighborhood, and for a young child, even the loss of a transitional object, such as a favorite blanket or stuffed toy. These examples may represent a major disruption and the severing of important bonds and attachment relationships. In the case of foster care, children "often are moved from home to home in the foster care system, sometimes on short notice, with little time to say adequate goodbyes. These children leave behind a trail of broken relationships and a huge reservoir of disenfranchised grief" (Crenshaw & Lee, 2010). These types of losses may result in complications related to trauma, grief, or both.

The Circumstance of Death

Doka (2002a) identified the circumstance of the death as a key factor influencing disenfranchised grief. In instances when death is stigmatized, such as suicide and abortion, support from others can be withheld and the bereaved may refrain from seeking consolation from fear of being judged. When children are affected by suicide, their questions can be dismissed because adults feel too uncomfortable talking about the subject as a result of their own feelings of shame or confusion. Furthermore, many adults believe children are not capable of understanding what suicide means despite the fact that "children as young as 6 know what it means to 'kill oneself,' even if they do not understand the word 'suicide'" (McCormack & Webb, 2010, p. 112).

Admittedly, explaining suicide to a child can be difficult, but it is important to speak openly to allow the child to process the loss without feeling excluded (McCormack & Webb, 2010). Teenage abortion is another example of loss that is disenfranchised because it is seen as a conscious choice rather than an unavoidable outcome. Abortion carries the added burden of judgement and social stigma at a time in an adolescent's life when fitting in socially is very important. As a result, "grief after elective abortion is uniquely poignant because it is largely hidden" (Angelo, 1996, p. 43).

The Nature of the Response

Ways in which individuals respond to significant loss can also be disenfranchised (Doka, 2002a; Corr, 2002). Individuals who express their pain openly may not receive sufficient comfort and empathy because those around them are uncomfortable with strong emotions. They may be told they need to "move on" or "get over it." When children release emotions in their effort to process the powerful feelings that accompany significant loss, they, too, are at risk of being misunderstood and shut down. In some cases, children may respond to loss by "acting out aggressively, making it difficult for parents to be attuned to the underlying pain of their grief" (Crenshaw & Lee, 2010, p. 93), and, therefore, providing the comfort and guidance needed. Conversely, individuals who respond by controlling emotions and keeping busy may have support withheld because they do not appear to be suffering. They may be admonished for not displaying an appropriate expression of genuine mourning. Likewise, avoidant behavior in children may be misinterpreted by family members to indicate an absence of grief, failing to understand that children may disengage in order to protect themselves when they are unable to tolerate the intense demands of grief (Crenshaw & Lee, 2010). The Dual Process Model, which outlines the fluctuations between *loss orientation* and *restoration orientation* (Stroebe & Schut, 1999), describes a natural oscillation between expressions of grief and engaging in everyday activities, which is helpful in observing how children grieve. Children tend to naturally alternate between these two orientations; however, this natural rhythm may be disrupted if there is a lack of understanding about how they are living with and expressing their unique experience of loss.

When a child loses someone close, a parent or sibling for example, the importance of continuing bonds and attachment to the deceased can also be overlooked, causing disenfranchised grief (Webb, 2010). In a study of children whose baby sibling died, Jonas-Simpson et al. (2015) noted the importance of an evolving sibling relationship even in the absence of a physical presence. "All the children connected with and integrated their deceased baby sibling into their lives in some way; parents confirmed this finding. The children described being attuned with their sibling's spirit through signs, symbols, and tangible objects" (2015, p. 246). The children and youth were able to navigate their experience of loss and make sense of it, particularly as they matured and revisited it with a greater understanding of death and the process of grief. One of the participants, an adolescent, talked about a continued relationship with the baby sibling who had died, and how comfortable it felt to acknowledge his presence in the context of his shared family story, but also how difficult it was to talk with others outside the family who were not able to acknowledge his feelings (Jonas-Simpson et al., 2014, 2015).

Self-Disenfranchised Grief

Building on the work of Doka, Kauffman (1989) identified *self-disenfranchised grief* as a form of grief precipitated by the bereaved individual rather than social forces. Self-disenfranchised grief is a way for children to protect themselves against *emotional flooding*, which is the fear that they might not be able to stop the flow if they begin to release feelings of sadness and pain (Crenshaw, 2002). Children may also fail to acknowledge their own feelings of pain to protect their parents or siblings if they sense that family members are not able to cope (Crenshaw, 2002). When children have experienced grief in the past that was not acknowledged, they may not want to risk exposing their feelings in order to avoid the shame that accompanies disenfranchised loss. This sets a dangerous precedent, particularly in childhood, that risks becoming a pattern of self-initiated disenfranchised grief when faced with subsequent losses later in life (Kauffman, 2002).

Social Forces Influencing Disenfranchised Grief in Children

When children do not feel sanctioned in their grief, "they are less likely to be able to influence their social environments than are bereaved adults" (Corr, 2000, p.8). Consequently, social forces, primarily the family context, but also the school environment and the broader cultural framework, have a significant effect in shaping children's experience of grief.

Family Context

Parents and other family members may be reluctant to share their own grief or talk about the death in an attempt to shield children from pain (Jonas-Simpson & Blin, 2015). Alternatively, parents, especially in the case of child loss, may be so wrapped up in their own grief they lack the energy and emotional strength to support their children's grief; in response, children may hide their feelings in order to minimize their parents' suffering. When parents and family members believe the child is too young to understand, "the child may have no one to ask questions about the deceased, or, in extreme cases, the name of the deceased family member may not even be mentioned in the presence of the child" (Crenshaw & Lee, 2010, p. 92).

Furthermore, children may be excluded from adult mourning rituals, such as funerals and memorial services, in order to protect them from witnessing painful emotions and as a way to avoid having to explain death. One bereaved father in Jonas-Simpson et al.'s (2015) research documentary rationalized the decision he and his wife made to exclude their two children, ages 2 and 5, from attending a small memorial service in honour of their brother who was stillborn, nor did they have the siblings come to the hospital to see their brother. At the time, the parents felt their young children might be overwhelmed, frightened, and confused. Years later, however, the father acknowledged that both siblings had expressed regret at not having had the chance to meet their baby brother. They had no memories of him despite the fact that he enjoyed a special place in the family narrative, a spiritual presence shared through conversation and personal rituals the family had created to honor him.

School Context

Once a child enters school, teachers and peers assume an important role in determining how grief is acknowledged and supported. Children, especially adolescents, do not want to appear to be different. Experiencing a significant loss sets them apart, particularly among their peers who may have little or no personal experience of death-related loss and who may or may not know how to respond in a supportive and understanding way. Unlike adults, who may seek comfort in talking with friends, bereaved children may feel trepidation about the idea of talking about their emotions with other children (Webb, 2010).

By contrast, adolescents tend to grieve with their peers rather than turn to their families, a coping strategy that is consistent with their developing sense of identity and autonomy (Crenshaw & Lee, 2010). When confronted with death, some teens intentionally hide their grief in order to appear more adult-like, but in doing so they risk sacrificing support from caring and well-intentioned adults who may assume their support is not needed. Furthermore, teens may unwittingly invite criticism from adults who fail to recognize their behavior as appropriate. The resulting "double jeopardy," a concept identified by Oltjenbruns (1996), serves to intensify the experience of disenfranchised loss and inhibits the grief process. Regardless of the age of the child, if teachers and staff are not knowledgeable about grief, comfortable talking about death, or sensitive to the emotional well-being of children and youth living with loss, it is difficult for them to moderate the effects of isolation and minimize the risk of disenfranchised grief. One of the challenges for schools is to ensure more consistent training to provide teachers with skills and confidence to talk about grief as well as support for more formal death education within school curriculums (Holland, 2008).

Cultural Context

In the broader cultural context, unique cultural aspects may accentuate disenfranchised aspects of mourning rituals and practices when the prevailing Western culture does not share in those beliefs. For youth from various ethnic backgrounds, the tensions caused as a result of straddling diverse cultures, that of their parents and the world of their peers, can add another layer of pain or stress (Crenshaw & Lee, 2010). Latin cultures are more open about expressing grief and more inclusive of children in their mourning traditions. In Mexican culture, for example, the lively and colourful celebration held on the Day of the Dead to honor the deceased has no equivalent in North American society in which funerals often mark the end of any formal remembrance ceremony for family members who have died.

What We Can Do to Support Grieving Children

Children witness death in some form from an early age even if it does not directly touch their lives. When we insulate children, we forego important opportunities to teach them in ways that can enhance their ability to cope when they face the death of a loved one (Silverman, 2000). By opening the channels of communication and personal expression, nurturing resilience, modeling grief, and offering the possibility of participating in ritual and commemoration, adults can support bereaved children by validating their experience as genuine and acceptable and by teaching them that death is a natural, if mysterious and sometimes painful, part of life.

Open Communication

Often, children's grief is disenfranchised as a result of our own uneasiness with the subject of death and dying. "Frequently, our difficulty in talking with children about death stems from the fact that we have never acknowledged our own anxieties and discomfort with these issues" (Silverman, 2000, p. 4). Death is not an easy topic to address. However, talking more transparently about our own feelings so that children are comfortable posing questions, answering their questions honestly, providing enough detail without over-whelming, and using straightforward language rather than euphemisms all help to validate children's grief. According to Silverman (2000), even the act of naming the experience is helpful to a grieving child. "A name legitimates and demystifies an event. It makes something real, gives a sense of owner-ship, and verifies for the child his or her ability as an observer and experience as a mourner and that sharing experiences and feelings is valued" (p. 2).

Communicating thoughts and feelings through creative expression is another helpful way for children to articulate their experience of grief and continuing bonds through art in a variety of forms (Jonas-Simpson et al., 2014, 2015). Adults can help offset feelings of disenfranchisement by inviting children to explore grief through artistic forms such as drawing, dance, journaling, and poetry writing. Younger children, who often find it difficult to talk about death, may find an outlet for their feelings through drawing or painting.

Nurturing Resilience

When adults are willing to engage in meaningful interactions about the topic of death, they help nurture resilience in children so that they are better able to tolerate the negative feelings they encounter. Children learn that they *can make choices* that help them maintain a positive worldview even as they struggle with difficult emotions. Furthermore, fostering resilience helps children acquire the knowledge, problem-solving skills, and good decision-making they need to come to terms with their grief and to face difficult times in the future with self-assurance. They learn that loss can lead to growth and transformation, and they discover in themselves a greater capacity for empathy and caring that can have a positive impact on their world (Goldman, 2005).

Modeling Grief

Children are keen observers. They learn from watching how adults behave. Adults can help by modeling grief and mourning openly, allowing children the opportunity to see that feelings of fear, anger, and sadness are normal responses to the pain and suffering that accompany significant loss (Silverman, 2000; Jonas-Simpson et al., 2015). When a child sees that it is "okay" to cry and "okay" to feel angry when they are grieving because they witness their parents openly expressing their own pain and when they see their parents comforting each other in grief, children learn how to accommodate loss, how to accept it, and how to support others. Realizing that adults have strong reactions they are comfortable conveying gives children confidence in trusting their own reactions when they, too, feel overwhelmed with grief. Seeing that grieving adults can laugh and smile despite their pain or withdraw in silence if they need space also teaches children that grief comes in many different guises.

Ritual and Commemoration

Ritual can also play an important role in helping bereaved children to feel enfranchised. Doka (2002b) defined *rituals* as "highly symbolic acts that confer transcendental significance and meaning on certain life events or experiences" (p. 135). Our rituals around death are typically collective experiences, such as funerals and memorial services, with defined protocols and expectations; but, they can also be highly personalized acts performed by a group of mourners or an individual. Limbo and Kobler (2013) discussed the healing nature of ritual when it echoes aspects of grief that resonate deep within. One example is the image of shifting sand to evoke the process of grief; one after the other, each participant places a handprint in the sand, side by side and overlapping each other, followed by a reflection on the meaning of what has been embedded and how the image of the finished design reflects a shared experience (Limbo & Kobler, 2013). Rituals benefit the grieving process because they provide structure for support within the community, a place to acknowledge the loss and to grieve publicly, a way to remember and honor the deceased, and a means for individual creative expression in so far as that is encouraged and supported.

Children are often excluded from participating in or even attending mourning rituals in order to protect them, but they can also benefit if adults are sensitive to their individual characters, the circumstances surrounding the loss, and their understanding of death. When attending funerals, children need information about what will take place and why; they need options so they can decide how much they want to participate and which aspects of the ceremony they may wish to avoid; and they need support from adults who can make themselves available to accompany the child, to engage him or her in conversation, or to leave the ceremony if necessary (Corr, 2000; Doka, 2002b). Funerals can help children come to terms with their own grief by witnessing adults grieving and providing support for each other.

Other personalized rituals and symbols that hold meaning for the bereaved can further enfranchise children who are trying to make sense of death. Families who have experienced the loss of a child often create rituals to honor their son or daughter, baking a cake to celebrate birthdays, releasing balloons, visiting the grave site, and attending memorial events alongside other bereaved families. When there are siblings involved, rituals help families share their journey through grief by marking important dates together, revisiting fond memories, and writing a family narrative that weaves the story of loss in a meaningful way. Rituals help siblings reexamine their own feelings from a new perspective as their view of the world and their understanding of death mature. As time passes, individual and family rituals can also evolve and new rituals can be introduced, transferring new meaning and restoring hope through the continuing relationship with the deceased. Acknowledging the unique aspects of a child's culture or ethnicity can also promote openness, genuine interest, and acceptance.

Case Study

A young man was 5 years old when his baby brother Jacob was stillborn. Family portraits he drew as a child always included Jacob, often with the other members of the family, but sometimes in the form of an angel or symbol. As an adolescent, the young man had difficulty recollecting his emotions at the time of the loss, although he remembered his parents' grief quite vividly. When he reached his mid-teens, he gained a deeper realization of the relationship he had lost and a yearning for some of the boyhood experiences the two brothers might have shared. He wanted to design a tattoo of his brother's name as a physical sign of their connection. Knowing others often cannot understand how he could grieve a brother he never met, he is selective about who he speaks to and much of his experience is internal and very personal. He wrote a poem in which he described holding his parents in their grief and sensing peace and happiness when he felt Jacob visiting him in the form of a butterfly.

His sister, 2 years younger, also found meaning through symbolism and was able to convey her ongoing sense of connection by creating a leather mask which incorporated the monarch butterfly as a symbolic representation of her little brother. The personal significance of her art was not always understood by her teachers and her fellow classmates. In this instance, she wanted her teacher to know why she had chosen the butterfly, but when she mentioned her deceased baby brother, her teacher quickly changed the topic, evidence of her discomfort and unwillingness to acknowledge the importance of the symbolism. On other occasions when she mentioned Jacob's death to high-school classmates, she encountered the same awkwardness and a sense that her peers thought she was just saying something to get attention. Although she made a conscious decision to avoid talking about Jacob at school, she continued to keep him present in her private life regardless of a resulting feeling of her loss not being legitimate to others.

Both siblings found meaning and opportunities for personal expression of grief through art. Their creative exploration helped them articulate growth and transformation through loss built on resiliency and a deepening spiritual awareness (Jonas-Simpson et al., 2014). What this case example illustrates is the need for such losses to be genuinely recognized by attuned adults. Accurate empathy, showing interest in the child's relationship to the deceased, or asking about a favorite memory are ways to support and validate the child's ongoing grief process.

Discussion Questions

1. What societal changes need to occur in order for grief to be less disenfranchised among children and adolescents?
2. How might a child or adolescent's grief response be misinterpreted by an adult?
3. How is childhood grief disenfranchised as a result of our inability to find the right language to talk about death?

References

Angelo, E. J. (1996). Post-abortion grief. *The Human Life Review, 22*(4), 43–46.

Attig, T. (2004). Disenfranchised grief revisited: Discounting hope and love. *OMEGA, 49*(3), 197–215.

Baker, J. E., Sedney, M. A., & Gross, E. (1992). Psychological tasks for bereaved children. *American Journal of Orthopsychiatry, 62,* 105–116.

Bowlby, J. (1960). Grief and mourning in infancy and early childhood. *Psychoanalytic Study of the Child, 15,* 9–52.

Corr, C. A. (2000). What do we know about grieving children and adolescents? In Kenneth J. Doka (Ed.), *Living with grief: Children, adolescents, and loss.* Washington, DC: Hospice Foundation of America.

Corr, C. A. (2002). Revisiting the concept of disenfranchised grief. In Kenneth J. Doka (Ed.), *Disenfranchised grief: New directions, challenges, and strategies for practice* (pp. 39–60). Champaign, IL: Research Press.

Crenshaw, D. A. (2002). The disenfranchised grief of children. In Kenneth J. Doka (Ed.), *Disenfranchised grief: New directions, challenges, and strategies for practice* (pp. 293–306). Champaign, IL: Research Press.

Crenshaw, D. A., & Lee, J. (2010). The disenfranchised grief of children. In N. B. Webb (Ed.), *Helping bereaved children: A handbook for practitioners* (pp. 91-108). New York, NY: The Guilford Press.

Doka, K. (Ed.) (1989). *Disenfranchised grief: Recognizing hidden sorrow.* New York, NY: Free Press.

Doka, K. J. (Ed.) (2002a). *Disenfranchised grief: New directions, challenges, and strategies for practice.* Champaign, IL: Research Press.

Doka, K. J. (2002b). The role of ritual in the treatment of disenfranchised grief. In Kenneth J. Doka (Ed.), *Disenfranchised grief: New directions, challenges, and strategies for practice* (pp. 135–147). Champaign, IL: Research Press.

Goldman, L. (2005). *Raising our children to be resilient: A guide to helping children cope with trauma in today's world.* New York, NY: Brunner-Routledge.

Holland, J. (2008). How schools can support children who experience loss and death. *British Journal of Guidance and Counselling, 36*(4), 411–424.

Jonas-Simpson, C. (Director, Producer and Principal Investigator). Research team: Steele, R., Granek, L., Davies, B., & O'Leary, J. (2014). *Always with me: Understanding bereaved children whose baby sibling died.* Toronto, ON, Canada.

Jonas-Simpson, C., & Blin, C. (2015). Mothering bereaved children after perinatal death: Implications for women's and children's mental health in Canada. In N. Khanlou & F. B. Pilkington (Eds.), *Women's mental health: Resistance and resilience in community and society* (pp. 357–374). New York, NY: Springer.

Jonas-Simpson, C., Steele, R., Granek, L., Davies, B., & O'Leary, J. (2015). Always with me: Understanding bereaved children whose baby sibling died. *Death Studies, 39*(4), 242–251. doi:10.1080/07481187.2014.991954

Kauffman, J. (1989). Intrapsychic dimensions of disenfranchised grief. In K. Doka (Ed.), *Disenfranchised grief: Recognizing hidden sorrow.* New York, NY: Free Press.

Kauffman, J. (2002). The psychology of disenfranchised grief: Liberation, shame, and self-disenfranchisement. In Kenneth J. Doka (Ed.), *Disenfranchised grief: New directions, challenges, and strategies for practice,* (pp. 61–77). Champaigne, IL: Research Press.

Klass, D., Silverman, P. R., & Nickman, S. L. (1996). *Continuing bonds: New understandings of grief.* Philadelphia, PA: Taylor & Francis.

Lang, A., Fleiszer, A. R., Duhamel, F., Sword, W., Gilbert, K. R., & Corsini-Munt, S. (2011). Perinatal loss and parental grief: The challenge of ambiguity and disenfranchised grief. *OMEGA, 63*(2), 183–196.

Limbo, R., & Kobler, K. (2013). *Meaningful moments: Ritual and reflection when a child dies.* La Crosse, WI: Gundersen Medical Foundation.

McCormack, C., & Webb, N. B. (2010). Suicide in the family: Helping child and adolescent survivors. In N. B. Webb (Ed.), *Helping bereaved children: A handbook for practitioners* (pp. 109–128). New York, NY: The Guilford Press.

Neimeyer, R. A., & Jordan, J. R. (2002). Disenfranchisement as empathic failure: Grief therapy and the co-construction of meaning. In Kenneth J. Doka (Ed.), *Disenfranchised grief: New directions, challenges, and strategies for practice* (pp. 95–117). Champaigne, IL: Research Press.

Oltjenbruns, K. A. (1996). Death of a friend during adolescence: Issues and impacts. In C. Corr & D. Balk (Eds.), *Handbook of adolescent death and bereavement* (pp. 196–216). New York, NY: Springer.

Piaget, J. (1954). *The construction of reality in childhood.* New York, NY: Basic Books.

Silverman, P. R. (2000). *Never too young to know: Death in children's lives.* New York, NY: Oxford University Press.

Stroebe, M., & Schut, H. (1999). The dual process model of coping with bereavement: Rationale and description. *Death Studies, 23,* 197–224.

Webb, N. B. (2010). The child and death. In N. B. Webb (Ed.), *Helping bereaved children: A handbook for practitioners* (pp. 3–21). New York, NY: The Guilford Press.

5 Death of a Parent in Childhood or Adolescence

Eunice Gorman and Carrie Arnold

The death of a parent for a child or adolescent is a defining moment that can create ripples that ebb and flow throughout their life. Within Western countries, it is estimated that approximately 4% of children and adolescents will experience the death of a parent by age 18 (Kaplow, Saunders, Angold, & Costello, 2010). The more emotionally significant and unique the relationship, the greater the effect will be on the developing young person. While some youth will experience resolution of grief symptoms within one year of the death without significant functional impairment (Melhem, Porta, Shamsddeen, Walker Payne, & Brent, 2011), parental death may also be associated with increased risk for psychiatric problems within 2 years following the loss (Cerel, Fristad, Verducci, Weller, & Weller, 2006). Clinicians and researchers continue to explore multifaceted dimensions that are associated with either a resolution of grief responses or indicative of prolonged distress (Melhem, Moritz, Walker, Shear, & Brent, 2006). At present, there is lack of consensus within the literature as to the defining conditions for these phenomena within the pediatric population (Dyregrov & Dyregrov, 2013; Melhem et al., 2006).

Children who have experienced the death of an important attachment figure will often feel sadness, loneliness, isolation, decreased energy, regression, and a need to make sense of what has transpired. Yamamoto, Davis, Dylak, Whittaker, Marsh, and van der Westhuizen (1996) reported that the death of a parent in childhood is the most stressful life experience. For some, parental death may have been preceded by a long illness where there would have been indefinite adjustments, hope for a cure, or ongoing disappointment. Illness likely influenced family functioning, shifting and changing relationships, and the day-to-day habits over a prolonged period of time (Davey, Kissil, & Lynch, 2016). That said, when the death is sudden, perhaps the result of a health event or an accident, the loss can result in additional feelings of shock, confusion, or even trauma. Within the literature on sudden versus anticipated deaths there is often an assumption that sudden deaths may be associated with increased risk of grief complications, more so than anticipated deaths (Schuurman, 2017; Dyregrov & Dyregrov, 2013). However, Schuurman (2017) stated that both types of deaths may be experienced as traumatic, particularly given that trauma is based on individual perception rather than just external events.

Children's reaction to the death of a parent will be influenced by their age and stage of development. Younger children may repeat stories associated with the loss to help make sense of it. Additionally, children tend to grieve in smaller doses or engage in episodic grief, allowing in just as much pain as they can handle before moving on to something else (Silverman, 2000). Predictability, routine, stability, nurturing, and comfort are needed; however, it is often challenging for the adults that are left behind to care for the bereaved child because they themselves are also grieving (Schuurman, 2003).

While children tend to naturally dose their grief (Webb, 2010), adolescents often feel alone, have a need for control, experience alienation and vulnerability, or feel more stress as they engage in ways to seek independence than they would typically have at this age and stage of their lives (Saldinger, Cain, & Porterfield, 2004). Over half of adolescents have experienced at least one adverse childhood experience, 22% have experienced two, and 17% have had three, including the death of one or both parents (Balistreri & Alvira-Hammond, 2016). Higher ACE (adverse childhood experiences) scores have long been associated with poorer emotional and physical health and well-being in adulthood (Tekeka, Hoertel, Dubertret, & LeStrat, 2016).

Adolescents require a significant amount of support yet they may not seek it out or appear indifferent. This could result in withdrawal, isolation, protective numbness, or aggression, as ways of managing their feelings. Oltjenbruns (2001) referred to this as *double jeopardy*, the tendency to silence one's grief when one needs support the most in order to not feel different from others. Moreover, because teens appear to be coping, the adults in their lives may fail to offer much needed support and comfort. Many will have offers of support from their peers, yet at the same time tend to prefer not to have it offered (Lafrenier & Cain, 2015), instead wishing to go back to the way they interacted with friends before the death.

A bereaved teen will typically experience a wide range of emotions, which are, in part, due to their developmental stage, but also due to the unique nature of their relationships with peers, family members, and the deceased. A developmental necessity for many children and adolescents is to fit in; being singled out as different because of the death of a primary attachment figure is often unwelcome in their efforts to individuate from their parent(s).

Alternately, adolescents who have lost an important person in their life may experience increased empathic capacities, maturity, cognitive awareness, health seeking, and clarification of values and views of relationships and what is important in life (Bylund-Grenklo, Furst, Nyberg, Steineck, & Kreicbergs, 2016). While adolescent responses will vary throughout the grief process, being attuned to the needs of an adolescent and his or her unique grief response is believed to be helpful in the process of meaning making (Neimeyer, Laurie, Mehta, Hardison, & Currier, 2008) and emotional regulation (Siegel, 2013).

Loss of a Parent

In the United States, 1.5 million children are living in single-parent families as a result of the death of a parent (Owens, 2008). Parents may provide safety and comfort within which children develop and receive emotional and psychological intimacy (Siegel, 2013). Attachment theory has delineated the primacy of the parent–child bond (Bowlby, 1953, 1969, 1973, 1980; Ainsworth & Wittig, 1969, 1971), and research that explores the connection between attachment and bereavement offers important insight into the nature of these bonds and the implications when they are affected by grief (Stroebe, Schut, & Stroebe, 2005). When the parent–child bond is loving and secure, it is easy to comprehend the anguish experienced by a child. Yet, even when the parent–child bond is characterized by fear, neglect, or abuse, the child still has an attachment to the primary caregiver (Cassidy, 2008) and this particular attachment style will influence the grief trajectory (Stroebe et al., 2005).

The response to the death of a parent is uniquely shaped by that particular parent–child bond. Subsequently, research findings vary with respect to outcomes. One study reported that 50% of children report a resolution of grief symptoms within 1 year of parental death, with 10% experiencing intrusive grief symptoms 3 years later (Melhem et al., 2011). The death of a parent may predict poorer adult health in later years and may cause the loss to resurface throughout the lifespan (Phillips & Carver, 2015).

Prior to the death of the parent, children's needs may be overlooked while the family attends to the needs of the dying member (Beale & Sivesind, 2004). This can be an unfortunate oversight, as children are often far more aware of what is happening than they are given credit for (Bugge, Helseth, & Darbyshire, 2008). While the child may be concerned about the critically ill parent, it is equally important that the connection to the well, or surviving, parent is maintained and fortified (Davenport & Macpherson, 2005). It is not unusual for children to feel guilt, worry, and helplessness in the face of parental terminal illness (Monroe & Kraus, 2010).

Of critical importance are the age of child, the quality of the relationship, previous experience with loss, and the nature of the death. For example, military families and families who experience murder or suicide may require special attention (Beale & Sivesind, 2004; Holmes, Rauch, & Cozza, 2013; Wood, Byram, Gosling, & Stokes, 2012). In the case of military families, death often comes after several other losses, including deployment, absences, or uncertainty regarding the actual cause of death given the circumstances of battle, war, or peacekeeping. When the cause of death is homicide or suicide, these deaths may result in what Doka (1989) referred to as *disenfranchised grief*, which causes additional stressors on the child and/or family.

Children respond in a variety of ways, many of which have been addressed in other chapters in this volume. It is not unusual for school performance to suffer (Berg, Rostila, Saarela, & Hjern, 2014; Masterson, 2012; Rostila & Saarela, 2011), or depressive episodes to occur (Appel et al., 2016; Gray,

Weller, Fristad, & Weller, 2011), posttraumatic stress symptoms to arise (Howell et al., 2015), and even for suicide risk to increase with children as young as 8 years old contemplating ending their lives in order to join their deceased parent (Renaud, Engarhos, Schleifer, & Talwar, 2015).

Additionally, there may be long-term effects on life satisfaction especially among young girls who have lost their mothers (Leopold & Lechner, 2015; Luecken & Roubinov, 2012). While not all children require complex or long-term interventions (Kennedy & Macintyre, 2008a; 2008b; Worden & Silverman, 1996), every child can benefit from a caring adult whether it is the surviving parent, grandparent, relative, or teacher who will continually assess and be on the lookout for signs that the child is struggling and requires support. Children can further benefit from those who show a willingness to become involved and offer age-appropriate interventions and supports (Christ, 2000; Corr & Balk, 2010).

Children will typically wonder what will happen to them or to their family, wonder whether they had something to do with the death of the deceased, and will ask about who will take care of them. Stated more simply: "Did I *cause* it?" "Can I *catch* it?" and "Who's going to take *care* of me?" These important questions are often referred to in the literature as *the three C's* of childhood bereavement (Krupnick & Solomon, 1988). Other issues to consider include the timing of the death in the child's life cycle; the nature of the death (e.g., sudden versus anticipated); the openness of the family system, including how communication occurs; and the position in the family held by the deceased member (Christ & Christ, 2006; Herz, 1980).

Children often look to their elders, such as parents, grandparents, teachers, faith leaders, or coaches to understand what this loss is evoking in other family members, and this can lead the child to express or repress his or her own feelings. Children who are as young as 1 year of age experience loss in ways that can undermine their coping capacities and delay their overall development (Bowlby, 1969; van der Horst & van der Veer, 2008), thus the presence of other caring, attuned adults helps to ensure positive grief outcomes.

Adolescents may be at greater risk and therefore need particular guidance and assessment around substance abuse, acting out, guilt, or isolation (Jacobs & Bovasso, 2009). They may also experience decreased academic performance (Cinzia et al., 2014). In the case of parental illness, adolescents, while able to reason that their parent is now released from their suffering, may not be willing to share their grief or this understanding with their remaining parent and may feel the need to take on more responsibility within the family (Sveen, Kreicbergs, Melcher, & Alavariza, 2016). However, despite this more mature awareness of death, adolescents are at increased risk for sleep disturbances, anger, irritability, low self-esteem, behavior problems, worries about financial issues, potentially poor parent–child relationships, and subsequent negative life events (Stikkelbroek, Bodden, & Reitz, 2016).

In a study of 622 bereaved adolescents, Bylund-Grenklo et al. (2016) found that 49% of adolescents interviewed 6 to 9 years after the death of a parent reported unresolved grief and problems with sleep, fatigue, depression, intrusive thoughts, and avoiding reminders of their deceased parent or the illness that took their life. The authors urge professionals to be alert to the vulnerability of teens given their desire for independence, the major transitions they are undergoing, and their risk for self-harm, numbing, or restricting feelings.

The Surviving Parent or Care-Giving Adult

Children's ability to adapt and cope is influenced by their own efforts as well as their dependence on the surviving parent's ability to be available and present. Other factors that affect the child's grief process include the way in which the child is informed of the death, participation in the funeral or rituals, and the type of support available to the child (Webb, 2010). Children may be affected by varying responses from the adults in their lives; they may receive support in a way that meets their unique needs, be encouraged to seek connection with the deceased parent, or experience adults' own death anxieties and subsequently become less available (Bugge, Darbyshire, Rokholt, Haugstevdt, & Helseth, 2014). Under optimal conditions, there is open communication in which children can ask questions, the family is flexible in meeting each person's needs, and the children's behaviors are noticed and addressed by a caring adult. In a phenomenological study composed of 39 experienced clinicians and researchers in the field of childhood bereavement, one respondent suggested that it would be useful to establish criteria that is indicative of healthy responses among families and, conversely, to "develop ways of identifying those parents who are at risk of increasing the likelihood of complicated grief in their children" (Dyregrov & Dyregrov, 2013, p. 299).

It is also necessary to consider that a surviving parent typically assumes the roles of the deceased spouse and will be unique within each family. Children may see their surviving parent being flexible and doing their best to adapt to new roles. By contrast, children may witness their surviving parent struggle to adapt or adjust. Children's grief needs to be considered within the context of their individual loss, as well as the multiple losses for the surviving parent (Dehlin & Mertensson, 2009). The parent's own grief may interfere with their ability to recognize their children's suffering (Karns, 2002) due to the increased responsibilities; periods of decreased social activity; or having less time, willingness, and energy to focus beyond their own sadness and loss (Kennedy & Lloyd-Williams, 2009).

Children need a safe environment (Gilroy & Johnson, 2004) and tend to have better grief outcomes when caring adults can model healthy grieving, enlist social supports, and create opportunities for physical expression of their grief in a nonjudgemental setting. While the surviving parent may attempt to maintain normality and be aware of their children's distress (Howell, Barrett-Baker, & Burnside, 2016; McPherson & Emelaus, 2007a, 2007b), they may in fact be overwhelmed in their attempts to deal with secondary losses associated with the loss of their partner including moving, financial difficulties, change in routines, loss of social support, returning to or leaving work, vulnerability, or shifts in their sense of identity (Schonfeld & Quackenbush, 2009).

The gender of the surviving parent may also have an effect on the expression of grief and the adjustment following the death of a parent. Mothers are often viewed as more child-centered and this parenting style after a loss can reduce negative outcomes (Saldinger, Porterfield, & Cain, 2004). Mothers are still viewed in many societies as the "hub" of the family, the nurturer, the communicator, and the one who is responsible for maintaining the emotional and kinship ties within the family system. Fathers on the other hand are often seen as strong, competent, protectors, providers, and problem solvers. However, it is misleading to adopt a strict gender binary view given the evolving nature of gender identities, family, partnerships, and parenting roles. As such, stereotypical "mothering" and "fathering" roles can be shared and assigned across and between genders.

Stepparents, Adoptive Parents, and Foster Parents

No conversation about the death of a parent would be complete without considering other important parenting roles. With respect to blended families, the stepparent–child relationship exists due to a prior separation either through death or divorce in the child's life. Stepfamilies make up 12.6% of Canadian families (Dell, 2012). The death of a stepparent represents yet another major loss in the life of the child or adolescent. If there has been a poor relationship with the stepparent, the younger child may feel that they somehow caused the death through magical thinking and may feel guilt ridden and/or relieved. If there was a healthy relationship, then the child is forced to once again live through the pain of permanent separation from an important attachment figure.

Regarding children who have been adopted, the child or adolescent has already experienced a permanent separation from his or her birth parents. Approximately 1 in 5 Canadians are touched by adoption (Adoption Council of Canada, 2016). There may have been abuse, neglect, developmental trauma, or multiple transitions in the life of an older adoptee that will not be present in a baby adopted at birth, and this prior experience will have an effect on the child's attachment, sense of safety, and grieving (Hodgdon, Blaustein, Kinniburgh, Peterson & Spinazzola, 2015). Possible wounds related to this type of separation may now be intensified in the event that the adoptive parent dies. Surviving children may struggle with feelings of abandonment, feeling unloved, unlovable, or in search of a mother or father figure to remain close to them and not leave them, either in death or through life circumstances (Fineran, 2012). Any existing attachment-related concerns would be best addressed by sensitive and attuned caregivers who are understanding of the layers of loss in the child's life. Children who have been brought into foster care because of the death of a parent may have even longer waits until adoption or permanency planning is complete (Shaw, Bright, & Sharpe, 2015), further complicating their attempts to adjust, make sense of their loss, and begin to heal.

The area of foster parents and foster children is a sphere that is typically unrecognized and underserviced in terms of the grief in the system for both foster parents and the children they support. In 2013, there were an estimated 62,428 children in out-of-home care across Canada (Jones, Sinha, & Trocmé, 2015). While a foster family may represent warmth and safety for a child, we must recognize that this is not always the case. In fact, some children and adolescents will experience less-than-ideal attention and nurturing, or even abuse, while in foster care, and this experience may add to the numerous losses they have encountered in their lives up to that point (Browning, 2015). In situations where a child suffers yet another loss or death in foster care, we cannot underestimate the cumulative impact of grief when loss is layered upon loss amidst grief that is potentially disenfranchised.

Additional Considerations

Over the last 25 years we have witnessed a growth in creative ways of addressing children's grief, including grief camps for children (McClatchey & Wimmer, 2014), centers where children can talk about their grief with their peers (Lafreniere & Cain, 2015), teacher education programs, family support groups (Dunning, 2006), and online-/Web-based support groups (Giesbers & Verdonck-De Leeuw, 2010). Additionally, there are organizations like The Lighthouse Program for Grieving Children, the Max and Beatrice Wolfe Centre at Mount Sinai Hospital in Toronto, creative legacy work including heart wills (e.g., Dougy Center, Portland, Oregon), Mummy Diaries (e.g., Winston's Wish, UK), and A Heroic Journey: Outward Bound for Grieving Teens and Young Adults. Lastly, creative modalities such as expressive arts therapy, bibliotherapy, storytelling, and memory books all represent innovative ways that children are supported.

Additionally, society's view of children attending funerals or participating in social conventions and rituals appears to be shifting (Softing, Dyregrov, & Dyregrov, 2015). The desire to stay connected with the deceased parent through continuing bonds (Klass, Silverman, & Nickman, 1996) can contribute to meaning making. A more recent understanding of the worth of linking objects (e.g., important objects that connect the child to the lost parent) can provide comfort to grieving children and adolescents. Another way that children and adolescents remain connected to their lost attachment figure is by becoming a living legacy, for instance, making a parent proud or internalizing the other in ways that carry forth into the future interests, hobbies, or characteristics of the deceased. For instance, a young girl who loses her mother, an excellent baker, becomes interested in a career as a chef.

Table 5.1 Example Items for a Memory Box

Memory Box
Include Anything That's Important to You or Your Child That Will Bring Comfort

---

- A special time you and your child shared together
- Favorite recipes
- Hopes and wishes for the future
- Notes to the surviving parent about what the child likes and dislikes
- Something you especially love about your child or about your relationship with them
- A sample of aftershave or perfume that you can use to trigger memories
- Letters, greetings, or stories about things you have done together
- Reminders of who in the family has more stories and can support the child
- A DVD recording with a message from you or camcorder videos
- Messages or your favorite music on an MP3 or other device
- A voice recording from your phone that can then be transferred on to a CD or transcribed
- Special books you liked to read together or games played together
- Baby books that you constructed together, scrapbooks
- DVDs that you enjoyed watching as a family
- Photographs with messages
- Scrapbooks
- Ideas for comforting activities alone, with friends, or with surviving caregivers and parent
- Small cards with messages: 'I love you because . . .,' 'Thank you for . . .,' 'When we're not together what I miss most about you is . . .,' or 'Remember when . . .
- Jewelry, cards, toys, or tickets from places you visited together that hold special memories
- A favorite childhood stuffed animal with your scent attached
- A piece of your clothing or a blanket
- Ethical wills
- Legacy work, for example, art work, scarves, prayer shawls, pillows, tapestries, quilting
- Personal histories
- Family trees
- Life story books available at bookstores to be completed by the parent

---

Note: Based in part on McMillan Cancer Support (UK), Winston's Wish (UK), The Dougy Center (U.S.), and The Max and Beatrice Wolfe Children's Centre and Dr. Jay Children's Grief Program at Mount Sinai Hospital Toronto resources.

Organized programs offer support, education, the opportunity to express grief, creative ways to remember the person who has died, and helpful information about communicating within the family. Furthermore, programs can show ways to continue the connection with the surviving parent and reinvest in life, thus predicting less anxiety and depression among grieving children (Koblenz, 2016). Children can meet others with similar experiences, demystify grief and death, reengage in life, have fun, and utilize skills of resilience, empowerment, taking back a sense of control, and learning healthy ways of coping with their emotions (Chowns, 2008; Koblenz, 2016; Siddaway, Wood, Schulz, & Trickey, 2015).

Case Study

Hassan is a 10-year-old boy who emigrated from a large city in Iran following the death of his father in the political unrest of the time when he was 6 years old. He lives with his mother in a small community of expatriates and asylum seekers in Toronto. Prior to coming to Canada, he and his mother lived with his maternal grandparents just down the street from his paternal grandparents. The families were relatively wealthy, but, given the climate of impending war and the death of Hassan's father, the two families felt it was important for Hassan and his mother to seek a better, safer life in Canada.

Hassan misses his grandparents and the familiarity of life in Iran but is slowly adjusting to life in a new country. He and his mother communicate regularly via email and FaceTime with their relatives back home. Hassan attends a local grade school where he has been thriving; he is walked to school daily by a neighbour who is 13 and stays at school for lunch so that his mother is able to work for a few hours each day outside the home. News of his maternal grandmother's illness and death takes both of them by surprise, as she had not been ill and there was no warning that her death was imminent.

Hassan responds to this latest loss in ways that are not unusual. He begins leaving his lunch, homework, or gym clothes at home and rushes back home as soon as he gets to school in order to check on his mother and avoid the other children who seem carefree. His room becomes messier and he refuses to accept playdates or stay after school for sports and activities he used to relish. He is reluctant to eat. He often climbs into bed with his mother after being woken by nightmares. He misses school because of previously unheard of headaches and stomach aches. When he is at school, he is unable to focus his attention and is often irritable and short tempered even with his best friends. His mother is broken hearted herself and is impatient with the extra attention and care needed by Hassan, a child who was in her words, "not even a bit of a problem before."

In desperation, Hassan's mother reaches out to Hassan's teacher following a brief meeting with the Imam at the Mosque she attends. The Imam suggests that she should seek help from people who understand children and will know more about what help might be offered. She explains her frustrations, impatience, and deep worry at his mounting problems with day-to-day life. His teacher encourages Hassan's mother to connect with a children's grief group at the local family health center and promises to reach out to him each day at school to support him in any way that she is able. Additionally, the Imam offers a program that helps with the losses associated with resettlement that they can both attend and suggests that this latest loss in a long line of changes and transitions may be very difficult for Hassan to cope with given his young age and limited support network. When several supports are instituted and Hassan begins to share his sadness and guilt at not being home with his grandmother, his behaviors slowly begin to shift and he starts to reengage in his favourite activities over the course of the next few months.

Conclusion

Children are remarkably resilient (Eppler, 2008; Fearnley, 2010). Families benefit from learning to balance consistency with the need to adapt by providing opportunities for rituals or creative strategies for meaning making (Biank & Werner-Lin, 2011; Pearlman, Schwalbe, & Cloitre, 2010; Werner-Lin & Biank, 2013). By giving the adults in a child's or adolescent's life empathy, stability, connection, opportunities for emotional expression, acceptance, and opportunities to address their own—and their child's—needs, we are more likely to see all members of the family reach some measure of adaptation, and adjustment after the devastating loss of a central attachment figure in their lives.

Discussion Questions

1. List ways that a child or adolescent might be supported following the death of a parent at home, school, or in their community.
2. How might we promote continuing bonds in families grieving the death of a central figure, particularly when not living in the same city/country, as in the case of Hassan?
3. When we care for grieving youth, we directly or indirectly care for their support system. How might we promote resilience within the remaining family members?

References

Adoption Council of Canada/Conseil d'adoption du Canada. (2016). *Myths and realities*. Retrieved from www.adoption.ca/myths-and-realities.

Ainsworth, M. D. S., & Wittig, B. A. (1969). Attachment and exploratory behaviour of one-year-olds in a strange situation. In B. M. Foss (Ed.), *Determinants of infant behaviour, volume 4*. New York, NY: Barnes & Noble.

Ainsworth, M. D. S., & Wittig, B. A. (1971). Individual differences in strange situation behaviour of one-year-olds. In H. R. Shaffer (Ed.), *The origins of human social relations* (pp. 17–57). London, UK: Academic Press.

Appel, C. W., Johansen, C., Christenberg, S., Oksbjerg, S., Dencker, A. B., & Dige, J. (2016). Risk of antidepressants among children and young adults exposed to the death of a parent. *Epidemiology, 27*(4), 578–585.

Balistreri, K. S., & Alvira-Hammond, M. (2016). Adverse childhood experiences, family functioning and adolescent health and emotional well-being. *Public Health, 132*, 72–78.

Beale, E. A., & Sivesind, D. (2004). Parents dying of cancer and their children. *Palliative & Supportive Care, 2*(4), 403–408.

Berg, L., Rostila, M., Saarela, J., & Hjern, A. (2014). Parental death during childhood and subsequent school performance. *Pediatrics, 133*(4), 682–689.

Biank, N. M., & Werner-Lin, A. (2011). Growing up with grief: Revisiting the death of a parent over the life course. *Omega, 63*(3), 271–290.

Bowlby, J. (1953). *Child care and the growth of love*. Harmondsworth, UK: Penguin.

Bowlby, J. (1969). *Attachment and loss: Attachment* (Vol. 1). London, UK: Hogarth.

Bowlby, J. (1973). *Attachment and loss: Separation* (Vol. 2). New York, NY: Basic Books.

Bowlby, J. (1980). *Attachment and loss: Sadness and depression* (Vol. 3). New York, NY: Basic Books.

Browning, A. S. (2015). Undertaking planned transitions for children in out-of-home care. *Adoption and Fostering, 39*(1), 51–61.

Bugge, K. E., Helseth, S., & Darbyshire, P. (2008). Children's experiences of participation in a family support program when their parent has incurable cancer. *Cancer Nursing, 31*(6), 426–434.

Bugge, K. E., Darbyshire, P., Røkholt, E. G., Haugstvedt, K. T. S., & Helseth, S. (2014). Young children's grief: Parents' understanding and coping. *Death Studies, 38*(1), 36–43.

Bylund-Grenklo, T., Fürst, C. J., Nyberg, T., Steineck, G., & Kreicbergs, U. (2016). Unresolved grief and its consequences: A nationwide follow-up of teenage loss of a parent to cancer 6–9 years earlier. *Supportive Care in Cancer, 24*(7), 3095–3103.

Cassidy, J. (2008). The nature of the child's ties. In J. Cassidy & P. R. Shaver (Eds.), *Handbook of attachment: Theory, research and clinical application* (2nd ed.). New York, NY: The Guilford Press.

Cerel, J., Fristad, M. A., Verducci, J., Weller, R. A., & Weller, E. B. (2006). Childhood bereavement: Psychopathology in the 2 years postparental death. *Journal of the American Academy of Child and Adolescent Psychiatry, 45*, 681–690.

Cinzia, P. A., Montagna, L., Mastroianni, C., Giuseppe, C., Piredda, M., & de Marinis, M. G. (2014). Losing a parent: Analysis of the literature on the experience and needs of adolescents dealing with grief. *Journal of Hospice & Palliative Nursing, 16*(6), 362–373.

Chowns, G. (2008). 'No, you don't know how we feel': Groupwork with children facing parental loss. *Groupwork, 18*(1), 14–37.

Christ, G. H. (2000). *Healing children's grief.* New York, NY: Oxford University Press.

Christ, G. H., & Christ, A. E. (2006). Current approaches to helping children cope with a parent's terminal illness. *CA: A Cancer Journal for Clinicians, 56*(4), 197–212.

Corr, C. A., & Balk, D. E. (Eds.) (2010). *Children's encounters with death, bereavement and coping.* New York, NY: Springer.

Davenport, D. S., & Macpherson, C. (2005). Telling children their ill parent is dying: A study of the factors influencing the well parent. *Mortality, 10*(2), 113–126.

Davey, M., Kissil, K., & Lynch, L. (2016). *Helping children and families cope with parental illness: A clinician's guide.* New York, NY: Routledge.

Dehlin, L., & Mertensson, R. G. (2009). Adolescents' experiences of a parent's serious illness and death. *Palliative and Supportive Care, 7*(1), 13–25.

Dell, P. (2012, September 19). *Stepfamilies make up 12.6% of Canadian families.* Retrieved from www.cbc.ca/news/canada/stepfamilies-make-up-12-6-of-canadian-families-1.1201217

Doka, K. (Ed.) (1989). *Disenfranchised grief: Recognizing hidden sorrow.* New York, NY: Free Press.

Dunning, S. (2006). As a young child's parent dies: Conceptualizing and constructing preventive interventions. *Clinical Social Work Journal, 34*(4), 499–514.

Dyregrov, A., & Dyregrov, K. (2013). Complicated grief in children—the perspectives of experienced professionals. *Omega, 67*(3), 291–303.

Eppler, C. (2008). Exploring themes of resiliency in children after the death of a parent. *Professional School Counseling, 11*(3), 189–196.

Fearnley, R. (2010). Death of a parent and the children's experience: Don't ignore the elephant in the room. *Journal of Interprofessional Care, 24*(44), 450–459.

Fineran, K. R. (2012). Helping foster and adopted children to grieve the loss of birth parents: A case example. *The Family Journal: Counseling and Therapy for Couples and Families. 20*(4), 369–375.

Giesbers, J., & Verdonck-De Leeuw, M. (2010). Coping with parental cancer: Web-based peer support in children. *Psycho-Oncology, 19*(8), 887–892.

Gilroy, C., & Johnson, P. (2004). Listening to the language of children's grief. *Groupwork, 14*(3), 91–111.

Gray, L. B., Weller, R. A., Fristad, M., & Weller, E. B. (2011). Depression in children and adolescents two months after the death of a parent. *Journal of Affective Disorders. 135*(1), 277–283.

Herz, F. (1980). The impact of death and serious illness on the family life cycle. In E. A. Carter & M. McGoldrick (Eds.), *The family life cycle: A framework for family treatment* (pp. 121–131). New York, NY: Gardner Press.

Hodgdon, H. B., Blaustein, M., Kinniburgh, K., Peterson, M.L., & Spinazzola, J. (2015). Application of the ARC model with adopted children: supporting resiliency and family well-being. *Journal of Childhood and Adolescent Trauma, 9*(1), 43–53.

Holmes, A. K., Rauch, P. K., & Cozza, S. J. (2013). When a parent is injured or killed in combat. *The Future of Military Children in Families, 23*(2), 144–162.

Howell, K. H., Barrett-Baker, E. P., & Burnside, A. N. (2016). Children facing parental cancer versus parental death: The buffering efforts of positive parenting and emotional expression. *Journal of Child and Family Studies, 25*(1), 152–165.

Howell, K. H., Barrett-Baker, E. P., Burnside, A. N., Wamser-Nanney, R., Layne, C. M., & Kaplow, J. B. (2015). Children facing parental cancer versus parental death: The buffering effects of positive parenting and emotional expression. *Journal of Child and Family Studies, 25*(1), 152–164.

Jacobs, J. R., & Bovasso, G. B. (2009). Re-examining the long-term effects of experiencing parental death in childhood on adult psychopathology. *The Journal of Nervous and Mental Disease, 197*(1), 24–27.

Jones, A., Sinha, V., & Trocmé, N. (2015). *Children and youth in out-of home care in the Canadian provinces.* CWRP Information Sheet #167E. Montreal, QC: Centre for Research on Children and Families, McGill University.

Kaplow, J. B., Saunders, J., Angold, A., & Costello, E. J. (2010). Psychiatric symptoms in bereaved versus nonbereaved youth and young adults: A longitudinal epidemiological study. *Journal of the American Academy of Child and Adolescent Psychiatry, 49*, 1145–1154.

Karns, J. T. (2002). Children's understanding of death. *Journal of Clinical Activities, Assignments & Handouts in Psychotherapy Practice, 2*(1), 43–50.

Kennedy, K. C., & Macintyre, R. (2008a). Supporting children and families facing the death of a parent: Part 1. *International Journal of Palliative Nursing, 14*(4), 162–168.

Kennedy, K. C., & Macintyre, R. (2008b). Supporting children and families facing the death of a parent: Part 2. *International Journal of Palliative Nursing, 14*(5), 230–237.

Kennedy, V. L., & Lloyd-Williams, M. (2009). How children cope when a parent has advanced cancer. *Psycho-Oncology, 18*(8), 886–892.

Klass, D., Silverman, P. R., & Nickman, S. L. (1996). *Continuing bonds: New understandings of grief.* Washington, DC: Taylor & Francis.

Koblenz, J. (2016). Growing from grief: Qualitative experiences of parental loss. *Omega, 73*(3), 203–215.

Krupnick, J., & Solomon, F. (1988). Death of a parent or sibling during childhood. In J. Bloom Feshbach & S. Bloom Feshbach (Eds.), *The psychology of separation and loss* (pp. 345–371). San Francisco, CA: Jossey-Bass.

Lafreniere. L., & Cain, A. (2015). Parentally bereaved children and adolescents: A question of peer support. *Omega, 71*(3), 245–271.

Leopold, T., & Lechner, C. M. (2015). Parent's death and adult well-being: Gender, age and adaptation to filial bereavement. *Journal of Marriage and Family, 77*(3), 747–760.

Luecken, L. J., & Roubinov, D. S. (2012). Pathways to lifespan health following childhood parental death. *Social and Personality Psychology Compass, 6*(3), 243–257.

Macpherson, C., & Emeleus, M. (2007a). Children's needs when facing the death of a parent from cancer: Part one. *International Journal of Palliative Nursing, 13*(10), 478–485.

Macpherson, C., & Emeleus, M. (2007b). Children's needs when facing the death of a parent from cancer: Part two. *International Journal of Palliative Nursing, 13*(12), 590–597.

Masterson, A. (2012). Retrospective reports of the lived school experience of adolescents after the death of a parent. *Journal of School Nursing, 29*(5), 370–377.

McClatchey, I. S., & Wimmer, J. S. (2014). Coping with parental death as seen from the perspective of children who attended a grief camp. *Qualitative Social Work, 13*(2), 221–236.

Melhem, N. M., Moritz, G., Walker, M., Shear, K., & Brent, D. (2006). Phenomenology and correlates of complicated grief in children and adolescents. *Journal of the American Academy of Child and Adolescent Psychiatry, 46*(4), 493–499.

Melhem, N., Porta, G., Shamseddeen, W., Walker Payne, M., & Brent, D. (2011). Grief in children and adolescents bereaved by sudden parental death. *Archives of General Psychiatry, 68*, 911–919. doi:10.1001/archgenpsychiatry.2011.101

Monroe, B., & Kraus, F. (2010). *Brief interventions with bereaved children.* Oxford, UK: Oxford University Press.

Neimeyer, R. A., Laurie, A., Mehta, T., Hardison, H., & Currier, J. M. (2008). Lessons of loss: Meaning-making in bereaved college students. *New Directions for Student Services, 121*, 27–39.

Oltjenbruns, K. A. (2001). Developmental context of childhood: Grief and regrief phenomena. In M. S. Stroebe, R. O. Hansson, W. Stroebe, & H. Schut, (Eds.), *Handbook of bereavement research: Consequences, coping, and care* (pp. 169–197). Washington, DC: American Psychological Association.

Owens, D. (2008). Recognizing the needs of bereaved children in palliative care. *Journal of Hospice and Palliative Nursing, 10*(1), 42–52.

Pearlman, M. Y., Schwalbe, K. D., & Cloitre, M. (2010). *Grief in childhood: Fundamentals of treatment and clinical practice.* Washington, DC: American Psychological Association.

Phillips, S. P., & Carver, L. (2015). Early parental loss and self-related health of older women and men: A population-based multi-country study. *PLoS ONE, 10*(4), e0120762. doi:10.1371/journal.pone.0120762

Renaud, S., Engarhos, P., Schleifer, M., & Talwar, V. (2015). Children's earliest experiences with death: Circumstances, conversations, explanations and parental satisfaction. *Infant and Child Development, 24*(2), 157–174.

Rostila, M., & Saarela, J. (2011). Time does not heal all wounds: Mortality following the death of a parent. *Journal of Marriage and Family, 73*(1), 236–249.

Saldinger, A. A., Cain, A., & Porterfield, K., (2004). Facilitating attachment between school-aged children and a dying parent. *Death Studies, 28*(10), 915–940.

Saldinger, A. A., Porterfield, K., & Cain, A. (2004). Meeting the needs of parentally bereaved children: A framework for child-centered parenting. *Psychiatry: Interpersonal and Biological Processes, 67*(4), 331–352.

Schonfeld, D., & Quackenbush, M. (2009). *After a loved one dies: How children grieve and how parents and other adults can support them.* New York, NY: New York Life Foundation.

Schuurman, D. (2003). *Never the same: Coming to terms with the death of a parent.* New York, NY: St. Martin's Press.

Schuurman, D. (2017, April). *An uneasy alliance? The integration of trauma and bereavement.* Presentation at the Association for Death Education and Counselling Annual Conference, Portland, Oregon.

Shaw, T. V., Bright, C. L., & Sharpe, T. L. (2015). Child welfare outcomes for youth in care as a result of parental death or parental incarceration. *Child Abuse and Neglect, 42,* 112–120.

Siddaway, A. P., Wood, A. M., Schulz, J., & Trickey, D. (2015). Evaluation of the CHUMS Child Bereavement Group: A pilot study examining statistical and clinical change. *Death Studies, 39*(2), 99–110.

Seigel, D. J. (2013). *Brainstorm: The power and purpose of the teenage brain.* New York, NY: Penguin Books.

Silverman, P. R. (2000). *Never too young to know.* New York, NY: Oxford University Press.

Softing, G. H., Dyregrov, A., & Dyregrov, K. (2015). Because I'm also part of the family: Children's participation in rituals after the loss of a parent or sibling. *Omega Journal of Death and Dying, 73*(2), 141–158.

Stikkelbroek, Y., Bodden, D. H. M., & Reitz, E. (2016). Mental health of adolescents before and after the death of a parent or sibling. *European Child and Adolescent Psychiatry, 25*(1), 49–69.

Stroebe, M. S., Schut, H., & Stroebe, W. (2005). Attaching in coping with bereavement: A theoretical integration. *Review of General Psychology, 9*(1), 48–66.

Sveen, J., Kreicbergs, U., Melcher, U., & Alvariza, A. (2016). Teenagers reasoning about a parent's recent death in cancer. *Palliative and Supportive Care, 14*(4), 349–357.

Tekeka, S., Hoertel, N., Dubertret, C., & LeStrat, Y. (2016). Parental divorce or death during childhood and adolescence and its association with mental health. *Journal of Nervous and Mental Disorders, 204*(9), 678–685.

van der Horst, F. C., & van der Veer, R. (2008). Loneliness and issues of separation. *Integrative Psychological and Behavioral Science, 42*(4), 325–335.

Webb, N. B. (2010). The child and death. In N. B. Webb (Ed.), *Helping bereaved children* (3rd ed.) (pp. 3–21). New York, NY: The Guilford Press.

Werner-Lin, A., & Biank, N. M. (2013). Holding parents so they can hold their children: Grief work with surviving spouses to support parentally bereaved children. *Omega, 66*(1), 1–16.

Wood, L., Byram, V., Gosling, A. S., & Stokes, J. (2012). Continuing bonds after suicide bereavement in childhood. *Death Studies, 36*(10), 873–898.

Worden, J. W., & Silverman, P. (1996). Parental death and adjustment of school-age children (Harvard Bereavement Study). *Omega, 33*(2), 91–102.

Yamamoto, K., Davis, O. L., Dylak, S., Whittaker, J., Marsh, C., & van der Westhuizen, P. C. (1996). Across six nations: Stressful events in the lives of children. *Child Psychiatry and Human Development, 26*(3), 139–150.

6   A Lifetime Loss
Death of a Sibling

Adam Koenig

In order to understand the experience of sibling loss, one must first understand the influence a sibling relationship can have on an individual. Seen as potentially one of the longest relationships in a person's life (Craft-Rosenberg, Montgomery, Hill, Kauder, & Eisbach, 2011), a sibling relationship can be a very unique and special bond between kin. At the same time, the relationship can also be a tumultuous experience for those involved. Described as one of the most ambivalent types of relationships (Edward, 2011), and involving an inherent competitive dynamic (Craft-Rosenberg et al., 2011), siblings can be seen playing cohesively one minute and then be involved in a verbal or physical conflict the next. Sibling pairs can even be inseparable during one part of their lives and then "distant ghosts" in another (Edward, 2011).

Although much variation can be found within sibling relationships, each child plays an important role within the social-cognitive development of their respective siblings (Whiteman, Bernard, & Jensen, 2011). Koehler (2010) discussed how children often seek out others to help them identify their own sense of being/identity. As siblings are often consistently present within a brother or sister's life, siblings offer their brother or sister a "mirror" to understand who he or she is. It is through this mirror children within a family can start to identify their uniqueness and develop separate identities from each other, as well as start to separate from their parents (Edward, 2011). The analogy of a mirror pays homage to Bandura's social learning theory.

Bandura (1977) theorized that humans acquire new skills and cognitive insights through observing others and social reinforcement. Considering siblings are often together, this relationship can serve as a way for children to learn about themselves and others. Research reviewed by Whiteman, McHale, and Soli (2011) indicated siblings influence each other by their interactions with one another, through being influenced by their social experiences with others outside the sibling interaction, and by observing how others interact within their family.

Another theoretical model that lends itself well to the sibling relationship is attachment theory (Bowlby, 1969). The belief is siblings may influence the internal working models of their respective brothers and sisters, especially if an older empathic sibling is present (Whiteman, McHale et al., 2011).

The sibling relationship does not negate the primary attachment with the parents, but can mirror the attachment type (i.e., secure or insecure; Volling, 2001). If one then thinks about the potential effect that siblings can have on a brother or sister, a sibling relationship can then be a significant positive or negative force in a child's development based on sibling interactions (Howe, Ross, & Recchia, 2011).

Longitudinal research conducted by Morgan, Shaw, and Olino (2012) sought to examine how temperament, specifically negative emotionality, and relationship quality with a sibling could moderate the potential development of internalization problems (e.g., anxiety, depression) and/or social skills in young boys. Morgan and colleagues found those boys who had high negative emotionality and more sibling conflict tended to have a higher likelihood of developing internalizing problems and limited social skills. Inherent in all sibling relationships is conflict, which can then lead to emotions of jealousy, rage, and frustration (Koehler, 2010). Empirical support has demonstrated siblings who were part of a conflictual relationship with one another often experienced higher internalizing and externalizing (i.e., aggression) problems (Buist & Vermande, 2014).

Looking more at the negative effect that siblings can have on one another, Tucker, Finkelhor, Turner, and Shattuck (2014) examined the victimization (i.e., psychological-, physical-, or property-related aggression) upon children (3–9 years old) and adolescents (10–17 years old) by their peers and siblings. Researchers found those children and adolescents who reported having been victimized by a sibling had greater odds of also reporting peer victimization and greater mental distress. The researchers discussed how the importance of the peer and sibling relationships during the child and adolescent years can have a negative effect on an individual's mental health if victimization occurs. It could also be said that victimization is a way siblings may attempt to establish control within their relationship; control is often a tactic used in the navigation of the sibling dynamic (Tucker, Updegraff, & Baril, 2010). As siblings age (i.e., getting closer to middle adolescence) there seems to be a decrease in the amount of control exerted by each sibling (Tucker et al., 2014; Tucker et al., 2010) with the exception being those siblings who are further apart in age (Tucker et al., 2010).

Conversely, sibling relationships can be a significant positive force in childhood and adolescent development. As siblings often serve as mentors, teachers, and friends to one another (Craft-Rosenberg et al., 2011), positive childhood sibling interactions have been shown to foster higher empathetic engagement between siblings as they become older (Lam, Solmeyer, & McHale, 2012). Sibling relationships can also serve as protective forces against various stressors, such as parental mental health issues (Keeton, Teetsell, Dull, & Ginsburg, 2015) and traumatic events (Perricone, Fontana, Burgio, & Polizzi, 2014); these relationships also help decrease the prevalence of internalizing and social problems in at-risk boys (Morgan et al., 2012).

Even though siblings are often born to the same parents, with the exception of blended families and adopted siblings, the family environment changes as each child is born or brought into the family. Dirks, Persram, Recchia, and Howe (2015) emphasized that the sibling dynamic must be evaluated within the network of other family relationships as they all can influence one another. Multiple variables, such as personality traits, parent–child dynamics, and cultural norms, are relevant and make each sibling experience different, and thus, each sibling relationship unique (Edward, 2011). Described as multidimensional, these relationships between brothers and sisters alike are shaped over time and place (Whiteman, McHale, et al., 2011), by themselves and their families, as well as extrafamilial factors (McHale, Updegraff, & Whiteman, 2012) such as peers (Tucker et al., 2014).

In short, the dynamics of each sibling relationship has to be uniquely considered when determining how each brother or sister is affected by his or her relationship with one another. Some can be mostly positive, some can be mostly negative, while others are in-between. As the sibling relationship can be a complex, ambivalent (Edward, 2011), and multidimensional (Whiteman, McHale et al., 2011) relationship, the need for unique consideration is then also important when determining how a child may react to, and be affected by, the death of his or her brother or sister. As sibling relationships can be significant social and developmental pillars in a child's life, understanding the child's relationship with his or her deceased sibling is just as important as understanding the child's grief process.

Sibling Bereavement

Approximately 3,245 children and adolescents die each year in Canada (Statistics Canada CANSIM Database, 2011), while 42,328 die in the United States (Center for Disease Control and Prevention, 2016). The grief reaction experienced by a child after the death of his or her sibling is influenced by various factors including developmental level and age, temperament and coping resources, the nature of the relationship with the sibling, the inner representation of the deceased sibling, the nature of the sibling's death, the family dynamics, parental reactions to the death (Edward, 2011; Koehler, 2010), spiritual beliefs, and ethnicity (Becvar, 2011). What is clear is that the surviving sibling is forever changed by his or her traumatic experience (Machajewski & Kronk, 2013; Marshall & Davies, 2011), even into adulthood (Sveen, Eilegård, Steineck, & Kreicbergs, 2014; Vollmann, 2014). When a sibling dies, the surviving child's worldview of safety can be called into question, which can negatively affect not only his or her current relationships with parents, family, friends, or other siblings but also future relational experiences and the ability to establish trust within them (Charles & Charles, 2006).

Various researchers have described the death of a sibling as a potential *double loss*, where not only does the sibling lose his or her brother or sister but also the emotional support from parents who may be preoccupied with their own grief (Avelin, Gyllenswärd, Erlandsson, & Rådestad, 2014; Becvar, 2011; Horsley & Patterson, 2006; O'Leary & Gaziano, 2011). If the sibling who died experienced a lengthy illness, parental physical and emotional resources may have been directed toward that child and thus unavailable for the healthy child during their sibling's illness and after their sibling's death. The disconnect between the surviving child's needs and parental ability to attend to those needs can then negatively effect the surviving child's well-being. Bereaved children and adolescents may even be discounted as significant grievers by their parents, family members, and peers (Balk, 2014; Edward, 2011; Seyda & Fitzsimons, 2010).

The term *disenfranchised grief* is used when one's grief is discounted by others for various reasons and can lead to isolation in one's bereavement and complicate one's grief work (Doka, 1999). For example, if a child's sibling dies before or during birth, individuals may not understand how a child could be affected since he or she never physically met the sibling (Seyda & Fitzsimons, 2010). Moreover, if children are very young, individuals might believe they would not understand death; therefore, it is assumed that young children would not be affected by a death in the family. Older children could also experience disenfranchised grief because when a child dies, much of the focus and support tends to go toward the parents rather than the children (Balk, 2014). Peers may not know what to say or how to interact with someone whose sibling has just died, making the surviving child feel different from his or her peers and thus abandoned (Jonas-Simpson, Steele, Granek, Davies, & O'Leary, 2015; Marshall & Davies, 2011).

The death of a child is impactful for all those involved. Even if a sibling's grief is being acknowledged, he (or she) may attempt to hide his grief reactions from his parents to prevent further emotional instability or hardship (Balk, 2014; Koehler, 2010; Malcolm, Gibson, Adams, Anderson, & Forbat, 2014). The death of a brother or sister, no matter how attentive parents are to the surviving child's grief, can be very significant to the surviving sibling(s). In order to better understand sibling bereavement, it is important to be aware of the various grief reactions that a surviving child may exhibit (see Chapter 3 for an overview of normative grief).

Sibling Responses

Many common grief reactions are exhibited by bereaved siblings, such as feelings of confusion, fear, anger, loneliness, depression, shock, guilt, numbness (Balk, 2014), injustice, sadness, helplessness, a sense of vulnerability (Avelin et al., 2014), irritability, and even jealously over the parents' preoccupation with the dying or diseased sibling (Koehler, 2010). Koehler (2010) described how children may even display signs of happiness at times, as other emotions may be too overwhelming for them to consistently cope with. Somatic symptoms can also be present where children's grief may be expressed through muscular tension, headaches, sleep disturbances, nightmares, loss of appetite, and lower immune functioning. According to Koehler, some children may even experience a delayed response, seeming fine after the death but then displaying grief symptoms later on. Erlandsson, Avelin, Säflund, Wredling, and Rådestad (2010) described child sibling reactions after the death of their stillborn brother or sister. Reactions noted included wanting to be physically close to the deceased and their parents, talking about their feelings, reading about hope and death, drawing the deceased, and pretending to play with them.

Another grief reaction could be one that comes even before the death of the sibling. Using open-ended interviews, researchers Nolbris, Enskär, and Hellström (2014) qualitatively investigated the experiences of 29 siblings whose respective brother or sister was diagnosed with cancer. A common theme of anticipatory grief was uncovered where siblings who were sampled described experiencing grief symptoms as soon as they learned of the diagnosis. Those sampled reported difficulty sleeping and experiencing anxiety, as well as wishing someone would have been there to talk to them about their dying sibling's treatment and impending death.

What is more unique about a bereaved sibling who experienced the death of a brother or sister during childhood or adolescence, compared to an adult's grief reaction, is how developmental changes can affect their grief reaction.

Developmental Influence

Machajewski and Kronk (2013) summarized research about how bereaved siblings can be affected according to their developmental level. As the bereaved siblings age, their understanding of death matures. With a deeper understanding of death comes an increase in the variety of potential reactions. According to Piaget (1972), younger children who are in the preoperational stage of development can experience a regression in their behaviors, an increase in aggressive behaviors, displays of anger, and attention seeking. Those children in the concrete operational stage can exhibit the same developmental reactions as their younger counterparts as well as increased anxiety, fear, depression, and loneliness. Downy (2005) even suggested that these younger children tend to show more behavioral and anxiety issues in their grief reactions.

Research by Barrera, Alam, D'Agostino, Nicholas, and Schneiderman (2013) used secondary analyses of qualitative interviews conducted with 20 bereaved families to investigate what parents observed within their surviving children after the death of a child. The researchers found parents reported the surviving siblings (i.e., under the age of 6) struggled with understanding the concept of death, experienced sadness, and were angry they no longer had their sibling as a playmate 6 months after the death of their brother or sister. As the surviving children aged, some parents also identified their child's growing understanding and awareness of death as evidenced through increased grief reactions at the 18-month post-death mark. These researchers also found adolescents in their sample displayed fears of dying, hid their sadness from their parents, experienced difficulty in their academics, and engaged in risk-related behaviors, such as getting piercings, tattoos, and alcohol use. Adolescents can even experience some of the same reactions as younger children but may also existentially question life's purpose and seek peer support rather than familial support (Downy, 2005).

Summarized Sibling Grief Reactions

Davies (1999) outlined four ways a child may respond to the death of a sibling: *I hurt inside, I don't understand, I don't belong,* and *I'm not enough. I hurt inside* can be characterized by emotions such as fear, sadness, anger, loneliness, and many other emotional reactions noted above. As the child may not have the verbal capacity to explain his or her feelings, he or she may withdraw, be aggressive, or experience a change in appetite. The *I hurt inside* reaction is developed though the pain of losing the bond with the deceased.

The *I don't understand* response can occur alongside feelings of being overwhelmed and anxious. This reaction can stem from children being confused about the death and not receiving information about the current situation or the future in a way they understand (Davies, 1999). Youngblut (2013) found that some parents who lost a child identified that their surviving child experienced difficulty comprehending their sibling's death, causing confusion (supporting Davies' reaction category).

I don't belong relates to a child feeling out of place in their family because of their grief reaction (i.e., as it may differ from other family members) or because they try and help the family but are not acknowledged for it (Davies, 1999). Adolescents reported when their grieving styles did not match that of their parents, they felt guilty and inadequate for not grieving as they should: The discrepancy then created distance between them and their caregivers (Avelin et al., 2014). Children on the other hand reported feeling unimportant and forgotten (Nolbris et al., 2014).

As the family's grief is so intense, it may change the equilibrium within the family causing the child to feel ignored (O'Leary & Gaziano, 2011). *I'm not enough* is about the surviving child feeling they are second to the deceased sibling. Surviving children may attempt to be good at everything they do in their lives in an attempt to demonstrate they are worthy of parental attachment and attention (Davies, 1999).

According to Davies and Limbo (2010), when children are exhibiting a number of different reactions that were not existent before the death of their sibling, this may be a sign that intervention is required. Reactions that persist for an extended period of time such as sadness, depression, irritability, anxiety, social withdrawal, low self-esteem, or eating or sleeping difficulties may also indicate intervention is warranted. Other evidence to suggest intervention may be required can be seen through the research conducted outlining the various consequences related to the death of a sibling.

Potential Outcomes

Parents may be preoccupied with their own grief over the loss of their child. This preoccupation can then affect the surviving child(ren) in negative ways. The adolescents sampled by Avelin and colleagues (2014) described feeling alone and noticing their family relationships were affected by the still-born death of a stepbrother or -sister. The bereaved siblings mentioned a feeling of losing the future they envisioned for the family after the death of their sibling. Those sampled described feeling a sense of exclusion from their ability to grieve (i.e., disenfranchised) and also noted feeling unsure of their identity after the death of their sibling. The uncertainty of identity was described as being related to the loss and acceptance of new roles within the bereaved family.

Edward (2011) postulated a change of roles can threaten a surviving child's sense of identity. Moreover, it can also negatively affect the optimistic nature of a child as well as confidence in him- or herself and others. Koehler (2010) also discussed this notion that if the relationship between siblings was extremely close, this can severely disrupt the bereaved child's sense of identity (e.g., he or she is no longer a brother or sister, role model, protector, etc.).

Mental Health and Wellness

Fanos, Little, and Edwards (2009) identified some adults in their sample who lost a sibling during childhood reported having experienced anxiety as a child. Of those sampled, respondents identified the anxiety experienced was related to concern for their parents. Gerhardt et al. (2012) also identified difficulties experienced by bereaved siblings compared to their non-bereaved peers. Young bereaved children in elementary school tended to be seen as having greater social difficulty than their non-bereaved peers, according to their teachers and classmates. These children were viewed as more sensitive, isolated, less prosocial, less accepted by their peers, and victimized; this perspective was particularly true for young boys. The authors speculated that the bereaved school children experienced social difficulties because their parents may not have been as emotionally present with their child in order to foster social development. This effect was not found in adolescents as the authors hypothesized teens have, and may seek more, peer support during their bereavement rather than parental support.

Looking at the effect on adolescents, Stikkelbroek, Bodden, Reitz, Vollebergh, and van Baar (2015) noted those who experienced the death of a parent or sibling were 4 times as likely to exhibit internalizing problems (i.e., mental health issues) compared to their non-bereaved peers. The authors also found factors such as low-socioeconomic status (SES) and being female were associated with greater chances of developing internalizing problems during bereavement. The probability of developing externalizing problems (e.g., anger, aggression) was also influenced by lower SES and bereavement but not gender.

Fletcher, Mailick, Song, and Wolfe (2013) also found a significant gender difference where adult females seemed to be at a disadvantage after the death of a sibling during childhood or adolescence. Examining two large datasets from the United States, the researchers found females who lost a sibling during childhood were more likely to drop out of high school, not attend college, have lower wage earnings, become pregnant as a teen, and access social programs. All of those factors were associated with a lower SES. Those surviving sisters whose respective sibling died suddenly due to illness were seen to be the most negatively affected when it came to educational attainment.

Fletcher et al. even found an association between marriage and sibling death. Sisters who experienced the death of an infant sibling were less likely to be married and those sisters who experienced the long-term illness of a sibling were more likely to never be married. When a sibling died during infancy, males tended to experience lower academic test scores but it did not seem to significantly influence their educational attainment. Only a sibling suicide was associated with a significant reduction in educational attainment for males.

Other research by Clarke, Tanskanen, Huttunen, and Cannon (2013) described the negative effect the death of a sibling or father during early childhood had on adult life. Results indicated a 1.6-fold increase in chances of developing bipolar disorder and a 1.3-fold increase of chances for developing schizophrenia if the father or sibling died suddenly or violently rather than due to illness during the subject's childhood. The authors suggested such early life stressors may negatively impact the child's neurodevelopment and thus increase the risk of developing a psychiatric disorder. Clarke et al. hypothesized the negative neurodevelopment could be the result of developing posttraumatic stress disorder (PTSD) as a child or even experiencing dysfunction of the hypothalamic-pituitary-adrenal axis, which is key in stress management. Mental health issues such as PTSD and complicated grief have been linked to childhood sibling bereavement mitigated by factors such as age of the deceased sibling, age of surviving child, support system availability, and timing of intervention, as well as family dynamics (Dickens, 2014).

Positive Outcomes

Looking at potential positive consequences, Jonas-Simpson et al. (2015) identified children who continued to have a bond with their deceased sibling often displayed traits of compassion, empathy, and increased resilience which could be framed as posttraumatic growth. Some parents of children sampled in one study perceived them to have experienced an increase in maturity after the death of their sibling. Some surviving siblings reported an increase in academic achievement (Foster et al., 2012). Furthermore, Gerhardt and colleagues (2012) described how bereaved siblings who were in grades 7 to 12 were more likely to be viewed as popular and possess leadership qualities by their peers and teachers after their sibling's death. Other research highlighted that some bereaved siblings enter into helping or health-care professions because of their experience (Fanos et al., 2009).

Although there are negative consequences and implications related to the experience of losing a sibling, there also appears to be some positive consequences. Ways to increase the potential development of these positive consequences and mitigate the negative ones can be attained through supporting the child in ways that will be discussed through the case study below.

Case Study

Joseph was a 9-year-old boy who was brought to counseling by his parents. Before the death of his sister Sarah a year ago, Joseph was described as an adventurous and outgoing child. Joseph's parents noted that since Sarah's death, he has been experiencing intense episodes of anxiety, is more interested in staying at home, and is having previously nonexistent academic difficulties. Joseph's parents also noted that Sarah's death was not the only child-related death experienced by the family.

Joseph's parents described having had a miscarriage a couple of years after Joseph was born. Moreover, when Joseph was 4 years old, his parents gave birth to a daughter named Autumn. Everything initially seemed to be fine with Autumn until various tests revealed she had a genetic disorder called spinal muscular atrophy-I (SMA-I). SMA-I is a debilitating recessive neurological disease that affects the muscles in the body (Iannaconne, Smith, & Simard, 2004). Both Autumn and Sarah had SMA-I and died due to SMA-I–related complications within a year of their respective births. Joseph's parents described the stressful environment of the household during the times when their daughters' conditions were deteriorating. The parents talked about nurses/support personnel coming in and out the house, supplies being delivered at various hours, and people coming to visit or drop off meals. On days where Autumn and Sarah seemed to be having difficulty, Joseph's parents would send him over to a neighbor's house. Joseph's parents emphasized they tried to have at least one of them with him when he was home but that it was not always possible. As a result, Joseph would often play alone.

Joseph's parents reported that his behavior after the death of Autumn was "pretty normal" and that he did not seem to be greatly impacted. His parents described being unsure of how to initially tell Joseph about Autumn's death but they told him directly and allowed him to spend time with his deceased sister. Joseph was always a kind child and so it did not surprise his parents that at Autumn's funeral he could be found talking to his cousins about his sister, asking if they would like to view the body, and demonstrating comforting behaviors toward them. However, Joseph's worry-free disposition changed after Sarah's death, seeming to be less assured of himself as well as of the safety of the world he lived in.

During play therapy sessions, Joseph discussed not remembering his parent's miscarriage nor if they had talked to him about it. Joseph described hazy memories of Autumn and how he remembered seeing his parents crying in their bedroom but not being sure why. He remembered enjoying the time he was able to spend with his parents after Autumn's death because he had them both to himself. Joseph also highlighted that lately he was having a particular fear of eating in restaurants and feeling overwhelmed by the noise, people, and smells associated with them.

Joseph went on to describe not really feeling like he experienced significant grief after the deaths of his sisters. He identified that he was saddened by their deaths but that they were young and so he was not really able to engage with them at his level of play. Joseph described not missing the sound of crying babies in the home and also mentioned not missing the sound of the suction machine his parents would have to use on his sisters to clear their throats of mucus (due to their weakened muscles). Joseph also discussed how a lot of his friends did not know what to say to him when he returned to school and that he felt like an outsider compared to his peers, "All I want is for them to treat me like they did before Sarah died."

Providing Support

When considering the case example of Joseph and his family, there are several important highlights:

- Understanding the sibling relationship is just as important as understanding the bereaved sibling's grief experience.
- Bereaved siblings can be both negatively and positively affected by the death of their brother or sister.
- There may be long-term implications in the surviving sibling's life if caregivers or other family members are not attentive to the child's needs.

Additionally, children's grief can be supported through communication, modeling, and making sense of the loss.

Communication

The need for clear and direct communication is vital in fostering family coherence and improving longitudinal family outcomes (Barrera et al., 2013). Information then needs to be presented in an open, honest, and developmentally appropriate way (Moore & Moore, 2010) to maximize the child's understanding of death. If the death is not communicated in these ways, Edward (2011) has described how younger children will often create their own realities/fantasies if information is not provided about their dying or deceased sibling. A climate conducive to family secrets can even develop as a result of limited communication around the death of a sibling (Fanos et al., 2009).

Balk (2014) described the importance of family communication and its effect on adolescents in bereaved families. Families viewed as experiencing greater coherency/connection allowed teens to feel comfortable to talk to their family members about the death of their sibling. By talking about their grief, the teens reported less fear, shock, numbness, and loneliness over time, as they were able to resolve their grief. In contrast, those adolescents in less coherent families initially tended to report guilt and anger which then led to confusion about the death. Teachers, grandparents, counselors friends, or family members can all be individuals who children seek comfort from: These adults should note that one of the most important parts of supporting a child in grief is to listen to what the child has to say without judgement (Jonas-Simpson et al., 2015).

Modeling

Jonas–Simpson and colleagues (2015) noted in their sample that parents who were emotionally open with their children served as grief models, illustrating that it was acceptable to cry, express emotions, and articulate how one felt. The vulnerability parents displayed then enhanced the child's feelings of vulnerability. Because parents were open with their feelings, it offered the child opportunities to develop resilience skills as he or she learned to accept and trust his or her own feeling over what others may think or say. It is important that if parents are overcome by their grief, other family members step in and serve as healthy grief models for the surviving child (Sood, Razdan, Weller, & Weller, 2006).

Making Meaning

There are countless ways children can conduct their grief work. Some children and adolescents may be fine working through it with receptive family members, while others may benefit from therapeutic intervention. Bereavement support groups can be a positive modality of intervention where children and adolescents learn they are not alone in their grief, are able to share their emotions in a safe and compassionate environment, and the group can normalize their grief in the shared bereavement experience (Balk, 2011). Research summarized by Dickens (2014) emphasized the importance of making meaning of the deceased sibling's life as well as the survivor's life during sibling grief. Doing so aided in the survivor's grief work and processing.

Processing a sibling's or one's own meaning in life could be something that is worked on in therapy. For example, De Preter and Hooghe (2012) discussed how bereaved children can benefit from developing a "Life Story" where they can collect and review all of their different experiences using words, pictures, drawings, and more. Conducting this exercise can help the child identify his or her support network, and that the large and small things he or she does in life matter. Supporting children in maintaining a continuing bond with the deceased through memory work, using things such as memory boxes or books, can also support meaning making (Goldman, 2012) as can bibliotherapy (i.e., the use of storybooks to help children find personal meaning in their grief; Robinson, 2012). All these activities can help children and adolescents not only process the death but also support post-death self-development and understanding.

Offering children some sense of normalcy by engaging in typical daily activities (Barrera et al., 2013) can also be a way to offer them some emotional stability. Fanos et al. (2009) noted in their sample of bereaved individuals how creating or maintaining family rituals was another way families helped maintain a sense of connection with the deceased. Some families reported visiting the grave of the deceased child on special days (e.g., birthdays, holidays), planting a special tree, or holding on to keepsakes of the deceased or photos. All offered opportunities for the child to continue their bond with their deceased sibling and this continuing bond helped facilitate familial communication among the bereaved.

Foster et al. (2011) highlighted various activities such as doing things the deceased child enjoyed doing, creating special events, honoring the deceased, and spending time where the deceased child used to spend time as ways bereaved families were able to maintain a bond with the deceased child.

In all, just as the sibling relationship is unique to each pair, so too is the sibling grief experience that follows the death of a brother or sister. It is then important to consider each child's situation uniquely when determining how best to support children in their bereavement.

Discussion Questions

1. Review the case study of Joseph and, based on the information presented in this chapter, discuss why his parents may have felt therapy would be helpful for him.
2. If your friend experienced the death of a child, what might you do to support them as well as their surviving child(ren)?
3. How might we better support siblings so that their grief is less disenfranchised?

References

Avelin, P., Gyllensward, G., Erlandsson, K., & Rådestad, I. (2014). Adolescents' experiences of having a stillborn half-sibling. *Death Studies, 38,* 557–562. doi:10.1080/07481187.2013.809034

Balk, D. E. (2011). Adolescence, sibling death, and bereavement. In J. Caspi (Ed.), *Sibling development: Implications for mental health practioners* (pp. 358–376). New York, NY: Springer.

Balk, D. E. (2014). *Dealing with dying, death, and grief during adolescence.* New York, NY: Routledge.

Bandura, A. (1977). *Social learning theory.* Englewood Cliffs, NJ: Prentice Hall.

Barrera, M., Alam, R., D'Agostino, N. M., Nicholas, D. B., & Schneiderman, G. (2013). Parental perceptions of siblings' grieving after a childhood cancer death: A longitudinal study. *Death Studies, 37*, 25–46. doi:10.1080/07481187.2012.678262

Becvar, D. S. (2011). Death and the grieving process in families. In M. Craft-Rosenberg & S. R. Pehler (Eds.), *Encyclopedia of family health* (pp. 278–280). doi:http://dx.doi.org/10.4135/9781412994071.n102

Bowlby, J. (1969). *Attachment and loss: Attachment* (Vol. 1). London, UK: Hogarth.

Buist, K. L., & Vermande, M. (2014). Sibling relationship patterns and their associations with child competence and problem behavior. *Journal of Family Psychology, 28*(4), 529–537. doi: http://dx.doi.org/10.1037/a0036990

Centre for Disease Control and Prevention, National Vital Statistics Report. (2016). *Deaths: Final data for 2013* (NVSR Volume 64, Number 2). Retrieved from www.cdc.gov/nchs/data/nvsr/nvsr64/nvsr64_02.pdf

Charles, D. R., & Charles, M. (2006). Sibling loss and attachment style: An exploratory study. *Psychoanalytic Psychology, 23*(1), 72–90. doi:10.1037/0736-9735.23.1.72

Clarke, M. C., Tanskanen, A., Huttunen, M. O., & Cannon, M. (2013). Sudden death of father or sibling in early childhood increases risk for psychotic disorder. *Schizophrenia Research, 143,* 363–366. doi:http://dx.doi.org/10.1016/j.schres.2012.11.024

Craft-Rosenberg, M., Montgomery, L. A., Hill, J. M., Kauder, J. K., & Eisbach, S. (2011). Sibling death/loss. In M. Craft-Rosenberg & S. R. Pehler (Eds.), *Encyclopedia of family health* (pp. 951–957). doi:http://dx.doi.org/10.4135/9781412994071.n311

Davies, B. (1999). *Shadows in the sun: The experiences of sibling bereavement in childhood.* Philadelphia, PA: Brunner/Mazel.

Davies, B., & Limbo, R. (2010). The grief of siblings. In N. B. Webb (Ed.), *Helping bereaved children: A handbook for practitioners* (3rd ed., pp. 69–90). New York, NY: The Guilford Press.

De Preter, M., & Hooghe, A. (2012). Documenting children's life stories. In R. A. Neimeyer (Ed.), *Techniques of grief therapy: Creative practices for counseling the bereaved* (pp. 193–195). New York, NY: Routledge.

Dickens, N. (2014). Prevalence of complicated grief and posttraumatic stress disorder in children and adolescents following sibling death. *The Family Journal: Counselling and Therapy for Couples and Families, 22*(1), 119–126. doi:10.1177/1066480713505066

Dirks, M. A., Persram, R., Recchia, H. E., & Howe, N. (2015). Sibling relationships as sources of risk and resilience in the development and maintenance of internalizing and externalizing problems during childhood and adolescence. *Clinical Psychology Review, 42,* 145–155. doi:10.1016/j.cpr.2015.07.003

Doka, K. J. (1999). Disenfranchised grief. *Bereavement Care, 18*(3), 37–39. Retrieved from www.tandfonline.com/doi/abs/10.1080/02682629908657467?journalCode=rber20

Downy, L. (2005). Children bereaved by parent or sibling death. *Psychiatry, 4*(9), 118–122. doi:10.1383/psyt.2005.4.9.118

Edward. J. (2011). *Sibling relationship: A force for growth and conflict.* London, UK: Rowman & Littlefield.

Erlandsson, K., Avelin, P., Säflund, K., Wredling, R., & Rådestad, I. (2010). Siblings' farewell to a stillborn sister or brother and parents' support to their older children: A questionnaire study from the parents' perspective. *Journal of Child Health Care, 14*(2), 151–160. doi:10.1177/1367493509355621

Fanos, J. H., Little, G. A., & Edwards, W. H. (2009). Candles in the snow: Ritual and memory for siblings of infants who died in the intensive care nursery. *The Journal of Pediatrics, 154*(6), 849–853. doi:10.1016/j.jpeds.2008.11.053

Fletcher, J., Mailick, M., Sung, S., & Wolfe, B. (2013). A sibling death in the family: Common and consequential. *Demography, 50,* 803–826. doi:10.1007/s13524-012-0162-4

Foster, T. L., Gilmer, M. J., Davies, B., Dietrich, M. S., Barrera, M., Fairclough, D. L., . . . Gerhardt, C. A. (2011). Comparisons of continuing bonds reported by parents and siblings after a child's death from cancer. *Death Studies, 35,* 420–440. doi:10.1080/07481187.2011.553308

Foster, T. L., Gilmer, M. J., Vannatta, K., Barrera, M., Davies, B., Dietrich, M. S., . . . Gerhardt, C. A. (2012). Changes in siblings after the death of a child from cancer. *Cancer Nursing, 35*(5), 347–354. doi:10.1097/NCC.0b013e3182365646

Gerhardt, C., Fairclough, D. L., Grossenbacher, J. C., Barrera, M., Glimer, M. J., Foster, T. L., . . . Vannatta, K. (2012). Peer relationships of bereaved siblings and comparison classmates after a child's death from cancer. *Journal of Pediatric Psychology, 37*(2), 209–219. doi:10.1093/jpepsy/jsr082

Goldman, L. (2012). Memory work with children. In R. A. Neimeyer (Ed.), *Techniques of grief therapy: Creative practices for counseling the bereaved* (pp. 240–242). New York, NY: Routledge.

Horsley, H., & Patterson, T. (2006). The effects of a parent guidance intervention on communication among adolescents who have experienced the sudden death of a sibling. *The American Journal of Family Therapy, 34*(2), 119–137. doi:10.1080/01926180500301519

Howe, N., Ross, H. S., & Recchia, H. (2011). Sibling relations in early and middle childhood. In P. K. Smith & C. H. Hart (Eds.), *The Wiley-Blackwell handbook of childhood social development* (2nd ed., pp. 356–372). Oxford, UK: Wiley-Blackwell.

Iannaccone, S. T., Smith, S. A., & Simard, L. R. (2004). Spinal muscular atrophy. *Current Neurology and Neuroscience Reports, 4*(1), 74–80. Retrieved from www.unboundmedicine.com/medline/citation/14683633/Spinal_muscular_atrophy

Jonas-Simpson, C., Steele, R., Granek, L., Davies, B., & O'Leary, J. (2015). Always with me: Understanding experiences of bereaved children whose baby sibling died. *Death Studies, 39,* 242–251. doi:10.1080/07481187.2014.991954

Keeton, C. P., Teetsel, R. N., Dull, N. M. S., & Ginsburg, G. S. (2015). Parent psychopathology and children's psychological health moderation by sibling relationships dimensions. *Abnormal Child Psychology, 43,* 1333–1342. doi:10.1007/s10802-015-0013-z

Koehler, K. (2010). Sibling bereavement in childhood. In C. A. Corr & D. E. Balk (Eds.), *Children's encounters with death, bereavement, and coping* (pp. 195–218). New York, NY: Springer.

Lam, C. B., Solmeyer, A. R., & McHale, S. M. (2012). Sibling relationships and empathy across the transitions to adolescence. *Journal of Youth and Adolescence, 41,* 1657–1670. doi:10.1007/s10964-012-9781-8

Machajewski, V., & Kronk, R. (2013). Childhood grief related to the death of a sibling. *The Journal of Nurse Practitioners, 9*(7), 443–448. doi:http://dx.doi.org/10.1016/j.nurpra.2013.03.020

Malcolm, C., Gibson, F., Adams, S., Anderson, G., & Forbat, L. (2014). A relational understanding of sibling experiences of children with rare life-limiting conditions:

Findings from a qualitative study. *Journal of Child Health Care, 18*(3), 230–240. doi:10.1177/1367493513485825

Marshall, B., & Davies, B. (2011). Bereavement in children and adults following the death of a sibling. In R. A. Neimeyer, D. L. Harris, H. R. Winokuer, & G. F. Thornton (Eds.), *Grief and bereavement in contemporary society* (pp. 107–116). New York, NY: Taylor & Francis.

McHale, S. M., Updegraff, K. A., & Whiteman, S. D. (2012). Sibling relationships and influences in childhood and adolescence. *Journal of Marriage and Family, 74*, 913–930. doi:10.1111/j.1741-3737.2012.01011.x

Moore, J., & Moore, C. (2010). Talking to children about death-related issues. In C. A. Corr & D. E. Balk (Eds.), *Children's encounters with death, bereavement, and coping* (pp. 277–291). New York, NY: Springer.

Morgan, J. K., Shaw, D. S. S., & Olino, T. M. (2012). Differential susceptibility effects: The interaction of negative emotionality and sibling relationship quality on childhood internalizing problems and social skills. *Journal of Abnormal Child Psychology, 40*, 885–899. doi:10.1007/s10802-012-9618-7

Nolbris, M., Enskär, K., & Hellström, A. (2014). Grief related to the experience of being the sibling of a child with cancer. *Cancer Nursing, 37*(5), E1–7. doi:10.1097/NCC.0b013e3182a3e585

O'Leary, J. M., & Gaziano, C. (2011). Sibling grief after perinatal loss. *Journal of Prenatal and Perinatal Psychology and Heath, 25*(3), 173–193. Retrieved from www.researchgate.net/profile/Cecilie_Gaziano/publication/216347672_Sibling_Grief_After_Perinatal_Loss/links/0912f508ffd0e79dfd000000.pdf

Perricone, G., Fontana, V., Burgio, S., & Polizzi, C. (2014). Sibling relationships as a resource for traumatic events. *SpringerPlus, 3*, 525–530. Retrieved from www.springerplus.com/content/3/1/525

Piaget, J. (1972). Intellectual evolution from adolescence to childhood. *Human Development, 15*, 1–12. Retrieved from www.karger.com/Article/PDF/271225

Robinson, J. C. (2012). Bibliotherapy with children. In R. A. Neimeyer (Ed.), *Techniques of grief therapy: Creative practices for counseling the bereaved* (pp. 306–308). New York, NY: Routledge.

Seyda, B. A. & Fitzsimons, A. M. (2010). Infant death. In C. A. Corr & D. E. Balk (Eds.), *Children's encounters with death, bereavement, and coping.* New York, NY: Springer.

Sood, A. B., Razdan, A., Weller, E. B., & Weller, R. A. (2006). Children's reactions to parental and sibling death. *Current Psychiatry Reports, 8*(2), 155–120. Retrieved from www.ncbi.nlm.nih.gov/pubmed/16539886

Statistics Canada CANSIM Database. (2011). *Death and mortality rates by age group and sex, Canada, Provinces and Territories, Annual* (#102-0504). Retrieved from www5.statcan.gc.ca/cansim/pick-choisir?lang=eng&p2=33&id=1020504#customizeTab

Stikkelbroek, Y., Bodden, D. H. M., Reitz, E., Vollebergh, W. A. M., & van Baar, A. L. (2015). Mental health of adolescents before and after the death of a parent or sibling. *European child & Adolescent Psychiatry*, March, 1–11. doi:10.1007/s00787-015-0695-3

Sveen, J., Eilegård, A., Steinck, G., & Kreicbergs, U. (2014). They still grieve—a nationwide follow-up of young adults 2–9 years after losing a sibling to cancer. *Psycho-Oncology, 23*, 658–664. doi:10.1002/pon.3463

Tucker, C. J., Finkelhor, D., Turner, H., & Shattuck, A. M. (2014). Sibling and peer victimization in childhood and adolescence. *Child Abuse & Neglect, 38*, 1599–1606. doi:http://dx.doi.org/10.1016/j.chiabu.2014.05.007

Tucker, C. J., Updegraff, K., & Baril, M. E. (2010). Who's the boss? Patterns of control in adolescents' sibling relationships. *Family Relations, 59,* 520–532. doi:10.1111/j.1741-3729.2010.00620.x

Volling, B. L. (2001). Early attachment relationships as predictors of preschool children's emotion regulation with a distressed sibling. *Early Education and Development, 12,* 185–207. Retrieved from http://journals2.scholarsportal.info.proxy1.lib.uwo.ca/details/10409289/v12i0002/185_earapoerwads.xml

Vollmann, S. R. (2014). A legacy of loss: Stories of replacement dynamics and the subsequent child. *OMEGA, 69*(3), 219–247. doi:http://dx.doi.org/10.2190/OM69.3.a

Whiteman, S. D., Bernard, J. M. B., & Jensen, A. C. (2011). Sibling influence in human development. In J. Caspi (Ed.), *Sibling development: Implications for mental health practioners* (pp. 1–15). New York, NY: Springer.

Whiteman, S. D., McHale, S. M., & Soli, A. (2011). Theoretical perspectives on sibling relationships. *Journal of Family Theory & Review, 3,* 124–139. doi:10.1111/j.1756-2589.2011.00087.x

Youngblunt, J. M. (2013). Parents' report of child's response to sibling's death in a neonatal or pediatric intensive care unit. *American Journal of Critical Care, 22*(6), 474–481. doi:http://dx.doi.org/10.4037/ajcc2013790

7   Using Expressive Arts Following the Death of a Friend

Sheila O'Donovan

Piglet sidled up to Pooh from behind.
"Pooh!" he whispered.
"Yes, Piglet?"
"Nothing," said Piglet, taking Pooh's paw. "I just wanted to be sure of you."
                              A. A. Milne, *The House at Pooh Corner* (1988, p. 130).

For most of us, friendship is undoubtedly central to our lives, as friendships play a vital role and take place alongside key developmental changes. The positive influence of social interaction, emotional satisfaction, cognitive enhancement, and self-esteem that results from childhood friendships sets the stage for overall emotional, physical, and spiritual wellness as well as satisfying relationships in adulthood (Noppe & Noppe, 2008). Therefore, when a friend dies it can feel as though a part of us has died, changing our life narrative in a way we could not have predicted.

Research has shown that 87% of young people will experience the death of a peer during adolescence (Schachter, 1991, Cook & Oltjenbruns, 2004). Adolescent girls are 23% more likely than boys to experience peer death within a 1-year time frame (Rheingold et al., 2004). These deaths are typically sudden, unexpected, often violent, and viewed as preventable, such as death by suicide (Barrett, 1996). Girls of minority race/ethnicity and adolescents from households with lower incomes are at the greatest risk for experiencing peer death (Johnson, 2010). After a peer dies, children and teens are confronted with the realities of death and their own mortality. When a friend dies, their entire world and beliefs are questioned, and they can feel disrupted to the core (Schuurman, 2003).

For most children, death is a new experience, thus young children often do not know what to expect when someone dies. Children will look to their caregiver for answers to understand their confusing feelings. While adults may not have all the answers to questions children may have, especially when the loss is traumatic, they can help children better understand the grieving process (Perry & Rubenstein, 2002).

For younger children, the first challenge is for them to understand the circumstances of death and the long-term implications (Cowan, 2010).

Unlike the adolescent who can think abstractly and understand the permanence of death, the younger child understands primarily that something has changed (Cowan, 2010). There is evidence to support the view that the majority of children do not actually experience serious emotional problems following bereavement (Dowdney, 2000; Haine et al, 2008). Research shows that 10–15% of grievers experience persistent and disabling grief symptoms following loss, and this percentage tends to be relatively consistent for both children and adults (Mancini, Griffin, & Bonanno, 2012). Rolls and Payne (2007) found that children who required additional support benefitted from speaking with someone who understood their experience; this could be someone who had experienced loss themselves or a professional trained in the field of grief and loss. Bull and Pengelly (2014) developed a four-session 3-hour grief group for children at the George Thomas Centre Hospice Care Centre in England. After attending these sessions, children provided feedback such as, "It was good to talk to others about the happy memories," "I learnt to share my feelings," and "I'm not the only one." Explaining death and understanding the grief process can be overwhelming for most people and therefore professional support can provide assistance to both the child and his or her family.

Caregivers supporting a bereaved child or teen may need to access a child therapist whose area of specialty is grief and loss. Creative art and play therapy have proven to be effective modalities of treatment. Ball's (2002) small but detailed long-term study of five severely emotionally disturbed children who participated in 50 sessions of individual art therapy provided evidence that art therapy treatment was a successful intervention for these children and suggested that art therapy may be an effective treatment for this population in other situations. Additionally, a meta-analysis of 42 studies on play therapy demonstrated that it is a viable and effective intervention for children with various additional emotional and physical needs (LeBlanc & Ritchie, 2001). A further meta-analysis of 93 play therapy studies concluded that play therapy is a worthwhile therapeutic intervention for a range of childhood problems (Bratton, Ray, Rhine, & Jones, 2005).

Creative Modalities of Treatment

Malchiodi (2014), an art therapist, explained that creative interventions have been formalized through the disciplines of art therapy, music therapy, dance/movement therapy, drama therapy or psychodrama, poetry therapy, and play therapy, including sandtray therapy. Each discipline has been applied in psychotherapy and counselling with individuals of all ages for more than 70 years. Art, music, dance, drama, and poetry therapies are referred to as *creative arts therapies* because of their roots in the arts and theories of creativity. Therapies that utilize self-expression in treatment are also called *expressive therapies* (Malchiodi, 2005, 2012, 2014). The expressive arts include a variety of creative processes to foster personal growth and awareness. The following is a description of what expressive art therapies are and how they invoke emotional growth and healing.

Art therapy is a health service profession that provides therapeutic intervention to those experiencing emotional difficulty. Art therapy can be used with children, adolescents, adults, and seniors. Children naturally express themselves through the use of art and play. Children and teens often do not have the words to articulate how they feel, especially with painful emotions, so the familiar cliché "a picture paints a thousand words" becomes much more meaningful when working with children because the process of creating and exploring their story through art becomes the conduit to healing and repair.

Art therapy functions on two levels, *process* and *product*. The process of creating art is inherently therapeutic, allowing for expression of emotions. The completed art product is used as the therapist guides the client in exploration of the work created and provides reflection on the thoughts and emotions that arise. Malchiodi (2012) stated that drawing provides children an impetus to tell their story and the ability to translate their experience into a narrative (Malchiodi, 2012). The act of drawing is a form of externalization, a visible projection of self, one's thoughts, and feelings (Riley, 1997).

Lusebrink, another art therapist, observed that images are "a bridge between body and mind, or between the conscious levels of information processing and the physiological changes in the body" (1990, p. 218). The capacity of art making to tap sensory material makes it a potent tool in grief and trauma intervention. In *The Handbook of Art Therapy*, Malchiodi (2012) explained that art making allows an individual to actively try out, experiment with, or rehearse a desired change through a drawing, painting, or collage through the use of a tangible object that can be physically altered. The process of creating art is inherently therapeutic, and, when processed with a qualified art therapist, the process can move people from passive victim to active survivor (Steele, 1997).

Play therapy is the systematic use of a theoretical model to establish an interpersonal process wherein qualified play therapists use the therapeutic powers of play to help clients prevent or resolve psychosocial difficulties and achieve optimal growth and development (Crenshaw & Stewart, 2014; Webb, 2007). Art and play therapy often go hand in hand. In play therapy, toys are like the child's words and play is the child's language (Landreth, 2002). Play therapy is especially appropriate for children ages 3 through 12 years old (Carmichael, 2006; Gil, 1991; Landreth, 2002; Schaefer, 2013). Teenagers and adults have also benefited from play techniques. Play-based interventions often involve the use of symbolic expression to help adolescents express themselves and allow clients to have a safe distance between themselves and painful reality (Bratton & Ferebee, 1999; Malchiodi, 2005).

Music therapy is the prescribed use of music to effect positive changes in the psychological, physical, cognitive, or social functioning of individuals with health or educational problems (American Music Therapy Association, 2014). Music is one of the primary ways that teenagers express their feelings, hopes, and dreams. Playing instruments and writing songs about personal experiences have been shown to provide a sense of relief in teens experiencing a loss (McFerran, Roberts, & O'Grady, 2010).

Drama therapy is the systematic and intentional use of drama/theater processes, products, and associations to achieve the therapeutic goals of symptom relief, emotional and physical integration, and personal growth. It is an active approach that helps the client tell his or her story to solve a problem, achieve catharsis, extend the depth and breadth of his or her inner experience, understand the meaning of images, and strengthen his or her ability to observe personal roles while increasing flexibility between roles (National Association for Drama Therapy, 2016).

Sandplay therapy is a creative form of psychotherapy that uses a sandbox and a large collection of miniatures to enable a client to explore the deeper layers of his or her psyche in a totally new format; by constructing a series of "sand pictures," a client is helped to illustrate and integrate his or her psychological condition (Malcholdi, 2012). Two recent research projects explored treatment effectiveness of group sandtray therapy. Mon-hsin & Ray (2007) determined that group sandplay is an effective treatment intervention for preadolescents with behavior problems. Shen and Armstrong (2008) showed how group sandplay with seventh-grade girls improved self-esteem in areas of academic competence, physical appearance, and global self-worth.

Integrative approaches involve two or more expressive therapies to foster awareness, encourage emotional growth, and enhance relationships with others. This approach distinguishes itself through combining modalities within a therapy session. Integrative approaches are based on a variety of orientations, including arts as therapy, arts psychotherapy, and the use of arts for traditional healing (Estrella, 2005; Knill, Levine, & Levine, 2005). Expressive arts therapies are a creative process of art making that can be used to transform grief. Individuals of all ages can learn to express, and make meaning of, their grief in a variety of ways through connecting creatively (Wood & Near, 2010).

When a Child Experiences the Death of a Peer

Preteens have a clearer understanding about the concept and permanence of death than is typically found in younger children (Cowan, 2010). Children ages 11–13 are faced with a tumultuous time of body changes and increased performance expectations; when a death loss is added to this time of upheaval and transition, children's sense of vulnerability and insecurity can intensify. Children are intermittent grievers, and as they move through their developmental stages, grief can resurface (Smith, 1999). Other losses can trigger unexpressed or suppressed feelings of grief to surface, often confusing the adults in their lives to think "they should be over this" (Cowan, 2010). To honor and recognize the reality that this age group does grieve and needs an opportunity to mourn, we will review a case study of an 11-year-old. This example illustrates not only the grief process, but the need for attuned and sensitive caregiving by Katie's parents.

Case Study

Katie was brought to an art therapist for counseling. Her parents described being worried about her since the death of her best friend, Emily, 6 months prior. Emily had been diagnosed with brain cancer a year prior to her death. Katie was an only child and her best friend Emily had been the closest relationship she had had. Katie had often referred to Emily as the sister she never had but had wished for. During Emily's illness, Katie was her biggest cheerleader, helping organize fundraisers to raise money for her medical costs and going along with Emily to appointments at the hospital. Since both of Katie's parents were top-level executives and often worked long hours, they were grateful that Emily's family included Katie so much in their activities. They felt that it gave Katie a sense of leadership and purpose to be by Emily's side while she was sick.

Prior to Emily's death, Katie's parents described Katie as outgoing, always happy, and ready to help anyone. However, since the death of Emily, Katie had become quiet and withdrawn. She rarely wanted to go out or see friends, and she had started expressing worries about her parents leaving the house, fearing that something bad might happen to them. She started talking back to her parents, which was unusual because she had always been "such a well-behaved girl." Additionally, Katie was a high achiever and her marks had always been reflective of that, achieving nothing less than an 80%. Since Emily's death, Katie's marks had slipped and she indicated that she could hear that the teacher was speaking but could not piece together what she was required to do most of the time.

During her art therapy sessions, Katie embraced the opportunity to express herself through creative modalities, primarily through the use of drawing and painting. During her first session, she drew things that told the therapist about who she was and how she was currently feeling. Katie drew a dark cloud with rain drops coming out of it which she said represented "death." Katie explained that she never used to think about death but now, most days, it was all she could think about. Further, she had drawn herself standing alone, looking sad. She included question marks all around the figure; she wrote "confused" beside this figure. Katie stated that she did not know who she was anymore without Emily in her life. She described that she was so used to being Emily's "side kick" but now did not know what to do or who she was to be now that Emily was gone.

At the direction of the therapist Katie drew how she saw herself, how she thought others saw her, and how she would like to be. Through this activity, she discovered that most of the time she wore a mask of happiness, but on the inside she often felt sad and worried. Through the processing of this drawing it was discovered that the wearing of these masks predated

Emily's death; however, since her death Katie found that it was becoming increasingly difficult to wear her "happy mask." Many of us wear masks throughout the day; often people do not realize that they put on masks when interacting with others. We wear masks to get through stressful times and when we are with our family members, friends, and coworkers. Sometimes we wear several different masks all within one day. At the directive of the therapist, Katie created two masks, the mask she wears most days to the outside world and the mask of grief, worry, and sadness she was feeling on the inside and often did not show to anyone.

This directive art therapy activity is designed to help clients become aware of the masks they wear and what they are actually feeling. It allows clients to become more aware of what is really going on behind the masks, assisting them in processing who they can show their internal masks to, why they may hide their feelings, and, finally, learn how to deal with their feelings in healthy ways. Katie was asked to process each mask, exploring who she feels safe enough to take her "happy" mask off with and show her true feelings of grief, sadness, and worry. Through this activity, Katie explored the relationship she had with her parents and discovered how she needed them to be more present in her life. Even prior to Emily's death, Katie often showed her parents the "happy mask," explaining it was because they expected so much of her, such as high marks, leadership, and what she coined as "perfection." She did not want to disappoint her parents, and therefore, often showed them her "happy mask," only taking this mask off at night when she was alone in her bed and felt safe enough to cry.

The processing of this creative art activity was a conduit to explore the attachment relationship between Katie and her parents. The Circle of Security framework developed by Powell, Cooper, Hoffman, and Marvin (2014) derived from attachment and object relations theories was then taught and processed with Katie's parents over a series of sessions. As a result, Katie's relationship with her parents changed in many positive ways. It was only after the attachment was more secure that Katie was better able to work through her feelings of grief.

Box 7.1   Circle of Security

Attachment theory provides a framework to comprehend children's fundamental relationship needs. The *Circle of Security*™ is a user-friendly map that was developed to teach attachment theory to parents.

- When children feel safe, their exploratory system or innate curiosity is activated and they need support (either verbally or nonverbally) for exploration;

- As they are exploring, sometimes they need their parents to watch over them, sometimes they need help, and sometimes they need their parents to enjoy with them;
- When they have explored long enough, (or if they get tired or anxious, or find themselves in an unsafe situation) they need their parents to welcome them back. When they return, they need their parents to comfort, protect, delight in, and/or organize their feelings. The focus on the last piece is because for many parents it is a new idea that children need help organizing their *internal* experience as well as the *external* environment.
- When the attachment system is terminated, children are ready to start the circle again.

Much of the training with parents (and therapists) entails helping them develop the observational skills to differentiate between exploration and attachment systems; it also involves differentiating among the specific needs within each system. With a clear understanding of attachment theory and enhanced observational skills, parents (and therapists) can sharpen their responses to further promote secure attachment.

For more information on the Circle of Security please visit: http://circleofsecurity.net/for-professionals/resources/treatment-assumptions/

We know that children experiencing grief can have regressive behaviors and often feel anxious. Since Katie was already anxious on most days, holding on to the fear of disappointing her parents coupled with the stress of the loss of her best friend had her feeling overly anxious and unable to cope with her day-to-day activities. Additionally, it was difficult to pay attention in class and to understand what she was supposed to be doing. These feelings dissipated once her parents became more attuned to her and more understanding of her attachment needs.

Schore (2000) explained that the need for emotional regulation is what drives attachment behaviors. Further, Graham, the author of the book *Bouncing Back* (2013), reminds us what Stern (2002) and Fonagy (2001) have amply demonstrated—that it is the need for empathy, the need to be seen, understood, and reflected, that drives the intersubjectivity that develops theory of mind. Graham eloquently explained that it is how parents use empathy, bonding, and reflection to regulate fear, anxiety, and shame to soothe the firing of the amygdala (which is in overdrive during times of stress) that helps the child discover who he or she is.

This serves as an important reminder that attunement and feedback are remarkably determinative of attachment patterns and are a crucial part of healing (Graham, 2013). Once Katie's parents were better able to have an accurate sense of who Katie was and to learn how to respond to her attachment needs, she was better able to emotionally regulate. This permitted her to become vulnerable enough to shed her "happy mask" and expose her feelings of sadness and grief to her parents. Katie's parents helped her discover who she was by seeing and accepting her.

This development then allowed Katie to work through her feelings of grief and loss. The workbook by American art therapist Marge Heegaard (1996), *When Someone Very Special Dies*, was used to assist her in creating and personalizing her story of grief. This workbook was designed for children ages 6–12. The book is organized to assist children in exploring their feelings of grief and learning healthy ways of coping with feelings of loss. With the assistance of an adult trained in grief and loss, children are invited to illustrate and personalize their loss through art (Heegaard, 1996).

In the event of a significant loss, it is necessary to be mindful of the significance of that person's role in our lives. In friendships, each individual plays out his or her role in their unique and specific nature (Toray & Oltjenbruns, 1996). These authors have indicated that secondary losses occur with the death of a friend. These losses include not only the roles that made up the friendship (confidante, companion, teammate) but also intangible losses (dreams, hopes, self-esteem). Katie described experiencing grief reactions indicative of secondary loss when she explained that she no longer knew who she was if she was not "Emily's sidekick." One of Emily's roles in their friendship was that of "the sick one," and one of Katie's roles was that of being "the cheerleader" to Emily. The art therapist helped Katie to identify the role of cheerleader, examining the pros and cons of this role, honoring the role yet also moving her through the grief process that was occurring with the death of this role. Further, she helped her to develop the new goals, dreams, and hopes that she wanted to aspire to now that Emily was gone.

When an Adolescent Experiences the Death of a Peer

According to the U.S. Department of Health and Human Services (2004), the rate of adolescent deaths has remained constant from 1990 to 2006. The average is 16,375 deaths per year for ages 12–19 (Minino, 2010). Of deaths among 12–19 year olds, 67% were due to accidents (unintentional injuries, 13%; homicide, 11%; suicide, 6%; cancer and heart disease, 3%; Minino, 2010). Motor vehicle accidents account for 73% of all deaths due to unintentional injury (Minino 2010). Statistics Canada (2010) indicated that the leading cause of death amongst children age 10–14 are accidents (unintentional injuries) malignant neoplasms, and suicide. Of deaths amongst 15–19-year-olds, the leading cause of death was accidents (unintentional injuries), suicide, and malignant neoplasm.

Common reactions described in literature regarding teens who are grieving the loss of a friend include but are not limited to:

* more reliance on friends than family,
* reckless or thoughtless behaviors,

- increased moodiness,
- difficulty concentrating,
- withdrawal or sadness,
- headaches and/or stomach aches,
- thinking that nobody cares,
- regressive behaviors,
- indifference towards death, and
- withdrawing/isolating from friends and family.

Teens who are struggling with the death of a peer need a support system they can rely on. In his book *Working with Children and Youth with Complex Needs: 20 Skills to Build Resilience*, Ungar (2015) wrote:

> The metaphor of people being like metal springs that bounce back after being squished is nothing more than a polite way of blaming people who don't succeed (who don't bounce back) for their being unable to change conditions beyond their control. To see resilience as a quality of the individual reflects that ideology of rugged individualism that has convinced us that because one individual "beat the odds" every other individual in similar circumstances should be able to do the same. This detestable idea is challenged by research with people who live in challenging contexts around the world, in both high-income nations, like the United States, Canada, and the UK, and those from low- and middle-income countries, like Cambodia and Brazil (Bell, 2011; Panter-Brick & Eggerman, 2012; Unger, 2007; Weine et al., 2012). For many, success is beyond people's reach until someone (a therapist, teacher, family member, friend, politician or significant other) makes mental health resources available and accessible.
>
> (pp. 8–9)

Through studying children and families all over the world, Ungar (2007) devised seven factors associated with resilience.

Table 7.1 Seven Factors Associated with Resilience

Resource category	Explanation
Relationships	Relationships with significant others, peers, mentors, and family members within one's community
Identity	A personal and collective sense of who one is that fuels feelings of satisfaction and or pride; sense of purpose to one's life; self-appraisal of strengths and weaknesses; aspirations; beliefs and values; spiritual and religious identification
Power and control	Experiences of being able to care for oneself and others; personal and political efficacy; the ability to effect change in one's social and physical environment in order to access resources; political power

Resource category	Explanation
Social justice	Experiences related to finding a meaningful role in one's community; social equality; the right to participate; opportunities to make a contribution
Access to material resources	Availability of financial and educational resources; medical service; employment opportunities; access to food, clothing and shelter
Cohesion	Balancing one's personal interests with a sense of responsibility to the great good; feeling as if one's part of something larger than oneself socially and spiritually; one's life has meaning
Cultural adherence	Adherence to everyday culture-based practices; assertion of one's values and beliefs that have been transmitted between members of different generations or between members of one generation; participation in family and community practices

Source: (Ungar, 2015, p. 13). Reprinted with permission.

Ungar (2005) indicated that people who cope well and overcome adversity succeed at two processes, navigation and negotiation. Resilience is the capacity to both navigate their way through resources and negotiate for resources to be provided in meaningful ways (Ungar, 2015).

Helping the Bereaved Adolescent

How can we help teens navigate and negotiate their way through a grief process in a meaningful way? Children need sufficient connections with the adults in their lives so that they are embedded within a working attachment framework with an adult at all times (Neufeld & Maté, 2013). Neufeld and Maté (2013) also stated that being an adolescent means being neither an adult nor a child, and adolescents still need and long for some adult attachment. Although teens need their parents just as much as a young child does when they experience the loss of a friend, they are much more apt to isolate themselves from their caregivers and try to make sense of the loss themselves. Studies suggest that experiencing the death of a friend complicates the adolescents' struggle for their own identity, often feeling like the world has let them down (Schuurman, 2003). The death of a peer, even someone they hardly knew, affects adolescents differently than the death of an older person. They must cope not only with the shock of life's unpredictability, but their own mortality (Doka, 2000). It is important for the adults in the adolescent's life to acknowledge that the teen is grieving.

Additionally, adults are encouraged to model healthy expression of their own feelings. Cowan (2010) echoed Ungar's (2007) research on resiliency when he emphasized that it is the role of the families, the school, and the community to help children and teens identify and express their feelings of grief and loss. Acknowledging the teen's loss of a friend is critical to his or her healing process. Involving the teen as an active participant in the funeral or celebration of life can help him or her feel respected as a validated mourner (Cowan, 2010). Further, this highlights Ungar's (2007) resource categories of social justice, identity, and relationships that are associated with resilience. Teens are often more apt to express themselves through creative outlets, such as journal writing, playing music, drawing, painting, and art making. If teens can participate in the funeral process it helps fosters cohesion and shape resiliency. Various forms of social media also provide opportunities for adolescents to express their grief (this topic is explored further in Chapter 13).

Peer support groups can provide teens with opportunities to connect to peers and mentors within their community, generating more opportunity to create significant relationships and initiating a greater capacity for resiliency building as outlined by Ungar (2015) in his seven factors associated with resilience. Akerman and Statham (2014) suggested there is a need for interventions supporting bereaved children and teens, reporting that even children and teens who do not exhibit clinical levels of distress may benefit in the longer term from programs that normalize grief and help to strengthen coping strategies. Groups are an important and intrinsic component of an adolescent's life, which makes participation in a group an effective treatment modality for adolescents confronting the death of a peer (Aronson, 2004).

Discussion Questions

1. Review Ungar's seven factors associated with resilience and create a circle graph that surrounds a child or teen with what they may need based on these seven factors to help them cope with the loss of a friend.
2. Discuss the importance of Katie's parents learning about her attachment needs and how that had to happen first before she could process her feelings of grief.
3. Discuss how you understand that creative/expressive arts can be beneficial when dealing with individuals who have experienced the death of a peer. What creativity activity would you implement and why?

References

Akerman, R., & Statham, J. (2014). Bereavement in childhood: The impact on psychological and educational outcomes and the effectiveness of support services. *Childhood Wellbeing Research, Working Paper No. 25*, 1–37.

American Music Therapy Association. (2014). *Music therapy makes a difference: What is music therapy?* Retrieved from www. musictherapy.org.

Aronson, S. M. (2004). Where the wild things are: The power and challenge of adolescent group work. *The Mount Sinai Journal of Medicine, 71*(3), 174–180.

Ball, B. (2002). Moments of change in the art therapy process. *The Arts in Psychotherapy, 29*(2), 79–92.

Barrett, R. K. (1996). *Adolescents, homicidal violence, and death.* In D. E. Balk & C. A. Corr (Eds.), *Handbook of adolescent death and bereavement* (pp. 42–64). New York, NY: Springer.

Bratton, S. C., & Ferebee, K. W. (1999). The use of structured expressive art activities in group activity therapy with preadolescents. In D. S. Sweeny & L. E. Homeyer (Eds.), *The handbook of group play therapy: How to do it, how it works, whom it's best for* (pp. 192–214). San Francisco, CA: Jossey-Bass.

Bratton, S., Ray, D., Rhine, T., & Jones, L. (2005). The efficacy of play therapy with children: A meta-analytic review of the outcome research. *Professional Psychology: Research and Practice, 36*(4), 376–390.

Bull, S., & Pengelly, M. (2014). I'm not the only one: A collaborative approach to developing a children and young person's bereavement group. *Bereavement Care, 33*(3).

Carmichael, T. (2006). *Play therapy: An introduction.* Upper Sadler, NJ: Pearson/Merrill Prentice Hall.

Cook, A., & Oltjenbruns, K. (2004). *Dying and grieving life span and family perspectives* (2nd ed.). Belmont, CA: Wadworth.

Cowan, D. S. (2010). Death of a friend during childhood. In D. E. Balk & C. A. Corr (Eds.), *Children's encounters with death, bereavement, and coping.* New York, NY: Springer.

Crenshaw, D., & Stewart, A. (Eds.) (2014). *A comprehensive guide to play therapy.* New York, NY: The Guilford Press.

Dowdney, L. (2000). Annotation: Childhood bereavement following parental death. *Journal of Child Psychiatry, 41*(7), 819–830.

Doka, K. J. (2000). *Living with grief: Children, adolescents, and loss.* New York, NY: Brunner-Routledge.

Estrella, K. (2005). Expressive therapy: An integrated arts approach. In C. A. Malchiodi (Ed.), *Expressive therapies* (pp. 183–209). New York, NY: The Guilford Press.

Fonagy, P. (2001). *Attachment theory and psychoanalysis.* New York, NY: Other Press.

Gil, E. (1991). *The healing power of play.* New York, NY: The Guilford Press.

Graham, L. (2013). *Bouncing back: Rewiring your brain for maximum resilience and well-being.* Novato, CA: New World Library.

Haine R. A., Ayers T. S., Sandler I. N., & Wolchik, S. A. (2008). Evidence-based practices for parentally bereaved children and their families. *Professional Psychology Research and Practice, 39*(2), 113–121.

Heegaard, M. (1996). *When someone very special dies: Children can learn to cope with grief.* Minneapolis, MN: Woodland Press.

Johnson, C. M. (2010). When African American teen girls' friends are murdered: A qualitative study of bereavement, coping and psychosocial consequences. *Families in Society: The Journal of Contemporary Social Services, 91*(4), 364–370.

Knill, P., Levine, E., & Levine, S. (2005). *Principles and practice of expressive arts therapy: Towards a therapeutic aesthetics.* London, UK: Jessica Kingsley.

Landreth, G. (2002). *Play therapy: The art of relationship,* New York, NY: Brunner-Routledge.

LeBlanc, M., & Ritchie, M. (2001). A meta-analysis of play therapy outcomes. *Counseling Psychology Quarterly, 12*(2), 149–163.

Lusebrink, V. B. (1990). *Imagery and visual expression in therapy.* New York, NY: Plenum Press.

McFerran, K., Roberts, M., & O'Grady L, (2010). Music therapy with bereaved teenagers: A mixed methods perspective. *Death Studies, 34*(6), 541–565.

Mon-hsin, W.F., & Ray, D. (2007). Effect of group sandtray therapy with preadolescents. *The Journal for Specialists in Group Work, 32*(4), 363–382.

Mancini, A. D., Griffin, P., & Bonanno, G. A. (2012). Recent trends in the treatment of prolonged grief. *Current Opinion in Psychiatry, 25*(1), 46–51.

Malchiodi, C. A. (2005). *Expressive therapies.* New York, NY: The Guilford Press.

Malchiodi, C. (2012). *Handbook of art therapy.* New York, NY: The Guilford Press.

Malchiodi, C. (2014). Creative arts therapy and expressive arts therapy. *Psychology Today.* Retrieved from https://www.psychologytoday.com/blog/arts-and-health/201406/creative-arts-therapy-and-expressive-arts-therapy.

Milne, A. A. (1988). *The house at Pooh Corner.* Toronto, ON: McClelland & Stewart.

Minino, A. M. (2010). *Mortality among teenagers aged 12–19 years: United States 1999–2006.* U.S. Department of Health and Human Services, Centers for Disease Control and Prevention. Retrieved from www.cdc.gov/nchs/data/databriefs/db37.html.

Neufeld, G., & Maté, G. (2013). *Hold onto your kids.* Toronto, ON: Random House.

Noppe, I. C., & Noppe, L. D. (2008). When a friend dies. In K. J. Doka & A.S. Tucci (Eds.), *Living with grief: Children and adolescents* (pp.175–192). Washington, DC: Hospice Foundation of America.

North American Drama Therapy Association. (2016). General questions about drama. *What is drama therapy?* Retrieved from www.nadta.org.

Perry, B. D., & Rubenstein, J. (2002). The child's loss, death, grief and mourning: How caregivers can help children exposed to traumatic death. Retrieved from www.childtrauma.org.

Powell, B., Cooper, G., Hoffman, K., & Marvin, B. (2014). *The circle of security intervention: Early attachment in early parent-child relationships.* New York, NY: The Guilford Press.

Rheingold, A. A., Smith, D. W., Ruggiero, K. J., Saunders, B. E., Kilpatrick, D. G., & Resnick, H. S. (2004). Loss, trauma, exposure, and mental health in a representative sample of 12–17 year old youth: Data from the National Survey of Adolescents. *Journal of Loss and Trauma, 9*(1), 10–19.

Riley, S. (1997). Children's art and narratives: An opportunity to enhance therapy and a supervisory challenge. *The Supervision Bulletin, 9*(3), 2–3.

Rolls, L., & Payne, S. (2007). Children and young people's experience of UK childhood services. *Mortality, 12*(3), 281–303.

Schachter, S. (1991). Adolescent experiences with the death of a peer. *Omega: Journal of Death and Dying, 24*(1), 1–11.

Schaefer, C. (2013). *The therapeutic powers of play: 20 core agents of change.* Hoboken, NJ: John Wiley & Sons.

Schuurman, D. (2003). *Teen grief.* Retrieved from www.grievingchild.org.

Shen, Y., & Armstrong, S. A. (2008). Impact of group sandtray therapy on the self-esteem of young adolescent girls. *Journal for Specialists in Group Work, 33,* 118–137.

Shore, A. (2000). Attachment and regulation of the right brain. *Attachment and Human Development, 2*(1), 23–47.

Smith, S. S. (1999). The forgotten mourners. In D. E. Balk, & C. A. Corr (Eds.), *Children's encounters with death bereavement and coping.* New York, NY: Springer.

Statistics Canada. (2004). *Leading causes of death of children and youth, by age group, 2006 to 2008* (Table 5.5). Retrieved from http://www.statcan.gc.ca/pub/11-402-x/2012000/chap/c-e/tbl/tbl05-eng.htm

Steele, W. (1997). *Trauma intervention program for children and adolescents: Short term intervention model.* Detroit, MI: TLC.

Stern, D. B. (2002). *The first relationship.* London, UK: Harvard University Press.

Toray, T., & Oltjenbruns, K.A. (1996). Children's friendships and the death of a friend. In C. A. Corr & D. M. Corr (Eds.), *Handbook of childhood death and bereavement* (pp. 165–178). New York, NY: Springer.

Ungar, M. (2005). Pathways to resilience among children in child welfare, corrections, mental health and educational settings: Navigation and negotiation. *Child and Youth Forum, 34*(6), 423–444. doi:10.1007/s10566-005-7755-7

Ungar, M. (2007). The beginnings of resilience: A view across cultures. *Education Canada, 47*(3), 28–32.

Ungar, M. (2015). *Working with children and youth with complex needs: 20 skills to build resilience.* New York, NY: Routledge.

U.S. Department of Health and Human Services. (2004). *Child health USA 2004.* Retrieved from http://mchb.hrsa.gov/mchirc/chusa_04/pages/0473am.htm

Webb, N.B. (2007). *Play therapy with children in crisis: Individual, group and family treatment.* New York, NY: The Guilford Press.

Wood, D. D., & Near R. L. (2010). Using expressive arts when counseling bereaved children. In C. A. Corr & D. E. Balk (Eds.), *Children's encounters with death and bereavement and coping* (pp. 373–394). New York, NY: Springer.

8 The Unique Needs of Children with Life-Limiting Illnesses

Lisa Pearlman

Many individuals struggle with the reality that death is not just for the elderly or sick but that children also die. The death of a child can be completely inconceivable, unnatural, and the tremendous loss of human potential. A child's death is far reaching, enduring, and one of the most painful losses that a parent or sibling will ever experience. While death is a natural part of life, childhood death can seem unacceptable in the midst of an unspeakably painful grief process.

Despite the best medical and technological care in preventing and treating disease and illness, children still die from congenital, genetic, neurodegenerative, malignant, or multisystem/multiorgan diseases. Death for this cohort of children most often occurs after a period of weeks to years of curative, supportive, and/or palliative care. Many children undergo numerous life-prolonging, life-threatening surgeries, invasive procedures, and lengthy stays in critical care units. Not all children will survive and those who do are at risk of intractable pain and suffering, which has great potential to be underestimated and negatively impact quality of life (QOL).

Caring for a child with a life-limiting illness (LLI) whose death is expected can be one of the greatest challenges professionals encounter; however, it is often one of the most meaningful. As a medical community, we are only starting to recognize that the dying child has unique needs that are often unmet, particularly in the last months of life (Association for Children's Palliative Care [ACT], 2009; Clement de Clety et al., 2016; Feudtner, 2007; Kaye et al., 2015; Wolfe, Klar et al., 2000).

The intent of this chapter is to address the needs of children with life-limiting illness where cure is not or no longer possible and death is expected. The chapter contains (a) an introduction to pediatric palliative care, (b) identification of the groups of children with LLI who would benefit from palliative care, (c) an examination of symptom burden and quality of life issues, and (d) an exploration of the complexity of communication during this time.

The Goal of Palliative Care

According to the American Academy of Pediatrics (2000), the goal of palliative care for children is "to add life to the child's years not simply add years to the child's life" (p. 353). The timing of introducing palliative care is critical to ensure that support is not reserved solely for the last days or weeks of life but in the preceding months when symptom burden increases.

Pediatric palliative care is an approach to the art and science of child-focused, family-oriented, and relationship-centered care aimed at enhancing quality of life and attending to suffering. Thus, there is an imperative of care throughout the continuum of a life-limiting illness, whether the child begins the dying process or transitions to end-of-life (EOL) (American Academy of Pediatrics, 2000; Bergstraesser, 2013; Feudtner, 2007; Himelstein, Hilden, Morstad Boldt, & Weissman, 2004; Kaye et al., 2015).

Palliative care also refers to clinically specialized hospital- or community-based services, including pediatric hospices that were created to meet the multiple needs of chronically ill and dying children and their families (Groh et al., 2013; Kaye et al., 2015).

The intent of specialized palliative care teams is to ease suffering by attending to the child's existential, physical, psychosocial, educational, and spiritual needs. Clinically specialized pediatric palliative care teams have an expansive mandate that includes (a) complex pain and symptom management no matter what stage of illness or disease, (b) early advance care planning, (c) coordination and continuity of care, (d) enhanced communication, (e) improved accessibility to care, (f) provision of psychological and spiritual support for the child and the entire family, (g) early opportunities to make memories and create a legacy, (h) respite care, and (i) bereavement care (Feudtner, 2007; Himelstein et al., 2004; Kaye et al., 2015; Wolfe, Klar et al., 2000).

Early integration of specialty palliative care services into the circle of care for a child with advanced cancer has been associated with numerous benefits, including improved management of distressing symptoms, fewer invasive procedures, improved communication and collaboration, parental satisfaction with decision-making, earlier recognition of prognosis, reduced hospitalizations, disposition for care, and improved attention to the psychosocial needs of all family members (Feudtner, 2007; Feudtner et al., 2011; Himelstein et al., 2004; Kang et al., 2014; Mack & Wolfe, 2006; Wolfe, Hammel et al., 2008; Wolfe, Grier et al., 2000). Specialized palliative care teams provide an additional layer of support with symptom management and communication with the primary oncology/health-care teams (Kaye et al., 2015; Pearlman, Zelcer, & Johnston, 2015; Wolfe, Grier et al., 2000).

Regardless of who provides the palliative care, the most central issue is early integration as close to the time of diagnosis as possible in order to optimize the child's quality of life, irrespective of the age of the child and the setting or community in which the child lives (Feudtner, 2007; Himelstein et al., 2004; Kaye et al., 2015; Mack & Wolfe, 2006; Wolfe, Grier et al., 2000). The reality is, however, that society continues to associate palliative care with *end-of-life (EOL) care only.*

Who Are the Children That Benefit from Palliative Care?

The Association for Children's Palliative Care (2009) services provides a template to assist clinicians, administrators, and policy makers to classify children who would benefit from palliative care into the following four groups or conditions.

Conditions for Which Treatment May Be Feasible But Can Fail

Children with cancer are most commonly included in this group. The goal of care for children with cancer is focused on cure, yet there remains a risk of returning disease and eventual death. In the last two decades, the number of deaths from cancer in children has dramatically decreased, due to extraordinary advances in science from multinational clinical trials, evidence-based medicine, and coordinated care. 20% of children die of progressive malignant disease and/or treatment-related complications, making cancer for children the leading cause of death from birth to 19 years old (Greenberg, Barnett, & Williams, 2015). Early integration of palliative care is fundamental to the care of children with distressing symptoms. Palliative care should be introduced early to ensure an approach that emphasizes quality-of-life, the best symptom management possible, and supports psychosocial well-being.

Conditions in Which Premature Death in Childhood or Early Adulthood Is Inevitable But the Child May Enjoy Long Periods of Participation in Normal Activities and Reasonable Quality-of-Life

Children with LLI receive active and supportive treatment including life-saving procedures and surgeries over a span of years prior to a decline in functioning, well-being, and quality-of-life. This category may include children with complex congenital heart disease, lung disease, liver and renal disease, solid organ transplants, cystic fibrosis, or HIV/AIDS (Steering Committee of the EAPC, 2007). Children with such conditions may become increasingly medically complex, fragile, and require escalating technology and, often, long hospitalizations to sustain decreased or lost function (Widger, Seow, Rapoport et al., 2017).

*Progressive Conditions Whereby Premature Death Is Inevitable and
Treatment from the Time of Diagnosis to Death Is Focused Purely
on a Supportive and Palliative Model of Care*

Progressive conditions may include (a) slow, progressive neurogenetic, neurometabolic, and neurodegenerative diseases; (b) lethal brainstem tumors, such as a diffuse intrinsic pontine glioma; and (c) rare life-threatening chromosomal abnormalities that are associated with multisystem congenital anomalies, such as Trisomy 13 and Trisomy 18 (Steering Committee of the EAPC, 2007).

*Irreversible But Nonprogressive Conditions Causing Likelihood
of Premature Death Through Susceptibility to Multiple
Comorbidities and Complications*

This is a broad category of children with extreme prematurity and hypoxic, ischemic, hemorrhagic, and traumatic brain injuries. The common thread in this category is that children with LLI have a high degree of neurological impairment and associated complex multiorgan and symptom burden (Steering Committee of the EAPC, 2007).

Symptom Burden and Quality of Life

There is an expansive range of symptom burden experienced by the dying child due to the diversity of perinatal, genetic, congenital, and acquired diseases of infancy, childhood, and adolescence. Children with cancer are at risk of suffering from what is often a debilitating symptom burden related to pain, fatigue, dyspnea, nausea, vomiting, anxiety, and cachexia (Houlahan et al., 2006; Pritchard et al., 2008; Wolfe, Hammel et al., 2008; Wolfe, Grier et al., 2000). Children living with incurable brain tumors experience a predictable trajectory related to loss of function and progressive neurological impairment leading to a high level of disability (Pearlman et al., 2015).

Children with degenerative neurological diseases typically experience (a) loss of cognitive function, which may progress to dementia; (b) intractable seizures; (c) progressive loss of motor function; (d) vision loss; and (e) bulbar weakness, leading to problems with feeding and swallowing. Disease progression presents a high level of technological dependence to maintain a patent airway, to optimize lung function, and to administer medically provided nutrition (Kang et al., 2014). Steele et al. (2014) conducted a prospective study of children with progressive, noncurable neurological conditions to determine symptom burden. The most common symptoms were pain, sleep problems, constipation, and feeding difficulties, which were found to be more prevalent in children with gastrostomy/jejeunostomy feeding tubes. Parents reported an average of three distressing symptoms in their children that were present daily (Steele et al., 2014).

When given the choice, children and their parents tend to prefer to have as much care, including EOL care, in the home (Feudtner, 2007). To date, there have been no evidence-based validated predictive tools to guide clinicians to help parents and children with their most pressing questions of *when?* and *how long?* Clinicians are challenged by the complexity and uncertainty to define the dying point, which is the period when the child transitions from living with a chronic LLI to approaching end of life.

Caregiving Burden

Suffering in the dying child negatively affects quality-of-life for every member of the family. Parents, particularly mothers, are at high risk of caregiving burden due to unmet psychosocial needs (Hurtado, 2015). Mothers are frequently the primary caregiver and coordinator of the child's medical plan of care, which includes keeping all the medical details straight, advocating for the child's goals of care, and providing direct nursing care 24/7. Maternal stress is compounded by the mother's inability to meet the needs of all family members, social isolation, poor quality and quantity of sleep, and the loss of income potential. Studies indicate that parents, most often mothers, are at high risk for psychological maladjustment, below-standard QOL, and altered relationship satisfaction (Remedios et al., 2015).

Both in-home and out-of-home respite services are recommended as an *essential support* for parents. However, the reality is that (a) parental decision-making regarding acceptance of respite is complex and multidimensional and (b) there is a significant disparity of availability and accessibility of services across geographical regions (Ling, Payne, Connaire, & McCarron, 2016). Caregiving burden is even more complicated when there is more than one child affected.

Complexity of Communication

The Child

The dying child is no ordinary child. More often, the dying child knows he or she is dying despite what parents and professionals believe. The dying child experiences increasing symptom burden, progressive loss of function, and increased technological dependence. This prevents the child from attending school, limits social integration, and frequently keeps the child housebound, if not bedbound (Hinds, Menard, & Jacobs, 2012). Additionally, the dying child is often aware of his or her impending death, and deserves opportunities to communicate and share perceptions and experiences. Children are astute at picking up verbal and nonverbal cues in addition to overhearing conversations that parents believe they are expert at hiding (Contro et al., 2004; Wolfe, 2004). Bluebond-Langner's (1980) early work on the private worlds of dying children confirmed that children knew that they were going to die regardless of whether they asked questions of their parents or physicians.

Information and Decision-Making

In today's digital and online age, the vast network of social media available to children puts them at risk for discovering or learning information that parents have gone to great lengths not to share. Exploring the dying child's *voice* in research studies is complex and denotes a limited number of studies often due to the hesitancy of physicians and research ethics boards to approach pediatric patients for participation.

EOL care is multifaceted within the context of the child's physical, emotional, cognitive, and spiritual development, yet dying children are seldom asked directly about their experiences (Bluebond-Langner, Bello Belasco, & DeMesquita Wander, 2010; Hinds, 2004; Hinds, Menard, & Jacobs, 2012; Weaver et al., 2015). Maturity and life experiences are relevant contributions to rational decision-making. Still, there remain many questions and uncertainties as to how, what, and when children and adolescents with LLI make EOL decisions.

Weaver et al. (2015) explored decision-making preferences of children with cancer ages 12 to 18 years old. Adolescents in this study wished to be actively involved in a template of collaborative decision-making that included parental presence, clinician guidance, and family insight (Weaver et al., 2015). Hinds (2004) engaged children and youth with advanced cancer, ages 10 to 20 years old, in a study to gain new knowledge into their decisions to discontinue active treatment. The children and adolescents communicated that their wishes to stop cancer targeted therapy and agree to a *Do Not Resuscitate* order was strongly associated with their wishes to limit suffering of those they loved and cared about the most (Hinds, 2004).

Memories and Leaving a Legacy

Children and adolescents have the right to create memories and inform others how they wish to be remembered. There is an expanding body of literature that illuminates the lack of timely advance care planning and goals of care discussions, particularly with malignant disease. Timing of EOL discussions frequently occurs very late in the child's illness trajectory, usually in the last week of life when there is more certainty of death as the outcome. The child or adolescent is then robbed of precious time to prepare psychologically for impending death, and has lost opportunities to create lasting memories or a legacy (Beale, Baile, & Aaron, 2005; Bell et al., 2010; Hinds, Menard, & Jacobs, 2012; Wolfe, Klar et al., 2000).

Wiener et al. (2012) surveyed adolescents and young adults with metastatic or recurrent malignancy or HIV infection in order to rank the most important elements and to gain their opinions using the widely used advance-planning workbook, *Voicing My Choices and My Wishes*. Results demonstrated that it was important for adolescents to be involved in decision-making regarding the kind of medical treatment they wanted and did not want, how they would like to be cared for as their disease progressed, important information they wished to share with friends and family, and how they would like to be remembered (Wiener et al., 2012).

Spirituality

Religion, faith, spirituality, culture, and ethnicity are significant influences for the dying child and may affect the child's perception of health, illness, and death. Religion and spirituality may come to the forefront as death draws near; however, engagement in discussions should not be reserved for only when death is imminent. Spiritual questions change with age and stage of development; children as young as 3 to 4 years old are able to engage in exploration of their own spirituality in a much more concrete way as they do not understand the permanence and irreversibility of death. Early school-age children have very clearly defined ideas about God and the natural world associated with religious, cultural traditions, and rituals in their home and community. Children are often unable to make distinctions about religion and spirituality until they reach mid to late adolescence when they are capable of increasingly abstract and multiperspective religious thinking (Barnes, Plotnikoff, Fox, & Pedleton, 2000; Fowler, 1981).

Hope

It is common for the dying child to speak about his or her hopes for the future. For parents and clinicians, this may precipitate worry and fears that the child, having been told the truth, is now in denial or perhaps did not fully understand what had been shared about the disease and the future. That is often not the case, and it is most important to recognize that holding on to hope provides comfort and a source of strength for the dying child. Hope presents in many dimensions of everyday life and normalizes the child's experiences. The dying child may also speak openly about death, about "being ready," while at the same time can express hope for many tomorrows, whether in the short- or long-term future (Barnes et al., 2000).

The Parent

Death is a topic that adults find hard to discuss among themselves, let alone when their child is approaching death. Some parents share only part of the diagnosis with their child and not the prognosis. Others solemnly believe that their child should not even know the diagnosis. There are parents who are steadfast in their belief that the dying child should not ever know the truth. Parents believe the truth will cause psychological harm and more physical pain as death approaches (Dunlop, 2008). Parents also worry that their truth-telling will take away the child's joy and hope. They fear their child will give up and that this will hasten death.

Telling the Truth

In the clinical setting, it is often difficult to convince parents who are un-wavering in their need to protect their child. It is important to educate and support parents around the fact that withholding truths risks the child being silenced by a dance of secrecy. This inevitably leads to increased stress and poor coping for the dying child. The child is then compelled to carry a heavy emotional burden to protect the parent(s) from knowing that he or she in fact knows the truth (Bluebond-Langner, 1980; Muris, Steerneman, Merckelbach, & Meesters, 1996; Underwood, 2006).

Child life specialists, clinical psychologists, and art therapists are specialists who provide psychosocial support directly to children to assist them with stress and coping along the illness continuum by integrating child play, art therapy, storybooks, and workbooks. These clinicians also represent a tremendous resource in coaching parents in the practicalities of how and what to say to their child (Eaton Russell & Bouffet, 2015). Hinds, Oakes et al. (2009) conceptualized the role of *a good parent* as being central to parental EOL decision-making. A *good parent* (a) makes informed and selfless decisions that are in the child's best interests, (b) is a constant presence at the child's bedside, (c) advocates on behalf of the child to prevent suffering, and (d) role-models and teaches their child important values and beliefs. The construct of being a good parent has been positively associated with the process of truth telling (Hinds, Oakes et al., 2009).

Prognosis and Decision-Making

Parents consider prognosis communication to be both difficult and yet necessary for EOL decision-making. Nyborn, Olcese, Nickerson, and Mack (2016) studied the responses of prognosis communication in 32 pairs of parents who had been informed that their child had either refractory or relapsed malignant disease. Prognosis was discussed in 88% of conversations when physicians met with parents. 69% of parents who found prognostic information upsetting believed that the authentic and frank communication fostered hope by relieving uncertainty and providing parents with direction for end-of-life decision-making (Nyborn et al., 2016).

Kreicbergs, Valdimarsdóttir, Onelöv, Henter, and Steineck (2004) explored parental decisions to talk about death with their child dying of advanced cancer. A significant factor that guided parents to talk about death was the *sense* that they got from listening and observing their child. Of 147 parents surveyed in the study, none who talked with their child about death regretted doing so. 27% of parents who sensed that their child was aware of his or her imminent death but chose not to talk with the child about death reported ongoing regret for not having had the conversation (Kreicbergs et al., 2004).

The Clinician

Most clinicians who work with dying children and their families recognize and advocate for honest and authentic truth-telling and communication as a foundation for both child and parental decision-making.

Communicating the Prognosis

Clinicians need to be patient, provide empathic and compassionate guidance to parents, and role-model the process of this delicate communication. Nevertheless, informing a child that he or she is going to die is a daunting task for the clinician. Sharing sensitive and potentially distressing information may stir up feelings of discomfort, reluctance, and/or a lack of confidence in how the clinician is going to manage the process and outcome of the communication. Clinicians may find themselves feeling vulnerable as they struggle with how to emotionally cope with the child's death and balance their own professional feelings of failure to save the child (Beale, Baile, & Aaron, 2005; Mack & Smith, 2012).

Mack and Smith (2012) described a number of underlying misconceptions that affect clinician ability to divulge prognostic information. Such misconceptions include that (a) it will make people distressed, (b) it will take away hope, (c) involving palliative care will shorten survival, (d) it is culturally inappropriate, and (e) the child's prognosis is uncertain. Clinicians should also be aware of common communication pitfalls, which may include overcommunicating, using euphemisms, becoming an "explainaholic," and communicating excessive optimism. These defense mechanisms may help with clinician discomfort but do little to alleviate the child or parents' underlying fears and worry (Boodman, 2015; Hinds, 2004; Kavanaugh, 1974; Mack & Smith, 2012; Nyborn et al., 2016).

Active Listening

Half a century ago, Kavanaugh (1974) provided us with words of wisdom that active listening is the key to telling the dying child about his or her own death. Decades later, this advice still holds true. It starts with an assessment of the child's awareness by listening carefully to what the child asks and how he or she responds (Brown, Ward, & Shribman, 2007). Kavanaugh (1974) posited that the child will do the *telling* when there is an open and honest environment for the child to do so. It is Kavanaugh's opinion that the child should know as soon as possible when prognosis/survival is poor and death is certain. This is highly contentious, as there is often a lack of consensus between and among parents and clinicians as to the timing of when is "as soon as possible."

Clinician presence, vulnerability, and authenticity create a safe environment for the child to speak freely. The importance of each question should be validated and it is appropriate for clinicians to clarify the child's questions to avoid misunderstandings or assumptions. When the dying child asks a question, he or she wants to know the answers. Our moral obligation is to respond to the child's questions and emotions calmly, with honesty and integrity, which will then deepen trust.

Spiritual Care

Pediatric palliative care, by nature of its commitment to meaning and quality of life, affirms the importance of spiritual assessment and support. An approach to spiritual care begins with clinician knowledge, comfort, and confidence in dwelling with, and engaging in, a spiritual journey with the child. For the child who is dying, spiritual care includes creating an environment for defining meaning, hope, and continued growth of the mind–body–spirit (Crisp, 2016; Foster, Lafon, Reggio, & Hinds, 2010). Foster et al. (2010) described the process of *spiritual care* as (a) a purposeful, active presence, (b) supporting the child and family's coping strategies, (c) affirming hope through kindness, (d) acknowledging the uncertainty of the journey, and (e) exploring the many dimensions and meaning of hope and suffering. Children may request that the clinician engage in prayer. Clinicians may wonder if this is in their legal and ethical scope of practice, while at the same time wish to honor the child's ritual and not deny the child's request.

Case Study

Dominique is a 14-year-old girl living in a small town in eastern Quebec with her single father and younger brother. Her mother died when Dominique was a toddler in a motor vehicle collision. Dominique's father was recently diagnosed with cancer and is undergoing chemotherapy. Two years ago, Dominique was diagnosed with a posterior fossa brain tumor called a *medulloblastoma*, which had a favorable prognosis following surgery, radiation, and chemotherapy. Dominique was very ill with a high symptom burden for months prior to the actual brain tumor diagnosis. Following surgery to remove the tumor, Dominique experienced overwhelming disability, which included a period of mutism, poor speech, and severe impairment in her ability to feed herself, swallow, and walk. A gastrostomy feeding tube was inserted to deliver nutrition and Dominique required a wheelchair for mobility and was mostly bedbound and housebound. Dominique's level of independence was greatly reduced and she now relied on her father and caregivers for all of her activities of daily living.

The palliative care team (PCT) was consulted in the postoperative period to assist with symptom management and to provide an added level of psychosocial and spiritual support given the dramatic changes to Dominique's functioning and independence, not to mention the stress related to her father's illness. The PCT continued to follow Dominique when she was at the hospital for clinic appointments in addition to seeing her at home in the community. Once discharged from hospital, Dominique received personal care support at home, nursing support, and an educational assistant at school. Dominique could no longer participate in her prior extracurricular activities. Many of her friends lost interest in being Dominique's friend.

Over a period of 5 days in mid-December, Dominique presented with progressive and excruciating headaches and neck pain that radiated down to her back and legs. She had new onset of eye deviation, double vision, and a facial weakness. She could no longer tolerate her gastrostomy feeds and began to vomit. Brain imaging confirmed multiple metastatic lesions in her brain and along her spinal cord. Given the extent of her disease, the medical team and father collaboratively made the decision to focus on a purely palliative approach and plan of care to ease Dominique's suffering and optimize her comfort. Dominique was not privy to these discussions. Her parents and clinicians agreed that Dominique should know the truth but not until after Christmas, which was 8 days away. They knew this would be Dominique's last Christmas.

The day after her admission to hospital, the PCT observed Dominique to be despondent and withdrawn. Dominique identified her most pressing symptom to be her inability to sleep. Further exploration revealed that Dominique knew the reason for her insomnia, but she could not say the words out loud to anyone. With presence, authenticity, and very gentle open-ended questions, the PCT was able to help Dominique say out loud that she thought her cancer was back and this time she would not survive it. She referred to the cancer as being *stronger* and *harder* than she was.

With tears in her eyes, Dominique asked the PCT if her father and brother were aware that the cancer was back and that she would die. Dominique was most worried about how her father would manage the news given his own journey with cancer. Dominique expressed to the PCT that she wanted to do everything she could to ensure that she did not put any undue stress on her father. The PCT informed Dominique that her father and brother did know about the cancer but wanted to protect her to ensure she would have a special Christmas. Dominique immediately responded that she could tell by the expressions and nonverbal behavior of every person who walked into her hospital room that the news was not good and that she was going to die.

The PCT facilitated a meeting with Dominique and her father whereby in her own way and on her own terms, Dominique informed her father what her needs were and how she wanted to live her remaining days and weeks. Dominique, her father, and younger brother spoke openly about their fears and looked to the PCT for answers to the questions of what death would look like including what and how her symptoms would be managed.

Prior to her discharge home from hospital, Dominique and the child life specialist planned a Celebration of Life party in her hospital room for the many hospital team members who cared for her over the years. Unbeknownst to her father and brother when Dominique was at home, she planned every detail of her funeral with her home care nurse whom Dominique gave strict instructions of what to do upon her death. Dominique was not afraid of death, and she had a spiritual determination to find meaning and peace in her life and in her death. She was most intrigued by the afterlife, since her own father was being treated for an aggressive form of cancer, and she was hopeful that if her father died she would be reunited with both her parents. This imagery and vision gave her hope and left her peaceful.

The funeral home was decorated in pinks, purples, and reds. There were lots of balloons and inspirational quotes that Dominique herself said she lived by. Dominique's home care nurse read the eulogy Dominique composed, which was a reflection of the gratitude she felt towards her parents and brother for giving her a great life.

Conclusion

When death is expected for the child with a life-limiting illness, it makes us question our own core values, beliefs, and faith. It is very difficult for surviving family members and clinicians to find meaning when a child dies. For clinicians, recognizing and attending to the unique and holistic needs of children and their families are first steps in easing suffering so that children can live well, be the best they can be, and enjoy life for as long as possible, regardless of the outcome. In the words of Mattie Stepanek, an 11-year-old boy with a rare form of muscular dystrophy who wanted to be forever remembered as a poet, peacemaker, and philosopher: "While we are living in the present, we must celebrate life every day, knowing that we are becoming history with every work, every action, every deed" (Stepanek, 2002).

Discussion Questions

1. In order to protect their daughter, Dominique's parents defer talking with her about the prognosis until after Christmas. What are the most common fears parents have about talking about death with their child?
2. What principles guide your communication about death with children and adolescents? What personal and/or professional challenges or barriers may impact your own communication?
3. Describe ways in which you would assist or facilitate the dying child or adolescent to engage in memory making and creating a legacy?

References

Association for Children's Palliative Care (ACT). (2009). *A guide to the development of children's palliative care services* (3rd ed.). Bristol, UK: Association for Children's Palliative Care. Retrieved from http://old.rcpcf.ru

American Academy of Pediatrics, Committee on Bioethics and Committee on Hospital Care. (2000). Palliative care for children. *Pediatrics, 106*, 351–357. Retrieved from http://pediatrics.aappublications.org/content/106/2/351.long

Barnes, L. L., Plotnikoff, G. A., Fox, K., & Pendleton, S. (2000). Spirituality, religion and pediatrics: Intersecting world of healing. *Pediatrics, 106*, 899–908. doi:10.1542/peds.106.4.S1.899

Beale, E. A., Baile, W. F., & Aaron, J. (2005). Silence is not golden: Communicating with children dying from cancer. *Journal of Clinical Oncology, 23,* 3929–3631. doi:10.1200/JCO.2005.11.015

Bell, C. J., Skiles, J., Pradhan, K., & Champion, V. L. (2010). End-of-life experiences in adolescents dying of cancer. *Supportive Care in Cancer, 18,* 827–835. doi:10.1007/s00520-009-0716-1

Bergstraesser, E. (2013). Pediatric palliative care—when quality of life becomes the main focus of treatment. *European Journal of Pediatrics, 172*(2), 139–150. doi:1007/s00431-012-1710-z

Bluebond-Langner, M. (1980). *The private worlds of dying children.* Princeton, NJ: Princeton University Press.

Bluebond-Langner, M., Bello Bealsco, J., & DeMesquita Wander, M. (2010). I want to live, until I don't want to live anymore: Involving children with life-threatening and life-shortening illnesses in decision making about care and treatment. *Nursing Clinics of North America, 45,* 329–343. doi:10.1016/j.cnur.2010.03.004

Boodman, S. (2015). Teaching doctors how to engage more and lecture less. *The Washington Post.* Retrieved from www.washingtonpost.com/national/health-science/teaching-doctors-how-to-engage-more-and-lecture-less/2015/03/09/95

Brown, E., Warr, B., & Schribman, S. (2007). *Supporting the child and family in paediatric palliative care.* London, UK: Jessica Kingsley.

Clement de Clety, S., Friedel, M., Verhagen, A. A. E., Lantos, J. D., & Carter, B. (2016). Please do whatever it takes to end our daughter's suffering! *Pediatrics, 137,* 1–6. doi:10.1542/peds.2015-3812

Contro, N. A., Larson, J., Scofield, S., Sourkes, B., & Cohen H. J. (2004). Hospital staff and family perspectives regarding quality of pediatric palliative care. *Pediatrics, 114,* 1248–1252. Retrieved from http://pediatrics.aappublications.org/content/114/5/1248.long

Crisp, C. L. (2016). Faith, hope, and spirituality: Supporting parents when their child has a life-limiting illness. *Journal of Christian Nursing, 33*(1), 14–21. doi:10.1097/CNJ.0000000000000202

Dunlop, S. (2008). The dying child: Should we tell the truth? *Pediatric Nursing, 20*(6), 28–31. Retrieved from http://journals.rcni.com/doi/pdfplus/10.7748/paed2008.07.20.6.28.c6628

Eaton Russell, C., & Bouffet, E. (2015). Profound answers to simple questions. *Journal of Clinical Oncology, 33,* 1294–1296. doi:10.1200/JCO.2014.59.6627

Feudtner, C. (2007). Collaborative communication in pediatric palliative care: A foundation for problem-solving and decision-making. *Pediatric Clinics of North America, 54,* 583–607. doi:10.1016/j.pcl.2007.07.008

Feudtner, C., Kang, T. I., Hexem, K. R., Friedrichsdorf, S. J., Osenga, K., Siden, H., . . . Wolfe, J. (2011). Pediatric palliative care patients: A prospective multicenter cohort study. *Pediatrics, 127,* 1094–1101. doi:10.1542/peds.2010-3225

Foster, T. L., Lafond, D. A., Reggio, C., & Hinds, P. S. (2010). Pediatric palliative care in childhood cancer nursing: From diagnosis to cure or end of life. *Seminars in Oncology Nursing, 26,* 205–221. doi:10.1016/j.soncn.2010.08.003

Fowler, J. W. (1981). *Stages of faith: The psychology of human development and the quest for meaning.* San Francisco, CA: Harper and Row.

Greenberg, M. L., Barnett, H., & Williams, J. (Eds.) (2015). January 2015. *Atlas of Childhood Cancer in Ontario, 1985–2004.* Toronto, ON: Pediatric Oncology Group of Ontario (POGO). Retrieved from www.pogo.ca/wp-content/uploads

Groh, G., Borasio, G. D., Nickolay, C., Bender, H.-U., von Lüttichau, I., & Führer, M. (2013). Specialized pediatric palliative home care: A prospective evaluation. *Journal of Palliative Medicine, 16*(12), 1588–1594. doi:10.1089/jpm.2013.0129

Himelstein, B. P., Hilden, J. M., Morstad Boldt, A., & Weissman, D. (2004). Pediatric palliative care. *New England Journal of Medicine, 350,* 1753–1762. doi:10.1056/NEJMra030334

Hinds, P. S. (2004). The hopes and wishes of adolescents with cancer and the nursing care that helps. *Oncology Nursing Form, 31,* 927–934. doi:10.1188/04.ONF. 927-934

Hinds, P. S., Menard, J. C., & Jacobs, S. S. (2012). The child's voice in pediatric palliative and end-of-life care. *Progress in Palliative Care, 20,* 337–342. doi:10.1179/174329 1X12Y.0000000035

Hinds, P. S., Oakes, L. L., Hicks, J., Powell, B., Srivastava, D. K., Spunt, S., . . . Furman, W. (2009). "Trying to be a good parent" as defined by interviews with parents who made phase I, terminal care, and resuscitation decisions for their children. *Journal of Clinical Oncology, 27*(35), 5979–5985. doi:10.1200/JCO.2008.20.0204

Houlahan, K. E., Branowicki, P. A., Mack, J. W., Dinning, C., & McCabe, M. (2006). Can end of life care for the pediatric patient suffering with escalating and intractable symptoms be improved? *Journal of Pediatric Oncology Nursing, 23*(1), 45–51. doi:10.1177/1043454205283588

Hurtado, M. R. (2015). *Pediatric palliative care: Unmet needs for mental health resources of parents of children with life-threatening diseases* (Master's thesis). Retrieved from http://scholarworks.lib.csusb.edu/etd/208

Kang, T. I., Munson, D., Hwang, J., & Feudtner, C. (2014). Integration of palliative care into the care of children with serious illness. *Archives of Disease in Childhood, 99,* 754–762. doi:10.1136/archdischild-2013-305246

Kavanaugh, R. E. (1974). *Facing death.* Baltimore, MD: Penguin Press.

Kaye, E. C., Rubenstein, J., Levine, D., Baker, J. N., Dabbs, D., & Friebert, S. (2015). Pediatric palliative care in the community. *CA: A Cancer Journal for Clinicians, 65,* 315–333. doi:10.3322/caac.21280

Kreicbergs, U., Valdimarsdóttir, U., Onelöv, E., Henter, J. I., & Steineck, G. (2004). Talking about death with children who have severe malignant disease. *New England Journal of Medicine, 351,* 1175–1186. doi:10.1056/NEJMoa040366

Ling, S., Payne, S., Connaire, K., & McCarron, M. (2016). Parental decision-making on utilization of out-of-home respite in children's palliative care: Findings of qualitative case study research—a proposed new model. *Child: Care, Health and Development, 42*(1), 51–59. doi:10.1111/cch.12300

Mack, J. W., & Smith, T. J. (2012). Reasons why physicians do not have discussions about poor prognosis, why it matters and what can be improved. *Journal of Clinical Psychology, 30,* 2715–2717. doi:10.1200/JCO.2012.42.4564

Mack. J. W., & Wolfe, J. (2006). Early integration of pediatric palliative care for some children, palliative care starts at diagnosis. *Current Opinion in Pediatrics, 18,* 10–14. doi:10.1097/01.mop.0000193266.86129.47

Muris, P., Steerneman, P., Merckelbach, H., & Meesters, C. (1996). The role of parental fearfulness and modeling in children's fear. *Behaviour Research and Therapy, 34*(3), 265–268. doi:10.1016/0005-7967(95)00067-4

Nyborn, J. A., Olcese, M., Nickerson, T., & Mack, J. W. (2016). Don't try to cover the sky with your hands: Parents' experiences with prognosis communication about their children with advanced cancer. *Journal of Palliative Medicine* (Advance online publication). doi:10.1089/jpm.2015.0472

Pearlman, L., Zelcer, M., & Johnston, D. L. (2015). Palliative care for children with brain tumors. In K. Scheinemann & E. Bouffet (Eds.), *Pediatric Neuro-oncology.* New York, NY: Springer.

Pritchard, M., Burghen, E., Srivastava, D. K., Okuma, J., Anderson, L., Powell, B., . . . Hinds, P. (2008). Cancer-related symptoms most concerning to parents during the last week and last day of their child's life. *Pediatrics, 121*(5), 1301–1309. doi:10.1542/ peds.2007-2681

Remedios, C., Willenberg, L., Zordan, R., Murphy, A., Hessel, G., & Philip, J. (2015). A pre-test and post-test study of the physical and psychological effects of out-of-home respite care on caregivers of children with life-threatening conditions. *Palliative Medicine, 29*(3), 223–230. doi:10.1177/0269216314560008

Steele, R., Siden, H., Cadell, S., Davies, B., Andrews, G., Feichtinger, L., & Singh, M. (2014). Charting the territory: Symptoms and functional assessment in children with progressive, non-curable conditions. *Archives of Disease in Childhood, 99,* 754–762. doi:10.1136/archdischild-2013-305246

Steering Committee of the EAPC. (2007). *IMPaCCT: Standards for pediatric palliative care in Europe. European Journal of Palliative Care in Europe, 14*(3), 109–114.

Stepanek, M. J. T. (2002). *Hope through heartsongs.* New York, NY: Hyperion.

Underdown, A. (2006). *Health and well-being in early childhood.* Maidenhead, UK: Open University Press.

Weaver, M. S., Baker, J. N., Gattuso, J. S., Gibson, D., Sykes, A. D., & Hinds, P. (2015). Adolescents' preferences for treatment decisional involvement during their cancer. *Cancer, 121,* 4416–4424. doi:10.1002/cncr.29663

Widger, K., Seow, H., Rapoport, A., Chalifoux, M., & Tanuseputro, P. (2017). Children's end of life and health care costs. *Pediatrics, 139,* 1–11. doi:10.1542/peds.2016-2956

Wiener, L., Zadeh, S., Battles, H., Baird, K., Ballard, E., Osherow, J., & Pao, M. (2012). Allowing adolescents and young adults to plan their end-of-life care. *Pediatrics, 130*(5), 897–905. doi:10.1542/peds.2012-0663

Wolfe, J., Hammel, J. F., Edwards, K. E., Duncan, J., Comeau, M., Breyer, J., . . . Weeks, J. C. (2008). Easing of suffering in children with cancer at the end of life: Is care changing? *Journal of Clinical Oncology, 26*(10), 1717–1723. doi:10.1200/JCO.2007. 14.0277

Wolfe, J., Grier, H. E., Klar, N., Levin, S., Ellenbogen, J. M., Salem-Chatz, S., . . . Weeks, J. (2000). Symptoms and suffering at the end of life in children with cancer. *New England Journal of Medicine, 342,* 326–333. doi:10.1056/NEJM200002033 420506

Wolfe, J., Klar, N., Grier, H. E., Duncan, J., Salem-Schatz, S., Emanuel, E., & Weeks, J. (2000). Understanding of prognosis among parents of children who died of cancer: Impact on treatment goals and integration of palliative care. *Journal of the American Medical Association, 284,* 2469–2475. doi:10.1001/jama.284.19.2469

Wolfe, L. (2004). Should parents speak with a dying child about impending death? *The New England Journal of Medicine, 351,* 1251–1253. doi:10.1056/NEJMe048183

9 Understanding Trauma and Grief Complications

Jenifer Freedy

For many, experiencing grief following a death-related loss can be difficult to fully understand, define, and process. North American culture remains largely undereducated, either formally or informally, about this very natural, universal, and necessary response to loss. While various cultures are accepting of, and adept at, creating rituals surrounding this process, there is often a struggle to understand grief and mourning and a reluctance to allow this vital process to unfold. Given that this reluctance typically occurs even when a loss is uncomplicated, it may be especially true when a death or a series of deaths occurs in a traumatic way, under conditions that not only trigger a prolonged interruption in the trajectory of the bereaved's mourning process but also his or her neuropsychological functioning. Moreover, particular attention must be paid when a traumatic loss occurs during childhood or adolescence because of the important emotional, psychosocial, and neurobiological (i.e., brain and nervous system) development that occurs during this life stage.

The Confluence of Grief and Trauma

The effect of loss and trauma are recognized in both academic and clinical realms; thus, it may be surprising that the formal study of grief and trauma *together* is relatively new (Neria & Litz, 2004). Moreover, that traumatic loss in childhood or adolescence could produce a distinct emotional, psychosocial, and neurobiological profile has been formally considered only in the last two decades (Neria & Litz, 2004). However, death occurring under any number of traumatic circumstances is not only a daily experience for children across cultures, but mainstream and social media now routinely expose youth to school shootings, horrific violence, intense forms of bullying, natural disasters, and acts of terrorism (Goldman, 2001). Therefore, the formal study of complications related to grief and trauma in childhood has become an increasing and necessary area of concern.

Terms and Definitions

As discussed in Chapter 3, there have been various schools of thought with respect to the confluence of trauma and grief. A variety of terms have been used that attempt to categorize the source and type of death, associated indicators, and duration of symptoms that occur following a traumatic loss. Given the relative novelty of the intersection between traumatology and thanatology, it behooves us to proceed with caution regarding the lens through which we view these overlapping phenomena and the way in which terminology and diagnoses are applied. When supporting youth who have been exposed to a death experienced as traumatic, it is advantageous to adopt a holistic treatment approach that addresses the emotional, psychosocial, and neurobiological implications of both trauma and loss. This type of integrated perspective may have the potential to transcend some of the current discrepancies in the literature, and possibly stimulate discussion regarding the universal need for safety, regulation, and attunement, regardless of the type of grief and/or trauma.

This chapter addresses the intersection between trauma and grief in children as both inherently contain elements of loss. Therefore, a distinction will be made between normative grief and one type of non-normative grief, referred to here as *childhood traumatic grief* (CTG). (An attempt to resolve the dialogue between the various conceptualizations and terminologies is beyond the scope of this chapter.) Given the widespread use of CTG, it will be used here to refer to a grief trajectory that has gone awry for a child or adolescent, thus requiring skilled and knowledgeable intervention. Moreover, we acknowledge that this type of conceptualization of loss and trauma is defined within a relatively new field of inquiry, is socially constructed, and requires ongoing research and development. Thus, for this chapter, it is necessary to offer a conceptualization for normative grief, trauma, and traumatic grief, prior to exploring the implications of childhood traumatic grief.

Normative Grief

Pearlman, Wortman, Feuer, Farber, and Rando (2014) defined *grief* as "the psychological, behavioral, social, and physical reaction to the experience of loss" (p. 20). These authors asserted that normative grief is a natural and expected reaction to an important loss, can be expressed in a wide variety of ways, and is often influenced by both person-related and event-related factors unique to the bereaved. Therefore, in normative grief, an *initial acute grief* reaction will eventually lead to a *process of mourning*, the necessary vehicle through which the integrating of the death will occur (Pearlman et al., 2014). Over time, this will allow for a return to a more typical sense of self and life for the bereaved, as well as a modified but continued relationship with the deceased (Pearlman et al., 2014) through continuing bonds. For children and teens, this return to baseline should also include a return to a normative developmental trajectory.

It is important to acknowledge that grief and the process of mourning are not static but change continually over time, not necessarily progressing in a linear fashion (Pearlman et al., 2014). This may be particularly true of bereavement during the stages of childhood or adolescence where understanding, experiencing, and integrating a death is dependent on various cognitive, emotional, and neurobiological abilities that are still under development. Therefore, a young and underdeveloped brain and nervous system can challenge a child or teen's ability to tolerate and regulate complex grief-related thoughts and emotions (Siegel, 1999). Younger children may also struggle to understand the permanence of death or its long-term consequences (Cohen & Mannarino, 2011). Further, comprehending that love and connection can transcend death can be difficult at certain developmental stages (Dyregrov & Dyregrov, 2013; Goldman, 2001).

What Can Normative Grief Look Like?

From very early life to later adolescence, normative grief can produce a wide variety of emotional, psychosocial, and neurobiological reactions, including stomachaches, nightmares, anxiety, failing grades, hostility toward family or friends, being the "class bully" or "class clown," or social withdrawal (Goldman, 2001). It can include a young child repeatedly asking when the deceased is "coming home," a sudden and in-depth sharing of details related to the death, or having recurrent and varied thoughts and memories of the deceased (John, 2014; Cohen & Mannarino, 2011; Goldman, 2001). Impaired concentration, bed wetting, difficulty sleeping, eating issues, and oscillations between overwhelm, shock, preoccupation, worry, and numbness, and then "seeming like himself again" are all typical of children after loss (John, 2014; Pearlman et al., 2014; Cohen & Mannarino, 2011; Goldman, 2001).

In a normative grief trajectory, both the child's inner and outer resources help him or her to accept the reality of the death and to process the cognitive and emotional aspects of grief and the tasks of mourning (Cohen & Mannarino, 2004). They also help the child adjust to a world without the deceased, eventually integrating a new connection with the deceased, as well as supportive others still in the child's world (Dyregrov & Dyregrov, 2013; Cohen & Mannarino, 2004). While the grief and mourning process can be painful and varied, it is widely acknowledged that most children and teens are eventually able to mourn and integrate a loss in a healthy way. Although life will be forever changed by the death, an adaptive and functional path is often rebuilt without the need for professional support (Lindemann, 1944; Parkes & Weiss, 1983 as cited in Neria & Litz, 2004).

Trauma

Confusion about what is meant by the term *trauma* is not uncommon. Over the years, numerous researchers and clinicians—including Bessel van der

Kolk, Daniel Siegel, Allan Schore, Peter Levine, Janina Fisher, Pat Ogden, and Stephen Porges, to name only a few—have contributed greatly to elucidating the complex and varied emotional, psychosocial, and neurobiological consequences that can occur after a traumatic experience.

Stated simply, *psychological trauma* is "the experience of an *actual or perceived* threat to the *life, bodily* or *psychic* integrity of an individual that *overwhelms* the individual's capacity to *integrate* the threat" (italics added; Pearlman et. al., 2014, p. 25). As a result, enduring changes and impairments to the individual's emotional, psychosocial, and neurobiological functioning can result (van der Kolk, 2014; Porges, 2011; Ogden, Minton, & Pain, 2006; Siegel, 1999). For example, traumatized individuals may experience ongoing symptoms of avoidance, intrusion, hyper- and/or hypoarousal, and negative mood and cognitions (L. Stelte, personal communication, November 14, 2015; Williamson, Porges, Lamb, & Porges, 2014; American Psychiatric Association, 2013). Additionally, the traumatic event may be persistently recalled only in fragments, feel consistently "alive" or "frozen in time," and may create enduring shame-and fear-based beliefs about others, the world, and the survivor himself, while emotional flooding and/or emotional numbing can become chronic and unpredictable (Pearlman et al., 2014; Levine, 2010; Ogden et al., 2006).

Trauma and the Polyvagal Theory

Recent research indicates that psychological trauma must not only be considered from an emotional or psychological perspective but also from the standpoint of neurobiological functioning. "Most people think of trauma as a 'mental' problem, even as a 'brain disorder'....Trauma is something that also happens in the body" (Levine, 2010, p. 31). In recent years, this assertion has been supported by the Polyvagal Theory (PVT), developed by Dr. Stephen Porges (2011). This theory has greatly influenced the understanding of trauma, not only during its actual occurrence but also immediately afterward and even for months and years to come.

Very simply stated, PVT asserts that when humans are faced with a real or perceived threat, *neuroception* (an unconscious "threat detection" function of the nervous system) will activate one of three defensive responses to confront that threat: (1) social engagement, (2) fight/flight, and/or (3) freeze/faint (Porges, personal communication, 2014, June 19; Porges, 2011; Levine, 2010; Ogden et al., 2006). The PVT also asserts that these three defenses typically activate in a hierarchal fashion from the "newest" or most recently evolved (social engagement) to the oldest and least evolved (freeze/faint; L. Stelte, personal communication, November 14, 2015; Porges, 2011; Levine, 2010; Ogden, et. al., 2006). Moreover, each defense is available to the individual only when its respective branch of the autonomic nervous system (ANS) is activated, which often occurs outside of the conscious choice and control of the individual (Porges, personal communication, June 19, 2014; Porges, 2011).

The Polyvagal Theory in Action: A Closer Look

The full capabilities of the human social engagement system (SES) are not available at birth; instead, they develop in more evolved regions of the brain and nervous system primarily through repeated positive attachment and attunement experiences from parents or caregivers during childhood (J. Fisher, 2014). Over time, the developing child becomes able to use these more highly evolved skills to effectively engage and connect with others. Therefore, when first met with a real or perceived threat, a well-adapted individual may use social engagement as an initial defensive response to this threat (Ogden et al., 2006). In other words, he or she may use relational capabilities to attempt to "talk down" the threat or solicit support from another individual to help eliminate the threat and return safety. Once the threat is over, the individual may then also use social engagement for support and processing (Ogden et al., 2006).

If the social engagement defense proves ineffective in reestablishing the individual's safety, the next defense in this hierarchal response system may activate. Here, the fight/flight response, initiated by an older and less evolved branch of the ANS called the *sympathetic nervous system* (SNS), will cause rapid neurophysical changes in the brain and body (Williamson et al., 2014; Porges, 2011; Ogden et. al., 2006). Such changes will help the individual's body to maximize strength and/or speed to either fight the danger or flee from it—again, aiding a potential return to safety (L. Stelte, personal communication, November 14, 2015; S. Porges, personal communication, June 19, 2014; Levine, 2010; Ogden et al., 2006). Fight/flight is considered a mobilizing defense, as it allows the threatened individual to use his or her increased emotional and/or physical action toward self-protection (Levine, 2010; Ogden et al., 2006).

In trauma theory, many consider it particularly crucial when neither social engagement nor the fight/flight defenses prove effective in returning an individual to safety (Levine, 2010; Ogden et al., 2006). In other words, the threatening situation is unresponsive to social engagement and is also "too big," "too strong," or "too fast" to combat or flee. As a result, the ANS will then typically activate the oldest and least evolved, "last resort," defensive response (Levine, 2010; Ogden et al., 2006). And, different from the first two, this defensive response, termed *freeze/faint*, creates either partial or total immobilization, a factor that may be crucial in influencing posttraumatic outcomes (L. Stelte, personal communication, November 14, 2015; S. Porges, personal communication, June 19, 2014; Levine, 2010; Ogden et al., 2006). In this freeze or faint state, the individual's neuroception has perceived a level of danger or life-threat that is inescapable. In response, the individual's neurobiology now becomes one of inaction, passivity, or collapse; in other words, "a complex pattern of surrender" (Krystal & Krystal, 1988, p. 116). Thus, a frozen, anesthetized, or dissociated state will rapidly occur, the purpose of which is to either stop any movement that could provoke further harm, or reduce the intensity of the suffering about to be endured (Levine, 2010; Ogden et al., 2006).

Case Study: Part One

Daniel is a 12-year-old boy who has completed his weekly karate lesson. After staying late to talk with his instructor, Daniel walks to the parking lot to meet his father, where both notice an older teenaged boy quickly approaching. As this teen is unfamiliar, Daniel's neuroception (his inner threat detector) begins to activate, causing Daniel to orient to this boy. When the teen approaches, he appears quite agitated and hurried and begins demanding money. When Daniel's father explains that he does not have his wallet, the stranger calls Daniel's father "a liar," becomes violent, and produces a gun; he then hits Daniel's father on the side of the head several times. Daniel's father falls to the ground, unconscious. Upon witnessing this, Daniel's nervous system registers not only the danger he is in but also the potential threat to his father's life. As a result, Daniel's nervous system activates the first defensive response, *social engagement*. Here, Daniel attempts to use eye contact, a stable tone, and reasoning to compel the agitated teen to leave. Daniel also explains that his karate instructor's car is still in the parking lot, indicating that further support will soon be arriving.

Despite this, the adolescent boy does not withdraw. Instead, he moves closer to Daniel, now threatening to assault him. As such, Daniel's nervous system activates the second defensive response, *fight/flight*. Here, Daniel's heart rate greatly increases, various neurobiological changes quickly allow his focus to become pointed, and Daniel experiences a sharp and sudden increase in physical energy. With this, Daniel attempts to run fast for help. In response, the teen chases Daniel and wrestles him to the ground, causing Daniel to then fight back by forcefully flailing his legs and fists at the teen. At this point, the teen again produces his gun and shows it to Daniel.

The perpetrator has responded to neither social engagement nor Daniel's fight/flight response; the teen is not open to influence, and is also too fast, too strong, and armed. As such, Daniel's nervous system now assesses his situation to be inescapable. Moreover, provoking the teen with further verbal or physical action could add further risk to Daniel's life or that of his father. As a result the third and final defensive response activates within Daniel—*freeze/faint*. Here, Daniel's body becomes immobilized; initially, he becomes very still and rigid but remains oriented and alert to the teen's every movement, as well as a possible escape option that might arise. However, as the teen puts the gun directly to Daniel's forehead, Daniel's nervous system registers both the serious threat to his life and his powerlessness to change this. Daniel's nervous system therefore determines complete surrender to be the best defense to minimize further harm and/or the pain he may now endure. As such, Daniel begins to feel "spacey" and disconnected, his hearing becomes muffled, and his body goes limp and numb. From here, Daniel perceives only fragments of the event until the distant sound of police sirens and his karate instructor's voice cause Daniel to reorient to the present moment. 2 weeks later, Daniel's father dies from brain injury complications.

The Development of Trauma

The development of a trauma disorder is not simplistic, and a number of factors (e.g., developmental stage, level of resiliency, attachment style, history of traumatic experiences) appear to contribute to both its formation and its type (L. Stelte, personal communication, November 14, 2015; L. Ferentz, personal communication, October 29, 2012; J. Fisher, personal communication, November 16, 2009; Herman, 1992). Moreover, although successful use of the first two defensive responses does not eliminate the possibility of developing a posttraumatic stress disorder, a successful social engagement or fight/flight defensive response that restores safety may allow for easier recovery than a terror-induced "last resort" immobilization response (L. Stelte, personal communication, 2015, November 14; S. Porges, personal communication, 2014, June 19; Levine, 2010).

Part of the reason for this may be that immobilization does not allow the survivor to experience any action characteristic of mastery, empowerment, or triumph during the threatening event (Ogden et al., 2006). In other words, whereas successful mobilizing (i.e., social engagement or flight/flight) can allow the individual a greater sense of resilience and self-advocacy, inescapable trauma and a resulting immobilization defense (i.e., freeze/faint) dampens this sense of efficacy (Ogden et al., 2006). Therefore, although immobilization can be very adaptive and protective in life-or-death situations, the survivor may mistakenly view himself as "weak" or "cowardly" for his perceived "inaction," inviting chronic guilt, shame, or even self-hatred to develop (J. Fisher, personal communication, November 8, 2010; Levine, 2010; Ogden et al., 2006). Moreover, if an immobilization defense activates during childhood (i.e., the period of nervous system development) or if it activates frequently in situations of ongoing childhood or adult trauma, this rudimentary freeze/faint state may become the nervous system's "default" or "go to" response for all perceived threats, even those where social engagement or fight/flight would be adequate (L. Stelte, personal communication, November 14, 2015; Levine, 2010; Ogden et al., 2006).

In addition, the neurobiological changes necessary for a freeze/faint activation require an intense amount of *mobilizing* energy (i.e., the type of energy initially needed for a fight/flight response) to be contained or "locked down" (L. Stelte, personal communication, November 14, 2015; Levine, 2010). However, if this energy has no option to release or "complete" either during the traumatic event or after, it can remain "encoded" in the nervous system (L. Stelte, personal communication, 2016, March 4). As a result, a chronic pattern of either *hypoarousal* (i.e., emotional or physical numbing, detachment from self and others, concentration issues, intense shame), *hyperarousal* (i.e., emotional overwhelm, agitation, anger, anxiety, chronic hypervigilance), or oscillations between the two can develop (Fisher, 2009; Ogden, et. al., 2006).

Furthermore, the neurobiological changes required to create a fight/flight or freeze/faint state can prevent the nervous system from *accurately* and *completely* "recording," in memory, the sensory information (i.e., sights, sounds, physical experiences) of the traumatic event (Levine, 2015; Siegel, 1999). When this happens, traumatic memories that remain fragmented or dissociated cannot consolidate into a larger, more accurate narrative of the event (Levine, 2015; L. Ferentz, personal communication, October 29, 2012; J. Fisher, personal communication, November 19, 2012; Siegel, 1999). Instead, the traumatic memory and the resulting "trauma story" may be incomplete or even faulty, leaving the survivor with a modified belief system such as, "I should have done something different; it was my fault," "The world is completely bad and unsafe," "I am powerless and broken," and "I can no longer trust myself or others."

Finally, when trauma occurs during childhood, the younger and less developmentally mature the child, the more likely he or she will first respond to threat using immobilization rather than active struggle (Siegel, 1999). However, because activating the rudimentary defenses of fight/flight and freeze/faint require significant alterations in the brain and body, these neurophysiological changes can greatly influence the still-developing brain and nervous system (J. Fisher, 2014; Siegel, 1999). In other words, left unresolved, the resulting hyperarousal patterns (i.e., fight/flight responses) or hypoarousal patterns (i.e., freeze/faint response) may not only become the child's standard response to daily life but they may also prevent the development of more mature capacities going forward (J. Fisher, 2014; Levine, 2010; Siegel, 1999). Therefore, without effective treatment, these problematic arousal responses, coupled with incomplete developmental milestones, may become embedded into the child's personality and persist well into adulthood (J. Fisher, 2014; L. Ferentz, personal communication, October 29, 2012; Ogden et al., 2006; Siegel, 1999; van der Kolk, McFarlane, & Weisaeth, 1996).

Types of Trauma

Posttraumatic stress disorder (PTSD) can result from any number of single-incident, traumatic events that may be more random in nature, occur outside the context of a relationship, and result in four core symptoms: 1) avoidance, 2) intrusion/reexperiencing, 3) arousal, and 4) negative mood and cognition (American Psychiatric Association, 2013; Pearlman et al., 2014). And while PTSD is often the "conventionally known" form of traumatic stress, additional types are also recognized. Some of these include complex posttraumatic stress (C-PTSD; Herman, 1992) and developmental trauma disorder (DTD; S. Fisher, 2014; Heller & LaPierre, 2012). It has also been suggested that within these types of posttraumatic stress there may be further subtypes depending on the defensive response(s) used during a traumatic event (S. Porges, personal communication, June 19, 2014).

In addition to the above, traumatic grief is now also recognized as a unique and prevalent form of traumatic stress. The remainder of this chapter focuses on a subtype of this form of trauma, childhood traumatic grief.

Childhood Traumatic Grief

"It is important to recognize that developing CTG is not normative for children who lose loved ones, even if the cause of death is objectively traumatic" (Cohen & Mannarino, 2004, p. 822). In the face of such events, most children and teens are resilient and experience little or no enduring posttraumatic symptomology (Mannarino & Cohen, 2011). However, for some, this is not the case and CTG does develop, particularly after deaths associated with intense fear, helplessness, and shock or horror (Mannarino & Cohen, 2011; Cohen & Mannarino, 2011). Furthermore, the resulting posttraumatic symptoms are not simply "outgrown" or resolved on their own; instead, the child's nervous system becomes "stuck" on the traumatic aspects of the loss, which then also disrupts his or her progression into an adaptive mourning process (Pearlman et al., 2014; Mannarino & Cohen, 2011; Mahoney, 2008; Cohen & Mannarino, 2004).

The Development of CTG

There are a number of event-related risk factors that may enhance a child or adolescent's risk of developing CTG. According to Pearlman et al. (2014), Dyregrov and Dyregrov (2013), Cohen and Mannarino (2011), Mannarino and Cohen (2011), and Mahoney (2008), some of these include:

- Deaths that are untimely, sudden, or unexpected
- Deaths that occur under unnatural, grotesque, or violent circumstances
- Deaths that are human-induced (and, therefore, perceived as having been preventable)
- Deaths that are random (and, therefore, impact a survivor's sense of control)
- Circumstances that involve multiple deaths
- A death that also involved threat to the survivor's life (e.g., a car accident)
- Deaths as a result of military combat
- Deaths resulting from disaster (natural or human-made)
- Death involving real or imagined physical or emotional suffering by the deceased before dying
- A death that holds a social stigma (e.g., drug overdose, domestic violence, AIDS, suicide, homicide)
- Witnessing the actual death or finding the body

Additionally, Pearlman et al. (2014), Dyregrov and Dyregrov (2013), Mannarino and Cohen (2011), and Goldman (2001) asserted that there are various person-related risk factors for CTG development:

- Death of a parent (particularly a mother) or a sibling
- Problematic family dynamics prior to the death
- A problematic relationship dynamic with the deceased prior to the death (e.g., the child had an excessive dependency on the deceased)
- Pre-death relationship with the deceased that was very positive and cherished
- Problematic coping or functioning in the surviving parent/caregiver
- Resulting secondary adversities or losses, including the family home, income, or having to relocate, change schools, or lose family or peers
- Children or teens with an avoidant, preoccupied, or disorganized attachment style
- Limited resiliency, optimism, or positive self-esteem within the child
- Gender (girls tend to internalize problems relative to their male counterparts, thereby increasing their risk for depression and/or anxiety. As well, when the death of a mother occurs, daughters are more likely to assume the maternal tasks such as household chores and the care of siblings)
- Previous exposure to other important losses or traumas or a history of developmental trauma (i.e., abuse, neglect, poverty, etc.)
- Surviving parent/caregiver lacks an understanding of the nature of traumatic loss, leading to inadequate or harmful responses to the child or teen's bereavement responses

What Can CTG Look Like?

A key feature of CTG involves the presence of four core trauma symptoms: chronic avoidance, intrusion/reexperiencing, arousal, and negative mood and cognitions (American Psychological Association, 2013). For youth experiencing CTG, these core symptoms may present as follows:

- *Avoidance:* chronic avoidance or numbing related to reminders of the deceased or the death (i.e., thoughts, feelings, memories, images, objects, places, rituals, people, and/or situations; John, 2014; Williamson et al., 2014). As such, tasks of mourning requiring recognizing, recollecting, and reexperiencing the deceased are overwhelming, and therefore avoided (Pearlman et al., 2014).
- *Intrusion or reexperiencing:* nightmares or bad dreams, flashbacks or intrusive memories that may be overwhelming or retraumatizing (Pearlman et al., 2014; Williamson et al., 2014). Neutral or even positive memories of the deceased may also trigger overwhelming or intolerable reminders of the death (Cohen & Mannarino, 2004).

- *Arousal:* hyperarousal symptoms (e.g., easily distressed, angry outbursts, anxiety or panic, difficulty sleeping, restlessness, problematic risk-taking, acting out, easily startled, busy thoughts, constant hypervigilance), and/ or hypoarousal symptoms (e.g., depressed feelings, physical and emotional numbing, limited motivation, attention and concentration issues, dissociation) (Williamson et al., 2014; John, 2014; Cohen & Mannarino, 2004, 2011; Fisher, 2009).
- *Negative mood or cognitions:* chronic low or depressed mood, toxic shame or a self-image of "badness" that can invade every part of a child's life, an inability to conceptualize key aspects of the traumatic death accurately or create an accurate narrative of self, others, and the world after the traumatic loss (Williamson et al., 2014; John, 2014; APA, 2013; Cohen & Mannarino, 2011; Levine, 2010; Cohen et al., 2004).

Additional trauma-related symptomology may also include the development of irrational fears or phobias, consistent rescue or revenge fantasies, various somatic symptoms that seem to have no medical cause, sudden mood or behavioral changes, or an overidentification with the deceased (John, 2014; Cohen & Mannarino, 2011; Mannarino & Cohen, 2011). It is also important to note that in children, especially young children, the effects of traumatic loss may be observed more so through behavior (John, 2104; Cohen & Mannarino, 2011).

In returning to Daniel and his case study, we find that his case provides a possible CTG presentation.

Case Study: Part Two

2 weeks after his attack in the parking lot, Daniel's father dies from brain injury complications. 5 months later, the funeral and a memorial ceremony have been completed and visits from various family members and friends have slowed. Daniel, his mother, and younger brother are attempting to resume a routine. Despite this, Daniel's mother has not been able to return to work. She has begun spending a great deal of time on the couch watching television, playing on her computer, or "napping." Prior to the death, Daniel's mother loved to cook and often prepared sit-down breakfasts and dinners for the family. Now, she orders take-out for the children and remains in bed most mornings when the boys are preparing for school. Daniel now assumes responsibility for getting his brother ready for the day and sometimes also completes his bedtime routine. Daniel has also noticed that his mother is drinking wine frequently, hardly leaves the house, and rarely talks directly about the death with the children. Because of this, the children rarely talk about it with their mother for fear of "upsetting her."

For Daniel, recalling what life felt like prior to his father's death is very difficult; he no longer feels "like himself" and feels very different from everyone else. Since the attack, Daniel has frequent, violent nightmares or bad dreams in which he cannot find his father. He now dreads bedtime, and will stay awake until exhausted. Daniel also has vivid visual, auditory, and somatic flashbacks almost daily. The sound of sirens, small spaces such as elevators, and older male teens trigger panic. As well, the sudden memory of his father's lifeless body in the hospital creates a visceral feeling of utter helplessness in Daniel. When these arise, Daniel will secretly scratch or pick the skin under his arms until he "feels nothing" or will bury himself in violent fantasy video games for hours. Daniel can also "get lost" in intense, vivid, and often violent fantasies of revenge toward his father's murderer.

Daniel often experiences surges of extreme guilt and shame related to his father's death. He reasons that if he had not signed up for karate, his father would not have been in the parking lot that fateful night. Daniel also believes he is a "weak coward" for immobilizing when the teen presented his gun; Daniel believes a "good son" would have fought harder to save his father sooner.

Daniel no longer attends karate and avoids anything to do with the sport. Since the attack, he resists going anywhere near the dojo and insists that his mother drive alternative routes to avoid this area of town. He also avoids even pleasant references to his father and no longer engages in activities he and his dad once enjoyed together. Moreover, Daniel senses that his friends now feel awkward around him, and because he does not want to talk about his father or the attack when at school, Daniel acts as if it never happened or often wears his earphones when around peers.

Daniel is now primarily either numb and "zoned out" or agitated and restless. There are moments when he feels great sadness, but this is over-whelming, and anxiety, flashbacks, or feelings of emptiness quickly follow. He has also been experiencing episodes of dissociation where things look "dreamy" and Daniel feels disconnected from everything. Moreover, Daniel has lost a sense of himself in the future; instead, he feels like time is "standing still" and his former aspirations seem distant and meaningless. Finally, Daniel has developed a persistent fear that something bad will happen to him or his family. Although he logically knows this is unlikely, he has begun to ruminate about this daily.

CTG Treatment

The treatment of CTG is often complex and varied, and this process typically involves moving through three fundamental processes: (1) resource development/stabilization, (2) trauma processing, and (3) healthy mourning (John, 2014; Pearlman et al., 2014).

A child suffering from CTG will have difficulty experiencing and/or managing the emotional, psychosocial, and neurobiological aftermath of the traumatic loss (John, 2014). He will not only struggle to engage in healthy symptom management and an eventual mourning process, but he may also find simply coping with activities of daily life overwhelming (John, 2014).

Because of this, both internal and external *resource development/stabilization* can be an important starting point in the therapy process. Here, building more adaptive abilities toward emotional, social, and neurobiological regulation can enhance stress management and affect tolerance, healthy use of external supports, supportive social and communication skills, and a greater sense of self-empowerment and safety (John, 2014; Pearlman et al., 2014; Cohen & Mannarino, 2011, Siegel, 1999). Additionally, age-appropriate psychoeducation for the child regarding CTG can also help to validate the various symptoms traumatically bereaved children often experience (John, 2014).

Because the core symptoms of avoidance, intrusion/reexperiencing, arousal, and negative mood and cognitions are often chronic for traumatically bereaved children, once resource development has enhanced the child's stabilization, the necessary next step of *trauma-processing* can then be tolerated (John, 2014; Pearlman et al., 2014). This can be a vital part of treatment, as traumatically bereaved children become so "stuck" on the traumatic aspects of the loss they are unable to endure the thoughts, feelings, and memories necessary for mourning (Pearlman et al., 2014; Cohen & Mannarino, 2011; Mahoney, 2008; Cohen, Mannarino, & Knudsen, 2004). Therefore, therapies designed to process the cognitive, emotional, and neurobiological consequences of the trauma can be skillfully used to reduce the symptoms preventing an adaptive mourning process. Such therapies may include Trauma-Focused Cognitive Behavioral Therapy (TF-CBT) or its derivative, Traumatic Grief-Cognitive Behavioral Therapy (TG-CBT; John, 2014; Mannarino et al., 2011). In addition, EMDR (Eye Movement Desensitization and Reprocessing) Therapy, various forms of Exposure Therapy, Neurofeedback Therapy, or somatic-based therapies such as Somatic Experiencing or Sensorimotor Psychotherapy (S. Fisher, 2014; John, 2014; van der Kolk, 2014; Levine, 2010; Ogden et al., 2006) can also be used. As well, incorporating play and art therapy techniques may also be a part of this healing process.

Finally, as the child's inner and outer resources grow and stabilize and her posttraumatic symptoms remit, a process of healthy mourning can be facilitated (Pearlman et al., 2014). The tasks of this work often involve the child more fully acknowledging and understanding the loss, experiencing the emotional pain of the death, dealing with ambivalence related to the deceased, revising old or problematic belief systems and narratives, recovering positive memories of both the deceased and life before the death, creating a new relationship with the deceased, and developing a new identity and a way of being in the world after the loss (Pearlman et al., 2014; Crenshaw, 2007; Brown & Goodman, 2005).

It is important to note that the above process of CTG treatment is rarely linear but instead typically occurs through a number of oscillations back and forth between each phase, particularly as new developmental stages present (Pearlman et al., 2014; Crenshaw, 2007; Siegel, 1999). Moreover, it is essential to tailor the therapy to both the developmental stage of the child at the time of the loss, as well as the family, cultural, and religious customs of the child.

The Role of Caregivers

There are valuable reasons for considering the caregiver role in CTG treatment, as limited parental functioning can increase negative outcomes for the traumatically bereaved child (John, 2014; Dyregrov & Dyregrov, 2013; Cohen & Mannarino, 2004). Interventions that support a parent's ability to offer warmth, attuned emotional responses, healthy routine and rituals, and appropriate child discipline appear not only protective but may also enhance the effectiveness of the CTG therapy (Dyregrov & Dyregrov, 2013; Cohen & Mannarino, 2004). This aspect is so vital to CTG treatment that support to parents in considered a priority (Dyregrov & Dyregrov, 2013).

It is often necessary to educate and coach parents about the importance of attunement to the child, how and when to talk about different aspects of the loss, how to distinguish true behavior infractions from CTG symptoms, and how to administer appropriate interventions/discipline in response (John, 2014). Of course, for surviving parents/caregivers who themselves are traumatically bereaved, securing appropriate parental, social, and/or therapeutic support can be a vital element of the CTG treatment process. Additionally, parents can be counseled to communicate the unique needs of the traumatically bereaved child to teachers, coaches, or other family members (Cohen & Mannarino, 2011).

Conclusion

Children and adults throughout the world are both directly and vicariously affected by death and loss on a daily basis. Due to the internet and various forms of social media, never in the history of humankind have we had such access to an onslaught of information and images that remind us of death every day. As Siegel (1999) so aptly asserts, the effects of unresolved loss or trauma can be powerfully disorganizing not only to the mind, body, and self of a developing child but ultimately to our future generations if left unnoticed or misunderstood. The growing insight into the potentially devastating and far-reaching consequences of this often unexpected and overpowering human experience compels us to pay close attention not only to its nature but also the path to its healing.

Discussion Questions

1. Given what the polyvagal theory of trauma indicates about the nervous system, what are some ways parents/family/teachers can help children experiencing traumatic loss complications?
2. Why might a "one size fits all" model of assessment and/or treatment not benefit a child experiencing traumatic loss complications?
3. What aspects of traumatic loss complications in childhood were most surprising or new to you? How might this shift your own thinking about trauma and loss in childhood and its potential long-term impact?

References

American Psychiatric Association. (2013). *Diagnostic and statistical manual of mental disorders* (5th ed.). Arlington, VA: Author.

Brown, E. J., & Goodman, R. F. (2005). Childhood traumatic grief: An exploration of the construct in children bereaved on September 11. *Journal of Clinical Child and Adolescent Psychology, 34*(2), 248–259.

Cohen, J. A., & Mannarino, A. P. (2004). Treatment of childhood traumatic grief. *Journal of Clinical Child and Adolescent Psychology, 33*(4), 819–831. doi:10.1207/S15374424jccp3304_17

Cohen, J. A., & Mannarino, A. P. (2011). Supporting children with traumatic grief: What educators need to know. *School Psychology International, 32*(2), 117–131. doi:10.1177/0143034311400827

Cohen, J. A., Mannarino, A. P., & Knudsen, K. (2004). Treating childhood traumatic grief: A pilot study. *Journal of the American Academy of Child and Adolescent Psychiatry, 43*(10), 1225–1233. doi:10.1097/01.chi.0000135620.15522.38

Crenshaw, D. A. (2007). An interpersonal neurobiological informed treatment model for childhood traumatic grief. *OMEGA, 54*(4) 319–335.

Dyregrov, A., & Dyregrov, K. (2013). Complicated grief in children—the perspectives of experienced professionals. *OMEGA—Journal of Death and Dying, 67*(3), 291–303. doi:10.2190/om.67.3.c

Fisher, J. (2014, April 8). *Changing the Paradigm 2014—Janina Fisher Keynote Address* [Video file]. Retrieved from https://www.youtube.com/

Fisher, J. (2009). *Psychoeducational aids for working with psychological trauma* (8th ed.). Watertown, MA: Center for Integrative Healing.

Fisher, S. (2014). *Neurofeedback in the treatment of developmental trauma*. New York, NY: W.W. Norton.

Goldman, L. (2001). *Breaking the silence: A guide to help children with complicated grief-suicide, homicide, AIDS, violence, and abuse*. Philadelphia, PA: Brunner-Routledge.

Heller, L., & LaPierre, A. (2012). *Healing developmental trauma*. Berkeley, CA: North Atlantic Books.

Herman, J. (1992). *Trauma and recovery*. New York, NY: Basic Books.

John, S. (2014, August 29). *Treating childhood traumatic grief* [Video file]. Retrieved from https://www.youtube.com/watch?v=nmDwCFiQVS4.

Krystal, H., & Krystal, J. H. (1988). *Integration and self healing: Affect, trauma, alexithymia*. Hillsdale, NJ: Analytic Press.

Levine, P. (2010). *In an unspoken voice*. Berkeley, CA: North Atlantic Books.

Levine, P. (2015). *Trauma and memory*. Berkeley, CA: North Atlantic Books.

Lindemann, E. (1944). Symptomatology and management of acute grief. *American Journal of Psychiatry, 101*, 141–148.

Mahoney, D. (2008). Childhood traumatic grief must be addressed. *Clinical Psychiatry News, 36*(1), 25. doi:http://dx.doi.org/10.1016/s0270-6644(08)70024-9

Mannarino, A. P., & Cohen, J. A. (2011). Traumatic loss in children and adolescents. *Journal of Child & Adolescent Trauma, 4*(1), 22–33. doi:10.1080/19361521.2011.545048

Neria, Y., & Litz, B. T. (2004). Bereavement by traumatic means: the complex synergy of trauma and grief. *Journal of Traumatic Loss, 9*(1), 73–87. doi:10.1080/15325020490255322

Ogden, P., Minton, K., & Pain, C. (2006). *Trauma and the body*. New York, NY: Norton.

Pearlman, L. A., Wortman, C. B., Feuer, C. A., Farber, C. H., & Rando, T. A., (2014). *Treating traumatic bereavement*. New York, NY: The Guilford Press.

Parkes, C. M., & Weiss, R. S. (1983). *Recovery from bereavement*. New York, NY: Basic Books.

Porges, S. (2011). *The Polyvagal Theory*. New York, NY: Norton.

Siegel, D. (1999). *The developing mind*. New York: The Guilford Press.

van der Kolk, B., McFarlane, A., & Weisaeth, L. (1996). *Traumatic stress*. New York, NY: The Guilford Press.

van der Kolk, B. (2014). *The body keeps the score*. New York, NY: Penguin Books.

Williamson, J. B., Porges, E. C., Lamb, D. G., & Porges, S. W. (2014). Maladaptive autonomic regulation in PTSD accelerates physiological aging. *Frontiers in Psychology, 5*. doi:10.3389/fpsyg.2014.01571

10 Suicide in Children and Adolescents

An Overview

Rebecca T. Machado

Stereotypes abound regarding the joys of childhood and adolescence. We envision children engaged in endless hours of play and adolescents spending carefree time with friends.

While most of us would acknowledge that such idealistic images are wishful thinking on the part of nostalgic adults, we recoil from considering certain experiences as real parts of childhood and adolescence. Suicide is one of these as over 2,400 youth (ages 5 to 19) die by suicide each year in Canada and the United States (Centers for Disease Control and Prevention, 2017; Statistics Canada, 2017). Scanning the news, we learn of children like Montana, who was 9 years old when he died by suicide. Ronin was 12 at the time of his suicide. Dajia was also 12. Jamie, Jordan, and Amanda completed suicide at the age of 15. Jack was 18 at the time of his self-inflicted death.

Perhaps this list of names is a provocative way to begin a chapter on suicide in childhood and adolescence. Indeed, most literature on the topic begins with a range of impersonal statistics that attempt to describe the scope of the issue. Yet, however passionately we present the numbers, it is far too easy to separate statistics from the reality of the problem they describe, as well as from the individual children and teens who have died or who may be at risk in the future.

Terminology and Statistics

In the study of suicidality, terminology is significant. The astute reader will have noticed that the individuals whose deaths were acknowledged above are described as having *died by suicide* or *completed suicide*. This language is preferred to the historically common statement that someone has *committed* suicide, which has generally been associated with criminal or sinful activity. Such phrasing is inaccurate, as suicidal behavior is related to health concerns rather than morality or legality. Additionally, the term *committed* holds an assumption about the nature of choice in the suicidal act, suggesting a free decision by a clear-minded, fully comprehending participant. While rational decision-making may be present to some degree in some deaths, factors that drive behavior, impair judgement, or limit understanding suggests that the common understanding of *choice* is often not applicable, especially among children and adolescents.

Suicide and Related Behavior

A variety of terms have been proposed for self-harming and suicide-related behaviors, creating confusion for researchers, clinicians, students, and the general public (Silverman, 2006, 2011). Thus, it remains necessary to define the terms used in any discussion of this topic.

Suicidal ideation refers to a pattern of thoughts about death as a potentially desirable option. Such thoughts may include a passive wish to be dead or extend to active thoughts of killing oneself. These ideas may include speculative plans for action (e.g., "If I was going to kill myself, I would use pills") or very specific intentions (e.g., "I have been saving pills for 2 weeks and I am going to kill myself tonight"). Suicidal ideation may be expressed aloud, in writing, via electronic media, or through creative expression (e.g., poetry, art). Some expressions may directly reference death (e.g., "I can't see living like this for much longer") while others may be difficult to recognize (e.g., "I'm just tired of everything") except in retrospect.

Suicidal ideation is relatively common among adolescents, with 17% of American high-school students surveyed indicating that they had "seriously considered attempting suicide" in the previous year, while 13.6% stated that they had made a plan (Kann et al., 2014, p. 11). A Canadian survey of slightly younger students between the ages of 12 and 15 noted approximately 8% reported thoughts of suicide in the previous year (Peter, Roberts, & Buzdugan, 2008), while 8% of male and 17% of female high-school students in British Columbia admitted to such thoughts in the previous year (McCreary Centre Society, 2014).

Suicide attempt refers to an intentional action that is expected to result in death. The reasons for survival may vary, including interruption by another person, a "change of heart" where the individual seeks help after taking potentially lethal action, or an incorrect assessment of lethality (e.g., a child who eats red crayons because he wants to die and believes these are poisonous would be considered to have made a suicide attempt, even though he is almost certain to survive). Like ideation, suicide attempts are more commonly reported by female youth in the United States and Canada. Among American high-school students, 10.6% of female and 5.4% of male students stated that they had made one or more suicide attempt in the past year (Kann et al., 2014). In British Columbia, Canada, 9% of female and 3% of male high-school students reported a suicide attempt in the previous year (McCreary Centre Society, 2014).

Non-suicidal self-injury is different, yet can be difficult to discriminate, from suicide-related behaviors. Cutting, scratching, or burning skin and self-harming behaviors are generally understood to represent coping efforts by the individual and do not have life-threatening intent (Hoffman & Kress,

2010; Muehlenkamp & Kerr, 2010). However, several researchers have noted a correlation between non-suicidal self-injury (NSSI) and suicidal behavior for some youth (Brausch & Boone, 2015; Hamza & Willoughby, 2013; Nock, Joiner, Gordon, Lloyd-Richardson, & Prinstein, 2006). Further exploration of possible suicide risk is important for youth who engage in self-injurious behavior, and, as an expression of distress, NSSI ought to garner attention and support.

Defining Suicide

The World Health Organization defines *suicide* as "the act of deliberately killing oneself" (2014, p. 12). Though this definition may be expanded by noting that "the act" can include passive behaviors (e.g., choosing to remain in the path of an oncoming vehicle) or placing oneself in a situation where others will take the lethal action (e.g., "suicide by cop"), it is otherwise adequate in acknowledging the four key elements of suicide: (a) the actor/decision-maker is the individual, (b) the individual forms an intent to die, (c) the individual takes action (active or passive) intended to bring about death, and (d) the action has a lethal outcome.

Any effective definition of suicide will highlight the essential components that discriminate suicide from both accidental death (the individual's intent to die), and homicide (the actor/decision-maker and decedent are the same person in suicide, but not homicide). In order to intend to die, one must, at minimum, understand the concept of death itself, including properties of nonfunctionality (i.e., all life functions cease) and irreversibility (i.e., it cannot be undone). For suicide, one must also understand causality (i.e., there are ways to make death happen). Speece and Brent (1996) noted that most children understood these basic concepts of death by 7 years of age, and Mishara (1999) found that most school-age children understood the concept of "killing oneself" and could provide at least one realistic example of how to do so as early as Grade 1 (6 years old).

Questions about children's understanding of death and suicide become legally relevant when the coroner/medical examiner classifies the manner of death because intent to die is the primary difference between a death that will be ruled accidental versus one that ought to be acknowledged as suicide. If the investigation is unable to confirm the individual's intent, the coroner may classify the death using a third option—undetermined. Such classifications account for an average of 30 deaths per year in Canadian youth and 177 in American youth; if all such deaths are, in fact, suicides, the annual total would increase by 8–10% (CDC, 2015; Statistics Canada, 2014).

Intent is less immediately relevant when considering prevention, since a child or teen may be at risk for self-inflicted death that *is* irreversible, whether he or she understands or intends it to be so (Tishler, Reiss, & Rhodes, 2007). Thus, a child's risk for suicide must be assessed based on his or her intent and capacity to take action that could be lethal and not seen as "less serious" if the child mistakenly believes he or she will wake up again later. Indeed, a young child who acts based on the expectation of surviving in some way might be at greater risk rather than less. This is due, in part, to the inability to understand the basic concepts associated with causality and irreversibility.

Child and Adolescent Suicide Statistics

Within Canada and the United States[1,2] information is available with individuals grouped into 5-year age bands. This discussion of childhood and adolescent suicide includes statistics for Children (5 to 9 years of age), Pre- and Early Adolescents (10 to 14 years of age), and Mid- and Late Adolescents (15 to 19 years of age). As no deaths are documented as suicide for individuals 4 years of age or younger in either country, this group will not be discussed further in this section. When using statistics to describe suicide within a population, perhaps the most commonly reported figure is the *number* of individuals who died by suicide. This statistic allows us to acknowledge each "1" that is part of the sum. Since populations vary, however, a larger number of deaths does not necessarily indicate that suicide is a necessarily larger problem in a given area (e.g., if two people in a tiny hamlet of 100 citizens die by suicide, this represents a larger percentage of the population than if three people in larger town of 10,000 do so). Thus, another commonly reported statistic is the *rate* per 100,000 individuals in that group[3].

The *ranking* of suicide as a mode of death (i.e., how common suicide is in comparison to illness, accidents, etc.) is also often reported. Caution must be used here, as this statistic says as much about other modes of death as it does about suicide, and changes in rankings must be viewed with caution. For example, a decrease in the accidental death rate could result in suicide becoming the "number one" mode of death for some groups without any change in the number of deaths by suicide.

Children: 5 to 9 years old

Suicide is quite rare in the youngest age group under review. During the most recent 5-year period for which statistics have been released (2009–2013; Statistics Canada, 2017), only two deaths were recorded as suicide for Canadian children under the age of 10. Both —one boy and one girl[4]—occurred in 2011, resulting in suicide rate of 0.1 per 100,000 for this age group during that year[5]. During 2011, suicide was ranked as the ninth leading cause of death for this age group. It is not typically in the "top 10" for children.

It is not surprising that the United States, with a population almost 10 times that of Canada, reports a greater number of deaths in every age and gender category. Between 2007 and 2013, the number of 5- to 9-year-olds whose deaths were classified as suicide varied between four (in 2007) and nine (in 2013). In more recent years, however, the Centres for Disease Control and Prevention has begun limiting their release of statistics about suicide in this age range, stating that data regarding children younger than nine "are suppressed based on a child's inability to form and understand suicidal intent and consequences" (CDC, 2017).

Pre- and Early Adolescents: 10 to 14 years old

In Canada, an average of 31.4 pre- and early adolescents die by suicide each year, and suicide is the third most common mode of death for youth between the ages of 10 and 14. There is near gender equality reported among this group, with 15.8 female and 15.6 male deaths classified as suicide each year. The average suicide rate between 2009 and 2013 has been 1.66 per 100,000.

The United States reports than an average of 361.6 pre- and early adolescents died by suicide each year between 2011 and 2015. A larger gender disparity exists in this country in comparison with Canada, with the deaths of 237.8 males and 123.8 females reported as suicide. Despite the larger number of deaths, the suicide rate for this group is near to the Canadian rate, at 1.75 per 100,000, and suicide is similarly ranked as the third most common mode of death.

Mid- and Late Adolescents: 15 to 19 years old

In Canada, suicide is the second most common mode of death for adolescents between the ages of 15 and 19. An average of 199.4 deaths were recorded as suicide each year between 2009 and 2011 (138.8 male, 60.6 female). Significant differences in death rates by gender begin at this age and persist throughout the life span. The suicide rate for this group is 9.0 per 100,000, blending rates of 12.2 deaths per 100,000 males versus 5.6 deaths per 100,000 females.

In the United States, suicide has risen to match the Canadian ranking as the second most common cause of death for this age group (ranked third prior to 2011). The average number of deaths reported each year—1846—is divided unequally by gender, and includes an average of 1419.6 males and 426.4 females each year. The suicide rate for this group is slightly lower than that reported in Canada, with 8.7 deaths per 100,000 (13.0 deaths per 100,000 males; 4.1 deaths per 100,000 females).

Talking to Young People About Suicide

Children—even very young children—are keenly aware of their own distress. Despite the adult tendency to minimize problems associated with childhood concerns, children may experience conflict with peers, failing grades, or being grounded as intensely meaningful. Unfortunately, adults may not always be good at noticing when a child is in distress. In one study of over a thousand 8-year-olds and the adults in their lives, only about a quarter of the children who acknowledged thoughts of suicide were correctly identified by their parents/caregivers, and only 10% of these children were identified by their teachers (Thompson et al., 2006). Given the important role of adults in facilitating children's access to support and resources, failure to notice these needs is a concern.

Adolescents may be more aware of their needs and possible resources. However, as a group, adolescents may be less likely to seek support from outside their peer network. Perhaps more worrying, youth at higher risk due to depression or previous suicidal behavior have reported *less* favorable attitudes toward help-seeking than their non-suicidal peers, and male adolescents (who, by gender, are at higher risk) are less likely than females both to seek help for themselves or to recommend that a friend access help (Klimes-Dougan, Klingbeil, & Meller, 2012). Despite knowing that teens *know* about supportive resources, the adults in their lives must play a role in connecting youth to the support they may require.

Given the uniqueness and complexity of suicidal behavior, the following is intended to support helpers in adopting an effective interpersonal stance when interacting with a child or adolescent who may be at risk for suicide. Medical or psychotherapeutic treatment providers ought to be consulted for further risk assessment, and in the case of immediate crisis, emergency services are recommended.

Being Present

The first—and possibly most important—step in addressing suicide risk with a child or adolescent is simply to be there: paying attention, noticing their distress, and taking time to talk and asking questions are all necessary initial conditions for engaging in a suicide-preventative interaction. The simplicity of presence, however, is confounded by the difficulty in doing so when anxiety about safety or feeling unprepared for the life-and-death question of suicide pull us away in our own minds. In order to "be there," we must find ways to reduce or manage our own anxiety in the situation. Being informed, consulting with colleagues, maintaining our own well-being, and accessing counseling support can be useful strategies.

Understanding Suicide as a Viable-Seeming Option

Gaining an accurate understanding of the young person's experience is essential. This includes understanding *their perception* of the problems and pain they are experiencing and their specific thoughts of suicide as a solution. Doing so requires us to set aside any preconceptions we may have about the individual's stage of life or their life circumstances, and about suicidal and self-harming behavior, as well as resisting any urge to dismiss talk of suicide as "attention seeking."

Developing our understanding is likely to involve asking questions. But is it okay to ask a child or adolescent if she is thinking about suicide? In short, yes! The belief that talking about suicide will increase risk or give an individual the idea is a myth that has been debunked (Mathias et al., 2012). Failure to ask this question, on the other hand, may be associated with increased risk since it prevents full understanding and response.

Many suicide prevention programs recommend asking the individual if he or she has made a plan for suicide. It *is* necessary to ask about plans for suicide, as affirmative answers will guide response strategies. However, it is important to not overestimate the value of a negative answer. While having a plan to kill oneself is associated with increased risk, we lack evidence that would prove that those who do *not* have a plan are safe/not at risk (Berman & Silverman, 2014). The rapidly changing nature of suicidal thought, the role of impulsivity, and the possibility of single-step, opportunistic action (e.g., running into traffic) all contribute to necessary caution; considering the lack of a plan as proof of "safety" may be dangerously incorrect.

Understanding and Helping to Solve the Other Problem(s)

Broadening from a laser-like focus on a child's thoughts of suicide, we must also attempt to understand the distress that has resulted in suicide becoming a viable option. In many cases, *this* is actually the more valuable component of understanding (Fiske, 2008) since the resolution of painful problems may eliminate the desire for suicide. Care must be taken to understand the issue *as experienced by the young person* and not minimized by adults. Additionally, suicide treatment is often viewed as an *individual* treatment in which a young person is assessed and treated for a psychiatric "disorder" (e.g., depression). Depending on the situation, this treatment may be appropriate as a starting point. However, a full evaluation of the challenges faced by the young person is likely to result in a broader domain of treatment, which may involve the family, school, or community (e.g., Multisystemic Therapy in Huey et al., 2004). Also, assisting a child or adolescent to develop more effective coping responses may generalize to future situations and reduce ongoing risk.

Address the Ongoing Risk of Suicide

Addressing contributing problems often takes time, while risk for suicide may be both immediate and erratic. Thus, personalized suicide-prevention strategies are an important part of the conversation. Safety planning[6] is an individualized process tailored to address the particular risks and available resources of a young person. Such plans are likely to involve supportive others who can help to monitor, encourage, soothe, prompt the use of coping or problem-solving strategies, and connect the youth with additional help if needed.

When working with adolescents, a safety plan may be written using if–then logic, providing a series of strategies for the young person to notice and respond to their own signs of risk for suicide by engaging resources that can help lessen that risk. For example "*If* I am thinking about suicide at school, *then* I will go right away to talk to Mr. Murphy in the guidance department." To be effective, these plans must be created collaboratively with the young person involved and include only strategies that are acceptable to the youth. After all, strategies are not helpful if the individual will not use them. At the same time, the creation of such a plan is not sufficient to guarantee safety; caring attentiveness by adults is important to mitigate the varied ways that suicide risk may overwhelm the good intentions of such a plan.

Continued Conversation After a Suicide Attempt

Children and adolescents who have recently made a suicide attempt must be considered "still at risk" for some time, and ongoing attention is generally recommended (Pfeffer, 2001; Wagner, 2009). Not only do the factors that contributed to the initial attempt remain relevant, but additional elements such as shame, fear or experience of stigma, and stress of re-entering the school/peer environment are a few of the challenges that may present difficulty for a young person after a suicide attempt.

Despite the continued risk for suicide after an attempt, "suicidal youth tend to keep fewer aftercare appointments than non-suicidal youth, and tend to drop out of treatment earlier than other youth receiving psychiatric treatment" (Daniel & Goldston, 2009, p. 254). A range of factors may discourage youth from participating in continued treatment, including a desire to put the event behind them, feelings of shame, and fear of being found out and seen as "different" from their peers. Parents may be complicit in this disengagement as well (Daniel & Goldston, 2009). Thus, strategies that support engagement will be important when supporting youth who have made a suicide attempt.

When Is the Conversation Finished?

Caring adults must be aware that denials of suicidal ideation, planning, or intent are not guarantees of safety. A range of factors—including shame or embarrassment, distrust or discomfort with the person asking questions, protectiveness of their "solution," and the transient and ambivalent nature of suicidal ideation—may influence demurrals that are not necessarily accurate reflections of recent past (or near future) states of mind. Thus, any conversation about suicide with a young person should be part of an ongoing dialogue. At the same time, the focus of such dialogue should include coping and resolution of the problems and pain in the child's life, in addition to directly addressing suicide risk.

Special Populations

Some groups are known to be at heightened risk for suicide, including youth who identify as gay, lesbian, or bisexual (LeVasseur, Kelvin, & Grosskopf, 2013); youth who are homeless (Hadland et al., 2015); or incarcerated youth (Casiano, Katz, Globerman, & Sareen, 2012). Also, youth among many indigenous populations have a risk of suicide that is significantly higher than that of the majority culture (Cwik et al., 2015; Harder, Rash, Holyk, Jovel, & Harder., 2012). It is important to note that membership in one or more of these groups is not a *causal* factor for suicide. Instead, associated experiences may be the more relevant risk factors for suicide, such as the bullying of sexual minorities or abuse at home that leads a young person to run away and results in homelessness.

Warning Signs

Common warning signs include direct communication about suicidal thoughts, indirect expressions of admiration (e.g., "liking" a social media post about suicide), or an overall fascination with death. Acts of farewell—such as giving away possessions, making a will, quitting clubs or teams—may demonstrate withdrawal from life in general. "Acting out" behaviors, such as starting fights, acting recklessly, cutting classes, and new or increased drug or alcohol use, are often overlooked as "behavioral problems" and are met with punishment rather than concern. It may be more appropriate to understand these as demonstrations of distress that reflect difficulty finding more effective ways to cope. The American Association of Suicidology recommends the mnemonic IS PATH WARM (ideation, substance abuse, purposelessness, anxiety, trapped, hopelessness, withdrawal, anger, recklessness, and mood changes; 2015) as a helpful tool to recall common warning signs of suicide.

Conclusion

Suicide by children and adolescents simply seems *wrong* to many of us. Perhaps because it contradicts the stereotype that this ought to be an exciting and uncomplicated time in their lives; perhaps because we note the large number of potential years of life lost when a young person dies; or perhaps because we feel a greater responsibility to care for youth in our societies. Yet, once we acknowledge that suicide is a real possibility in the lives of young Canadians and Americans, there are few who would deny the importance of understanding and responding to this issue.

Our desire to understand and to respond, however, is confounded by the fact that suicide rates and patterns of behavior differ significantly across time, place, age, gender, culture, and other factors. As well, each child and adolescent has a wealth of experiences, beliefs, and perspectives that are uniquely his or her own. When we are able to blend what we know about statistics and risk factors with the information presented by a young person, we will find ourselves in the best possible position to help him or her resolve the problems for which suicide appears to be a viable solution.

Discussion Questions

1. Given that the topic of suicide makes many adults feel worried or ill-equipped, how might you support parents who have a child or teen at risk of suicide?
2. What would assist you, as a professional, in supporting children and teens who are in distress and discussing suicide?
3. What kind of social change is needed to reduce the stigma associated with suicide?

Notes

1. For an overview of global suicide rates, readers are invited to access records collected by the World Health Organization (www.who.int/mental_health/prevention/suicide/suicideprevent/en/)
2. Canadian national statistics are available up to 2013 (CANSIM database, Statistics Canada, 2017). We will refer to data for the 5-year period spanning 2009 to 2013 unless otherwise specified. During that time, Canada has reported an average of 3,943 deaths by suicide per year, a suicide rate of 11.4 per 100,000 people, and ranked suicide as the ninth most common cause of death within the population. Statistics for the United States are available up to 2015 (WISQARS, Centers for Disease Control and Prevention, 2017). From 2011 to 2015, the United States has reported an average of 41,657 deaths by suicide per year, a suicide rate of 13.2 per 100,000 people, and ranked suicide as the tenth most common cause of death within the population.
3. For example, the rate of 1.5 per 100,000 reported for American youth ages 10 to 14 indicates that 1.5 out of every 100,000 10–14-year-olds died by suicide in the given time period. If there were 200,000 youth in that age group, we would anticipate that there were 3 deaths by suicide.
4. Important note regarding discussion of gender: Please note that gender is a variable commonly included in both collecting and analysing statistics. However, we acknowledge that gender is not recognized as a dichotomous classification for many individuals, and also that the gender that is recorded on a birth or death certificate may or may not correspond with the experience of the individual. Since statistics are collected and grouped in this way, and since significant social forces make gender (however defined) an important element of individual experience, the recorded male–female statistics will be reported and discussed in this chapter. This is not intended to discount the relevant experience of transgender and gender fluid individuals.
5. All rates in this section are calculated based on very small numbers (<20 cases) and should be used with caution.
6. Safety plans are distinct from no-suicide contracts, wherein a young person is required to agree not to attempt suicide for a particular period of time. Readers are advised that the preponderance of evidence suggests that no-suicide contracts are not an effective intervention (McMyler & Pryjmachuk, 2008).

References

American Association of Suicidology (2015). *Know the warning signs of suicide.* Retrieved from http://www.suicidology.org/resources/warning-signs.

Berman, A. L., & Silverman, M. M. (2014). Rethinking suicide risk assessment and risk formulation. In S. H. Koslow, P. Ruiz, & C. B. Nemeroff (Eds.), *A concise guide to understanding suicide: Epidemiology, pathophysiology, and prevention* (pp. 32–41). Cambridge, UK: Cambridge University Press.

Brausch, A. M., & Boone, S. D. (2015). Frequency of nonsuicidal self-injury in adolescents: Differences in suicide attempts, substance use, and disordered eating. *Suicide and Life Threatening Behavior, 45*(5), 612–622.

Casiano, H., Katz, L. Y., Globerman, D., & Sareen, J. (2012). Suicide and deliberate self-injury in juvenile correctional facilities: A review. *Journal of the Canadian Academy of Child and Adolescent Psychiatry, 22*(2), 118–124.

Centers for Disease Control and Prevention (2017). Web-based Injury Statistics Query and Reporting System (WISQARS) [Online database]. Retrieved from: www.cdc.gov/ncipc/wisqars

Cwik, M., Barlow, A., Tingey, L., Goklish, N., Larzelere-Hinton, F., Craig, M., & Walkup, J. T. (2015). Exploring risk and protective factors with a community sample of American Indian adolescents who attempted suicide. *Archives of Suicide Research, 19*(2), 172–189.

Daniel, S. S., & Goldston, D. B. (2009). Interventions for suicidal youth: A review of the literature and developmental considerations. *Suicide and Life-Threatening Behavior, 39*(3), 252–268.

Fiske, H. (2008). *Hope in action: Solution-focused conversations about suicide.* New York, NY: Routledge.

Hadland, S. E., Wood, E., Dong, H., Marshall, B. D. L., Kerr, T., Montaner, J. S., & DeBeck, K. (2015). Suicide attempts and childhood maltreatment among street youth: A prospective cohort study. *Pediatrics, 136*(3), 440–449.

Hamza, C. A., & Willoughby, T. (2013). Nonsuicidal self-injury and suicidal behavior: A latent class analysis among young adults. *PloS One, 8*(3), e59955. doi:10.1371/journal.pone.0059955

Harder, H. G., Rash, J., Holyk, T., Jovel, E., & Harder, K. (2012). Indigenous youth suicide: A systematic review of the literature. *Pimatisiwin, 10*(1), 125–142.

Hoffman, R. M., & Kress, V. E. (2010). Adolescent nonsuicidal self-injury: Minimizing client and counsellor risk and enhancing client care. *Journal of Mental Health Counseling, 32*(4), 342–347.

Huey, S., Henggeler, S., Rowland, M. D., Halliday-Boykins, C. A., Cunningham, P. B., Pickerel, S. G., & Edwards, J. (2004). Multisystemic therapy effects on attempted suicide by youths presenting psychiatric emergencies. *Journal of the American Academy of Child and Adolescent Psychiatry, 43*(2), 183–190.

Kann, L., Kinchen, S., Shanklin, S. L., Flint, K. H., Hawkins, J., Harris, W. A., Lowry, R., . . . Zaza, S. (2014). Youth risk behavior surveillance—United States, 2013. *MMWR Surveillance Summaries, 63*(4), 1–168.

Klimes-Dougan, B., Klingbeil, D. A., & Meller, S. J. (2012). The impact of universal suicide-prevention programs on the help-seeking attitudes and behaviors of youths. *Crisis, 34*(2), 82–97.

LeVasseur, M. T., Kelvin, E. A., & Grosskopf, N. A. (2013). Intersecting identities and the association between bullying and suicide attempt among New York City youths: Results from the 2009 New York City Youth Risk Behavior Survey. *American Journal of Public Health, 103*(6), 1082–1089.

Mathias, C. W., Furr, M., Sheftall, A. H., Hill-Kapturczak, N., Crum, P., & Dougherty, D. M. (2012). What's the harm in asking about suicidal ideation? *Suicide and Life Threatening Behavior, 42*(3), 341–351.

McCreary Centre Society (2014). *From Hastings Street to Haida Gwaii: Provincial results of the 2013 BC Adolescent Health Survey.* Vancouver, BC: Author. Retrieved from http://www.mcs.bc.ca/pdf/From_Hastings_Street_To_Haida_Gwaii.pdf

McMyler, C., & Pryjmachuk, S. (2008). Do "no-suicide" contracts work? *Journal of Psychiatric and Mental Health Nursing, 15*, 512–522.

Mishara, B. L. (1999). Conceptions of death and suicide in children ages 6–12 and their implications for suicide prevention. *Suicide and Life-Threatening Behavior, 29*(2), 105–118.

Muehlenkamp, J. J., & Kerr, P. L. (2010). Untangling a complex web: How non-suicidal self-injury and suicide attempts differ. *The Prevention Researcher, 17*(1), 8–10.

Nock, M. K., Joiner, T. E., Gordon, K. H., Lloyd-Richardson, E., & Prinstein, M. J. (2006). Non-suicidal self-injury among adolescents: Diagnostic correlates and relation to suicide attempts. *Psychiatry Research, 144*, 65–72.

Peter, T., Roberts, L. W., & Buzdugan, R. (2008). Suicidal ideation among Canadian youth: A multivariate analysis. *Archives of Suicide Research, 12*(3), 263–275.

Pfeffer, C. R. (2001). Diagnosis of childhood and adolescent suicidal behavior: Unmet needs for suicide prevention. *Biological Psychiatry, 39*(12), 1055–1061.

Silverman, M. M. (2006). The language of suicidology. *Suicide and Life Threatening Behavior, 36*, 519–532.

Silverman, M. M. (2011). Challenges to classifying suicidal ideations, communications, and behaviors. In R. C. O'Connor, S. Platt & J. Gordon (Eds.), *International handbook of suicide prevention: Research, policy, and practice* (pp. 9–25). Malden, MA: John Wiley & Sons.

Speece, M. W., & Brent, S. B. (1996). The development of children's understanding of death. In C. M. Corr & D. M. Corr (Eds.), *Handbook of childhood death and bereavement.* New York, NY: Springer.

Statistics Canada (2017). Table 102-0561—Leading causes of death, total population, by age group and sex, Canada, annual, CANSIM [database]. Retrieved from www5.statcan.gc.ca/cansim/a47.

Thompson, R., Dubowitz, H., English, D. J., Nooner, K. B., Wike, T., Bangdiwala, S. I., . . . Briggs, E. C. (2006). Parents' and teachers' concordance with children's self-ratings of suicidality: Findings from a high-risk sample. *Suicide and Life Threatening Behavior, 36*(2), 167–181.

Tishler, C. L., Reiss, N. S., & Rhodes, A. R. (2007). Suicidal behavior in children younger than twelve: A diagnostic challenge for emergency department personnel. *Journal of Academic Emergency Medicine, 14*(9), 810–818.

Wagner, B. M. (2009). *Suicidal behavior in children and adolescents.* New Haven, CT: Yale University Press.

World Health Organization (2014). *Preventing suicide: A global imperative.* Retrieved from www.who.int/mental_health/suicide-prevention/world_report_2014/en/

11 Grief and Loss Among First Nations and African American Youth

Tashel C. Bordere and James A. Larsen

First Nations and African American youth and families share parallel experiences with grief around unprecedented numbers of externally imposed sudden, violent, and intentional death and non-death losses as a function of ethnocentrism, pervasive forms of discrimination (racial and ethnic profiling), and systemic oppression. The narratives of these youth and families have largely been unrecognized or have been framed from deficit, survivor-blaming perspectives that have not accounted for the roles of privilege or unearned advantages (Johnson, 2006), disenfranchisement, nor acknowledgment and consideration for grief (Doka, 1989) as a normal response to ongoing socially imposed losses.

Often, losses that are unacknowledged within the larger culture are also understudied in the scholarly literature and are then justified with other-blame as "hard to reach" populations (Bordere, 2016a) with few or no explanations of efforts employed to reach the less studied groups (Curtis et al., 2004). Thus, not surprisingly, an important yet understudied area in death-loss and non-death-loss literature is that of individual and collective grief for First Nations and African American youth and families around social injustices related to historical and present day experiences with ethnic and race-based trauma (Bryant & Ocampo, 2005a; Sanchez-Hucles, 1998) and loss, in deaths by suicide, "medical racism" (Rosenblatt & Wallace, 2005, p. 10), and those framed as "color-coded" deaths (Holloway, 2003, p. 3).

As a researcher (Tashel Bordere) who has been entrusted with access to the loss-and-grief stories of African American youth (e.g., Bordere, 2009b, 2014), my hope is to provide a humanized, culturally informed narrative. In doing so, we (Bordere and Larsen) hope to disrupt negative, stereotypical, and misinformed images contributing to the dehumanization of First Nations and African American children and teens and to reduced services specifically designed to meet their bereavement needs. More specifically, in this chapter, we present historical and present-day experiences with loss and varied forms of grief associated with narratives of social injustice for First Nations and African American youth. Concrete implications for research and programming, grounded in social justice and culturally conscientious practice, are also presented. We draw from Bell's (1997) definition of *social justice*, which includes "a vision of society in which the distribution of resources is equitable and all members are physically and psychologically safe and secure" (p. 3).

Oppressive Contexts of Loss and Grief

Oppression is described as a sense of being caught between two negative and opposing alternatives (Frye, 1998) and occurs when one group takes advantage of another group for its own gain (Hardiman & Jackson, 1992, p. 2). We see oppression in the historical and present-day experiences of both First Nations and African American youth. The intersecting forces of systemic oppression create multiple, cumulative losses that complicate grief for these youth and families. We explore elements of loss-and-grief journeys first with First Nations youth of Canada and then with African American youth.

First Nations Youth

The number of suicide attempts and completed suicides among First Nations youth and families is astounding. One population highlighted in the media for its distressingly high rate of attempted and completed suicides, in the absence of appropriate grief-related support, is the Attawapiskat First Nation. In this small population of 2000, a startling 101 individuals have attempted suicide, with one completion, within only a 7-month period (CBC News, 2016a). Individuals attempting suicide ranged in age from pre-adolescence (age 11) to 71. Representing a growing trend among youth, a group of five adolescent females who overdosed on drugs are included in this number.

The rates of suicide attempts are indeed what is commonly called a public health concern in that the well-being and life expectancy of large numbers of people are impacted. However, this issue should also be framed through a lens of accountability as a "population injustice concern." To look at the plight of First Nations youth and families without serious attention to the social issues and systemic factors contributing to the current conditions (suicide, attempts, poverty) is likely to further oppress already marginalized Aboriginal communities.

Historical Contexts: Dehumanization, Violence, and Death

Although the issue of suicide is appropriately highlighted in discussions of First Nations populations, their historical narrative, prior to having their land seized and culture violently dismantled, is not one grounded in high rates of self-harm leading to large numbers of intentional deaths. Thus, in understanding issues around life, loss, trauma, and grief for First Nations populations, the historical contexts of these youth and families must be explored. For thousands of years, Canada's indigenous peoples were free to celebrate a culture characterized by unity and harmony with the natural world ("First Nations in Canada," n.d.). Their daily lives, practices, values, and beliefs were rooted in the beauty and affordances of Canada's diverse landscapes. The intergenerational transmission of culture and knowledge was achieved through a rich oral tradition characterized by an unwavering love and respect for all creation (Steckley & Cummins, 2010). Survival was dependent on a keen sense of the environment in conjunction with sociocultural traditions used to govern the allocation of land and resources. This way of life was largely undisrupted until the onset of European colonization in the sixteenth and seventeenth centuries ("First Nations in Canada," n.d.).

It was not long before the early trade agreements between European settlers and First Nations evolved into military alliances driven by competition for the dominion over the vast expanse of natural resources (Dickason & McNab, 2009). Over time, land was seized from the indigenous populations by the settlers. Simultaneously, British colonists engaged in ethnocentrism, imposing their own societal beliefs and practices on First Nations (Steckley & Cummins, 2010). By the late 1800s, the British had put in place several policies intended to restrict the civil rights and ban the traditional practices of indigenous people. First Nations youth were among the primary targets for forced assimilation ("First Nations in Canada," n.d.), and this was primarily accomplished through forced attendance at residential schools.

Between the late nineteenth to the early twentieth century, the department of Indian Affairs removed generations of Aboriginal youth from their families and homes and through Canada's residential school system (Elias et al., 2012; "First Nations in Canada," n.d.). These children suffered multiple losses through assimilation processes in boarding schools. They were stripped of their cultural heritage—including traditional garbs, native languages, spiritual beliefs, and they were physically altered (hair cut) with their culture-bound daily practices forbidden—and Eurocentric values were enforced ("First Nations in Canada," n.d.). Additional losses included isolation from the security and protection of families, communities, and cultural narratives.

In addition to being forcibly removed from their homes, families, and having everything familiar to them taken away at such a vulnerable developmental stage of life, the physical, psychological, social, and emotional traumas experienced by First Nations youth during this period of history is unfathomable. Children were physically, sexually, and emotionally abused. Roughly 50,000 youth who were forced into the residential school system are believed to have died as a result of abuse and the outbreak of diseases such as tuberculosis (Richardson & Nelson, 2007). Multiple generations of youth and families were forcibly cycled through residential schools and the devastation that accompanied life and death within these settings.

The residential school system has been linked to a wide range of negative outcomes, such as substance abuse, increased rates of suicide, and the continued victimization of those who survived (Elias et al., 2012). Suicide rates for First Nations youth vary by geographic region.

First Nations youth ages 10–19 are differentially impacted by suicide loss with male youth eight times more likely to die of suicide than non-Aboriginal youth (MacNeil, 2008). Comparatively, in the geographic region occupied by the Attawapiskat First Nation, rates of suicide attempts and completed suicides have created a state of emergency. Grief related deaths due to suicide can be complicated by social stigma and suicide contagion. Suicide may also complicate grief as youth and families are often left with few explanations about the death, and may thus perform "psychological autopsies" (Jordan, 2009), recreating their vision of their cared-about-person's last moments in their quest to understand.

Before the residential school policies came to an end in 1996, a new platform of oppression and forced assimilation was established to continue the "aggressive civilization" of First Nations people (Richardson & Nelson, 2007). In the late twentieth century, amendments to the *Indian Act* made it possible, once again, for the Canadian government to legally remove scores of First Nations children from their families and place them into the welfare system. In the "60s scoop," thousands of First Nations youth were removed from their homes and put into adoptive households (Fanshel, 1972; Fournier & Crey, 1997). Similar to the residential schools of the nineteenth and twentieth centuries, the welfare system is an engine for "whitewashing" indigenous youth and creating losses by severing their familial and communal ties, often permanently (Richardson & Nelson, 2007). It is not uncommon for First Nations youth to experience dozens of losses and transitions between foster and adoptive homes. Unsurprisingly, this ongoing cycle of trauma has been linked to similar outcomes as those seen in the wake of the residential school system, such as disproportionate rates of substance abuse, low academic achievement, and negative physical and mental health outcomes (Morris, 2007; Richardson & Nelson, 2007) in the absence of available and accessible support for their grief experiences.

The forced displacement of First Nations youth from their land involved significant non-death losses and represents the lynchpin for a grand umbrella of ongoing social and cultural genocide. First Nations youth have been faced with numerous "ambiguous" non-death losses, or losses that are unclear, caused by an external force, and that may be traumatic (Boss, 2010). There is the historical and present day ambiguity or lack of certainty about their personal safety and that of family members and friends. Unearned entitlements (McIntosh, 2007), such as the right to choose one's own identity, culture, educational path, and to reside with one's own family, were revoked through policies such as the *Indian Act* and remain ambiguous losses or losses with no clear resolution or answers (Boss, 1999, 2010; Boss, Roos, & Harris, 2011).

First Nations youth are often dehumanized and negatively stigmatized as a societal burden by much of the dominant culture. This, too, stems largely from policies, including the *Indian Act,* which considered First Nations as "wards" of the State (Kirmayer et al., 2003). As such, the grief of First Nations is disenfranchised by negative stereotypes and sentiments that indigenous populations are somehow responsible for their continued plight. Well-documented symptoms of oppression, such as increased rates of substance abuse and suicide, have often been attributed by dominant factions of society to cultural flaws among First Nations populations (Palmater, 2011). This pattern of victim-blaming, however, has been dismantled by an insurgence of research demonstrating that it is, in fact, the disruption and *losses* of elements of cultural identity, traditions, and family/community support and the feelings of hopelessness associated with this traumatic grief that can be directly connected to ongoing social issues.

African American Youth: Stigma, Loss, and Race-Based Traumatic Grief

As with First Nations Youth, African American youth also share in a rich cultural heritage marred by profound death and non-death losses and "race-based trauma" (Bryant-Davis, 2007; Bryant-Davis & Ocampo, 2005b) related to historical and present-day systemic injustices.

Among several recent and highly publicized violent deaths of African American youth is that of Tamir Rice, a 12-year-old African American male. The child was at a park playing with a toy gun when a police officer, perceiving him as a threat, shot Tamir two times within only 2 seconds of the officer's arrival at the scene (Williams & Smith, 2015). The officers were not charged.

The highly publicized deaths of African American youth are undoubtedly tragic, but these are not a new lived experience for African American individuals and families. As a function of parental socialization practices, African American youth are exposed to present-day violence, and also maintain historical memories (Gillis, 1994, p. 7; Kansteiner, 2002) of racialized violence and deaths occurring in the forced immigration, enslavement, and dehumanization of African American children and families. Assaultive violence and sudden death were common conditions of slavery along with an absence of just practices to ensure the safety and survival of African American children and teens. Enslaved youth experienced what is described by King (2011) as a "stolen childhood." The period of adolescence was an especially difficult time of loss and grief for families, as it was during this time that youth, particularly male youth, were sold away on auction blocks like products, and, in many cases, never again to see their families.

The historical patterns of sudden, violent death and dehumanization look shockingly similar to deaths occurring in contemporary society at the hands of privileged entities (police/law enforcement officers) who should be assuring their safety. Within the last few years, several highly publicized deaths of multiple young African American males—Trayvon Martin (Barry, Kovaleski, Robertson, & Alvarez, 2012), Michael Brown (Buchanan et al., 2014) and Tamir Rice—have yielded decisions in which African American youth and families have experienced revictimization around the injustice of the verdicts (Lawson, 2012). Surviving youth (friends, peers, dating partners) are left to contend with both individual grief and collective race-based grief and trauma around loss.

High rates of homicide loss, both at the hands of other marginalized youth and among individuals who should be serving protective functions, create realistic fears about the potential deaths of cared-about persons. This worry is particularly salient concerning potential deaths of African American male youth and contributes to anticipatory grief, or grief in anticipation of a loss, and anxiety among these youth and families. The grief of these youth is met with diminished spaces for mourning practices and "suffocated grief," or penalties around their grief expressions, which are often misread, devalued, or improperly labeled ("acting out" versus physically expressing grief; Bordere, 2014, 2016b). The city of New Orleans (U.S.) is a notable exception in which teens in one study highlighted the value of the celebratory second-line ritual in their otherwise stigmatized and suffocated grief experiences with homicide loss (Bordere, 2009b). Further, the grief experiences of African American youth with anxiety may be under- or overdiagnosed (Kilgus, Pumariega, & Cuffe, 1995) or pathologized (e.g., as paranoia) and medicalized (Granek, 2016).

Dehumanized within the larger culture, Goff et al. (2014) found that African American male youth are viewed as older and less innocent than their white peers. As a consequence of this form of racial bias (perceived as older and less innocent) and the resulting disparities, African American youth are more likely to be perceived as a risk and harmed through gun violence at the hands of law enforcement officers. They are also less likely than majority youth to benefit from "unearned entitlements," or basic rights that everyone should experience (McIntosh, 2007), such as police protection, protection from police victimization, and justice in cases of victimization by law enforcement.

Implications for Research and Practice

As researchers and practitioners, it is our ethical and social responsibility to maintain an awareness of dominant discourses around First Nations and African American youth coping with historical and present day losses, trauma, and bereavement. It is our charge to be sure that we are not duplicating narratives that will further disenfranchise and contribute to ongoing "suffocated grief" (Bordere, 2016b) or penalization of the grief expressions of already marginalized bereaved youth. A condition of effective research and practice is one in which First Nations and African American youth are viewed in human ways, with dismantled notions of these youth as invaluable or desensitized, viewing them instead as individuals who are thinkers, possessing both present day and historical memories of death and violence and a myriad of feelings around individual and collective trauma and loss.

In practice with First Nations and African American youth, it is central to assist children and teens in establishing language to name and label their social experiences, cognitive processes, physiological responses, and emotions and to do so in connection to grief and loss. Naming and validation are especially important for disenfranchised youth and families coping with grief and ethnic and/or "race-based trauma" (Bryant-Davis, 2007) in cultural contexts in which their narratives are glaring for them yet alarmingly invisible or invalidated by privileged populations. This leaves youth to question their realities amid ongoing losses that are met with verdicts in legal proceedings, for example, which are experienced as unjust. All too often, underrepresented male youth are especially left out of places and spaces for naming and acknowledgement of experience with loss or are silenced by suffocated grief or penalties around their grief expressions (Bordere, 2014, 2016b). Both male and female First Nations and African American youth must have these opportunities.

In one Snuneymuxw First Nations community, creating ways for youth to connect to the community and culture has served protective functions in providing support and decreasing the suicide rate among youth (CBC News, 2016b). This observation is consistent with research examining factors related to suicide prevention as perceptions of "community caring" (Mota et al., 2012) and "cultural continuity" (Chandler & Lalonde, 1998, 2008) were found to contribute to reduced suicide rates among First Nations youth.

In *culturally conscientious practice*, these youth should be approached with an openness to evolving knowledge about the similarities and unique aspects of their life, loss, and grief narratives related to their specific social locations (e.g., gender, religion, spirituality, socioeconomic status, race, ethnicity, school location, resources; Bordere, 2009a). The Five A's of culturally conscientious care (Bordere, 2016a, p. 78) include the following:

Acknowledge

> African American Youth—"I can see from your poem today how scary it must be for you when you are unjustly followed by the police, given the historical deaths and the recently highlighted shooting deaths of other African American children and teens that you have written about in your poem."
>
> First Nations Youth—"I can see from the words used in your story how scary it must be for you to cope with so many suicide attempts and deaths of your family members and friends."

Ask

> African American Youth—"Can you tell me more about the ideas described in your poem? I am especially interested in what you were thinking and feeling when the verdict was handed down in which the police officer was not charged with the shooting death of Tamir Rice (12-year-old African American male), who you wrote about in your poem."
>
> First Nations Youth—"I can see that you were very angry and sad when you heard about the deaths of your close friends. Can you tell me

more about what were you thinking, what thoughts were going through your mind, when you learned that five of your friends died together by suicide? What would you want people to know about what this means to you?

Accept

Accept that the child or teen thinks and feels as he or she does regarding the social circumstances and the death. Rosenblatt (2016) highlighted the internal challenges that may be faced by researchers and practitioners of privilege (e.g., white male, heterosexual, Christian) when confronted with the notion that the interviewee or client is disenfranchised by the privilege of these professionals who engage with them.

Align (where privilege or power differentials are operating)

"Please know that I am your advocate and will also be writing a letter to the Legislature/Canadian government about injustices occurring with African American teens/First Nations teens. I will emphasize how important it is for you and your friends and family to be supported and have programs to keep you feeling connected to your communities and cultural values as you cope with the many deaths and losses that feel very unfair to you."

Apologize (if needed)

"I am sorry that I made an incorrect assumption about your poem with my first read of it. It is a powerful and creative way to express your grief and a constructive way to bring about social action and change."

Further, researchers and practitioners should also enter interactions with marginalized youth educated and informed about ethnic- and race-related trauma (see Byant-Davis, 2007) and grief. Additionally, central to socially just research and programming is a continuous commitment not only to "other knowledge," or knowledge about other diverse groups, but also to self-reflective practices (Bordere, 2016a; Goodman et al., 2004). Consistent practices that involve self-reflection facilitate increased awareness and self-knowledge of personal privilege and marginalization and the roles they play in rapport building, the framing of our questions and hypotheses, youth participant retention rates, and analysis and interpretation of First Nations and African American youth narratives and the dissemination of results. Findings from our research and practice must be disseminated to communities beyond our academic and clinical colleagues to communities that directly serve marginalized youth, such as educational settings, youth program directors and staff, medical offices, and religious and spiritual communities (Bordere, 2016a). It is when we engage in these practices that we further social justice efforts in grief and loss for First Nations and African American youth.

Discussion Questions

1. How can helping professionals develop a culturally conscientious practice?
2. In what ways can each of us as helping professionals contribute to social change with respect to racism, stigma, and discrimination?
3. How might you support youth who are grieving both death and non-death losses that have arisen from racism or discrimination?

References

Barry, D., Kovaleski, S. F., Robertson, C., & Alvarez, L. (2012). Race, tragedy and outrage collide after a shot in Florida. *New York Times, 1*. Retrieved from www.nytimes.com/2012/04/02/us/trayvon-martin-shooting-prompts-a-review-of-ideals.html

Bell, L. A. (1997). Theoretical foundations for social justice education. In M. Adams, L. Bell, & P. Griffin (Eds.), *Teaching for diversity and social justice: A sourcebook* (pp. 3–15). New York, NY: Routledge.

Bordere, T. C. (2009a). Culturally conscientious thanatology. *The ADEC Forum, 3*(2), 1, 3–4.

Bordere, T. C. (2009b). 'To look at death another way': Black teenage males' perspectives on second-lines and regular funerals in New Orleans. *Omega, 58*(3), 213–232.

Bordere, T. C. (2014). Adolescents and homicide. In K. Doka & A. Tucci (Eds.), *Helping adolescents cope with loss*. Washington, DC: Hospice Foundation of America.

Bordere, T. C. (2016a). "Not gonna be laid out to dry": Cultural mistrust in end of life care and strategies for trust-building. In D. Harris & T. C. Bordere (Eds.), *Handbook of social justice in loss and grief: Exploring diversity, equity, and inclusion* (pp. 75–84). New York, NY: Routledge.

Bordere, T. C. (2016b). Social justice conceptualizations in grief and loss. In D. Harris & T. C. Bordere (Eds.), *Handbook of social justice in loss and grief: Exploring diversity, equity, and inclusion* (pp. 9–20). New York, NY: Routledge.

Boss, P. (1999). Ambiguous loss: Living with frozen grief. *Harvard Mental Health Letter, 16*(5), 4–6.

Boss, P. (2010). The trauma and complicated grief of ambiguous loss. *Pastoral Psychology, 59*(2), 137–145. doi:10.1007/s11089-009-0264-0

Boss, P., Roos, S., & Harris, D. (2011). Grief in the midst of ambiguity and uncertainty: An exploration of ambiguous loss and chronic sorrow. In R. A. Neimeyer, D. L. Harris, H. R. Winokuer, & G. F. Thornton (Eds.), *Grief and bereavement in contemporary society: Bridging research and practice* (pp. 163–176). New York, NY: Routledge.

Brown, J., Higgitt, N., Wingert, S., Miller, C., & Morrissette, L. (2005). Challenges faced by Aboriginal youth in the inner city. *Canadian Journal of Urban Research, 14*(1), 81–106.

Bryant-Davis, T. (2007). Healing requires recognition: The case for race-based traumatic stress. *The Counseling Psychologist, 35*(1), 135–143.

Bryant-Davis, T., & Ocampo, C. (2005a). Racist incident-based trauma. *The Counseling Psychologist, 33*(4), 479–500.

Bryant-Davis, T., & Ocampo, C. (2005b). The trauma of racism: Implications for counseling, research, and education. *The Counseling Psychologist, 33*(4), 574–578.

Buchanan, L., Fessenden, F., Lai, R., Park, H., Parlapiano, A., Tse, A., ... & Yourish, K. (2014). What happened in Ferguson? *New York Times*. Retrieved from www. nytimes.com/interactive/2014/08/13/us/ferguson-missouri-town-under-siege-after-police-shooting.html

Chandler, M. J., & Lalonde, C. (1998). Cultural continuity as a hedge against suicide in Canada's first nations. *Transcultural Psychiatry, 35*(2), 191–219. doi:10.1177/136346159803500202

Chandler, M. J., & Lalonde, C. (2008). Cultural continuity as a protective factor against suicide in First Nations youth. *Horizons, 10*, 68–72.

CBC News. (Producer). (2016a, April 9). *Attawapiskat declares state of emergency over spate of suicide attempts*. Retrieved from www.cbc.ca/news/canada/sudbury/attawapiskat-suicide-first-nations-emergency-1.3528747

CBC News. (Producer). (2016b, April 18). *For First Nations facing suicide crisis, the solution is rooted in the community*. Retrieved from www.cbc.ca/news/aboriginal/suicide-first-nations-snuneymuxw-1.3536821

Curtis, K., Roberts, H., Copperman, J., Downie, A., & Liabo, K. (2004). "How come I don't get asked no questions": Researching "hard to reach" children and teenagers. *Child & Family Social Work, 19*(2), 167–175.

Dickason, O. P., & McNab, D. (2009). *Canada's first nations: A history of founding peoples from earliest times* (4th ed.). Ontario, Canada: Oxford University Press.

Doka, K. J. (1989). *Disenfranchised grief: Recognizing hidden sorrow*. Lexington, MA: Lexington Books.

Elias, B., Mignone, J., Hall, M., Hong, S. P., Hart, L., & Sareen, J. (2012). Trauma and suicide behaviour histories among a Canadian indigenous population: An empirical exploration of the potential role of Canada's residential school system. *Social Science & Medicine, 74*, 1560–1569. http://doi.org/10.1016/j.socscimed.2012.01.026

Fanshel, D. (1972). *Far from the reservation: the transracial adoption of American Indian children*. Metuchen, NJ: The Scarecrow Press.

First Nations in Canada. (n. d.). Retrieved from https://www.aadnc-aandc.gc.ca/eng/1307460755710/1307460872523

Fournier, S., & Crey, E. (1997). *Stolen from our embrace: The abduction of First Nations children and the restoration of Aboriginal communities*. Vancouver, Canada: Douglas & McIntyre.

Frye, M. (1998). Oppression. In P. S. Rothenburg (Ed.), *Race, class, and gender: An integrated study* (4th ed.). New York, NY: St. Martin's Press.

Gillis, J. R. (Ed.) (1994). Memory and identity: The history of a relationship. *Commemorations: The politics of national identity* (p. 7). Princeton, NJ: Princeton University Press.

Goff, P. A., Jackson, M. C., Allison, B., Di Leone, L., Cullotta, C. M., & DiTomasso, N. A. (2014). The essence of innocence: Consequences of dehumanizing Black children. *Journal of Personality and Social Psychology, 106*(4), 526–545.

Goodman, L. A., Liang, B., Helms, J. E., Latta, R. E., Sparks, E., & Weintraub, S. R. (2004). Training counseling psychologists as social justice agents: Feminist and multicultural principles in action. *The Counseling Psychologist, 32*, 793–837. doi:10.1177/0011000004268802

Granek, L. G. (2016). Medicalizing grief. In D. Harris & T. Bordere (Eds.), *Handbook of social justice in loss and grief: Exploring diversity, equity, and inclusion* (pp. 111–124). New York, NY: Routledge.

Hardiman, R., & Jackson, B. (1992). Oppression: Conceptual and developmental analysis. In M. Adams, P. Brigham, P. Dalpes, & L. Marchesani (Eds.), *Social diversity and social justice: Diversity and oppression: Conceptual Frameworks* (pp. 1–6). Dubuque, IA: Kendall/Hunt.

Holloway, K. (2003). *Passed on: African American mourning stories: A memorial.* Durham, NC: Duke University Press.

Johnson, C. (2006). We can't heal until the wounding stops. In A. Johnson's (Ed.), *Privilege, power, and difference* (2nd ed., pp. 66–67). Boston, MA: McGraw Hill.

Jordan, J. R. (2009). After suicide: Clinical work with survivors. *Grief Matters: The Australian Journal of Grief and Bereavement, 12*(1), 4–9.

Kansteiner, W. (2002). Finding meaning in memory: A methodological critique of collective memory studies. *History and Theory, 41*(2), 179–197. doi:10.1111/0018-2656.00198

Kilgus, M. G., Pumariega, A. J., & Cuffe, S. P. (1995). Influence of race on diagnosis in adolescent psychiatric inpatients. *Journal of the American Academy of Child and Adolescent Psychiatry, 34*, 67–72.

King, W. (2011). *Stolen childhood: Slave youth in nineteenth-century America.* Bloomington, IN: Indiana University Press

Kirmayer, L., Simpson, C., & Cargo, M. (2003). Healing traditions: Culture, community and mental health promotion with Canadian Aboriginal peoples. *Australasian Psychiatry, 11*(1), S15–S23.

Lawson, T. F. (2012). A fresh cut in an old wound–a critical analysis of the Trayvon Martin killing: The public outcry, the prosecutors' discretion, and the stand your ground law. *University of Florida Journal of Law and Public Policy, 271.*

MacNeil, M. S. (2008). An epidemiologic study of Aboriginal adolescent risk in Canada: The meaning of suicide. *Journal of Child and Adolescent Psychiatric Nursing, 21*(1), 3–12.

McIntosh, P. (2007). White privilege: Unpacking the invisible knapsack. In P. S. Rothenberg (Ed.), *Race, class, and gender in the United States* (7th ed.). New York, NY: Worth.

Morris, K. (2007). Re-examining issues behind the loss of family and cultural and the impact on Aboriginal youth suicide rates. *First Peoples Child & Family Review, 3*(1), 133–142.

Mota, N., Elias, B., Tefft, B., Medved, M., Munro, G., Sareen, J., & Swampy Creek Suicide Prevention Team (2012). Correlates of suicidality: Investigation of a representative sample of Manitoba First Nations adolescents. *American Journal of Public Health, 102*(7), 1353–1361.

Palmater, P. D. (2011). *Beyond blood: Rethinking Indigenous identity.* Saskatoon, SK: Purich Publishing.

Richardson, C., & Nelson, B. (2007). A change of residence: Government schools and foster homes as sites of forced Aboriginal assimilation—A paper designed to provoke thought and systemic change. *First Peoples Child & Family Review, 3*(2), 75–83.

Rosenblatt, P. (2016). Cultural competence and humility. In D. Harris & T. C. Bordere (Eds.), *Handbook of social justice in loss and grief: Exploring diversity, equity, and inclusion* (pp. 67–74). New York, NY: Routledge.

Rosenblatt, P., & Wallace, B. (2005). *American American grief* (pp. 7–18). New York, NY: Routledge.

Sanchez-Hucles, J. (1998). Racism: Emotional abusiveness and psychological trauma for ethnic minorities. *Journal of Emotional Abuse, 1*, 69–87.

Steckley, J. L., & Cummins, B. D. (2010). *Full circle: Canada's First Nations* (2nd ed., [Nachdr.]). Toronto, Canada: Prentice Hall.

Williams, T., & Smith, M. (2015). Cleveland officer will not face charges in Tamir Rice shooting death. *New York Times*. Retrieved from www.nytimes.com/2015/12/29/us/tamir-rice-police-shootiing-cleveland.html

12 Loss and Resilience in Gender and Sexual Minority Youth

Kip G. Williams

The legal and cultural context for gender and sexual diversity in the United States and Canada has shifted dramatically over the last 2 decades. Most notably, Canada enacted the Civil Marriage Act in 2005, and the U.S. Supreme Court guaranteed the fundamental right to marry to same-sex couples in 2015. Both countries have embraced other rights and protections for gender and sexual minorities (GSM), and the lives and identities of GSM individuals are much more visible throughout society. Still, a disproportionate number of GSM youth are experiencing homelessness in both the U.S. (Keuroghlian, Shtasel, & Bassuk, 2014) and Canada (Abramovich, 2012), and family rejection is the most frequently cited contributing factor (Durso & Gates, 2012). A growing body of empirical literature[1] demonstrates that GSM youth—especially those who do not conform to gender role expectations—are at increased risk for victimization during adolescence (Toomey, Ryan, Diaz, Card, & Russell, 2010) and for psychological problems including posttraumatic stress, suicide ideation and attempts, substance abuse, depression, and anxiety (D'Augelli, Pilkington, & Hershberger, 2002).

Many GSM youth have lost their lives to suicide or hate crimes, but these studies point toward the kinds of losses that many GSM youth experience—losses of safety, support, belonging, well-being, family, and even housing. These losses, in turn, influence the psychological development of GSM youth, who often are subjected to societal discrimination and prejudice before they develop awareness of their own gender and sexual identities. The result of this developmental order of events is that they have already learned stigmatizing attitudes by the time they begin to recognize themselves as members of a minority group (Malyon, 1982). This conflict often leads to concealment, self-hatred, and self-harm behaviors (McDermott, Roen, & Scourfield, 2008). This points toward another important loss that many GSM youth experience: the loss of compassion, love, and respect for oneself.

It is important to note that sex, gender, and sexual orientation are three distinct aspects of an individual's identity. *Sex* refers to the biological and physiological characteristics of an individual's reproductive anatomy. The general term *intersex* applies to those individuals who are born with a reproductive anatomy or genetic makeup that does not fit classification within the rigid *male–female* binary. *Gender* refers to the socially constructed identities and roles that are typically correlated with biological sex. The term *cisgender* refers to those individuals who experience congruence between biological sex and gender identity. Various terms such as *gender variant* or *gender nonconforming* refer to individuals who do not experience this congruence, and *transgender* refers to those individuals who change their gender identity to align it with their private experience or felt sense of gender. The construct *sexual orientation* categorizes individuals on the relationship between biological sex and erotic or romantic attraction.

These definitions are necessarily imperfect and imprecise because (a) the assumption of binary categories is not scientifically accurate, (b) binary classifications do not align with many people's biology or experience, and (c) the organization of sexual identity and gender roles is arbitrary and socially constructed. The broader, more inclusive term *gender and sexual minorities* is used throughout this chapter to refer to all individuals who are not cisgender and heterosexual. Various acronyms are used to refer to lesbian, gay, bisexual, transgender, queer, and intersex (LGBTQI) individuals to maintain fidelity to the research studies that are cited.

GSM can be considered as a group because they face similar challenges and overlapping forms of discrimination. For example, a young effeminate boy might be called a "fag" in school but identify as a heterosexual trans-woman as an adult. Similarly, a butch lesbian and a heterosexual transman might both experience discrimination for not conforming to expectations regarding how women should present themselves. One cannot do justice, however, to the unique individual and subgroup experiences of such a diverse group. In a spirit of humility, this chapter (a) reviews various theories that attempt to explain the complex interactions between societal discrimination, psychological distress, self-harm or risk-taking behaviors, and increased risk of completed suicide; (b) considers the incredible resilience of GSM youth; (c) examines and critiques the disorder model for its role in contributing to stigma and legitimizing harmful practices that target GSM youth; and (d) summarizes practical guidelines for educators and helping professionals.

Social Stigma

Conceptualizing Stigma

Weinberg (1972) suggested the term *homophobia* to describe the irrational fear of being near a homosexual. Today, the term is applied broadly to all negative attitudes and acts of discrimination or violence against lesbians and gay men (Greene, 2000). The original intent was to frame stigmatizing attitudes as a kind of personal pathology, similar to agoraphobia or claustrophobia. Empirical evidence does not support this conception of homophobia as an individual pathology (Herek, 1996), but the term has persisted in both scholarly and popular discourse. Similarly, *transphobia* has been used to describe all negative attitudes and acts of discrimination or violence against transgender people. Given the diversity of gender identity and expression, transphobia might also refer to stigma against a broader class of people who do not conform to conventional gender roles but do not identify as transgender.

Heterosexism is a related construct that refers to the ideological system that rewards and privileges heterosexuality while devaluing and punishing non-heterosexuality (Sears, 1997). This alternate view holds that stigma against GSM is not an individual pathology but, rather, a form of sociopolitical oppression similar to racism (Herek, 2000). Heterosexism functions to suppress gender and sexual diversity. According to various theoretical perspectives, heterosexism also functions to uphold the rigid gender binary system and to maintain the dominance of men over women (Pharr, 1997). Support for this position comes from empirical evidence that gender nonconforming LGB youth are at higher risk for victimization than their gender conforming LGB peers (Toomey et al., 2010). Although homophobia and heterosexism often are used interchangeably, this chapter includes the use of the term heterosexism because it is more consistent with empirical evidence and it emphasizes that stigma against GSM is a social and political problem that can be improved through advocacy, education, and activism.

Mechanisms of Heterosexism

Like other forms of oppression, heterosexism is enacted throughout society in various ways: interpersonal processes, such as bullying, harassment, physical violence, microaggressions, and intentional acts of discrimination; cultural processes, such as social customs and negative representations in popular media; and institutional processes, such as discrimination by governments, businesses, and churches. Since the focus of this chapter is on GSM youth, we consider several mechanisms of heterosexism that especially impact children and adolescents: school victimization, hate crimes, and family rejection.

School Victimization

Jamie Hubley, an openly gay 15-year-old student in Kanata, Ontario, took his own life on October 14, 2011. His goodbye letter made it clear that bullying and harassment in school had contributed to his decision (Boesveld, 2011). Unfortunately, his story is not unique. It is impossible to know the exact rate of completed suicides by GSM youth because many GSM youth conceal their identities. Recent studies showed that the rate of suicide attempts is 4 times greater for LGB youth than for their heterosexual peers (Kann et al., 2016) and that nearly 25% of transgender youth report having made a suicide attempt (Grossman & D'Augelli, 2007).

According to a recent national study in the United States, GSM students reported hearing words like *fag*, *dyke*, and *tranny* frequently at school in a negative context (Kosciw, Greytak, Palmer, & Boesen, 2013). Nearly 75% of

GSM students reported that they were verbally harassed at school. More than 36% were physically harassed (e.g., pushed, shoved), and 16.5% were physically assaulted (e.g., punched, kicked, injured with a weapon). More than 60% of students who reported an incident said that school staff did nothing to respond. Similar problems are prevalent in Canada as well (Anderson, 2014).

Comprehensive data on effective school intervention are not available, but the National Association of School Psychologists reported that more than two-thirds of students believe that adult help is infrequent and ineffective and estimated that teachers intervene in only 4% of bullying incidents (Cohn & Canter, 2003). These data demonstrate that schools can be hostile environments and that GSM youth often cannot depend on adults to intervene.

School victimization has been linked empirically to academic difficulties and negative learning outcomes, such as increased delinquency and drop-out rates (Barker, Arseneault, Brengden, Fontaine, & Maughan, 2008). It is also highly correlated with substance abuse, suicide ideation, and suicide attempts (Fedewa & Ahn, 2011). For gender nonconforming youth in particular, school victimization is correlated with higher depression and lower satisfaction with life in young adulthood (Toomey et al., 2010). When one considers the prevalence and impact of bullying and harassment—and the silence and complicity of school officials—it becomes clear that school victimization is one of the primary mechanisms of enacting heterosexist oppression. As a result, many GSM youth lose a sense of safety in their learning environment and face ongoing psychological difficulties into adulthood.

Religious Trauma

Religious discrimination often is classified in the broader category of institutional discrimination. A growing body of scholarship is examining the unique and harmful psychological influence of a perceived conflict between one's religious affiliation and one's gender or sexual identity. Many religious institutions continue to condemn or devalue GSM identities despite social progress, and the resulting psychological conflict often leads to shame, depression, and even suicide ideation (Schuck & Liddle, 2001). In one study of sexual minority youth experiencing depression and suicidality, more than half of youth cited religious beliefs as a contributing factor to rejection by their families (Diamond et al., 2011). As a result of these experiences, some GSM individuals come to see themselves as *sinners* (Kubicek et al., 2009), and qualitative research on adult gay men has elicited narratives about childhood religious experiences that suggest posttraumatic stress:

> I was always in a state of panic.... Cause I felt so guilty about how I was. Um, my religion was a very negative experience for me as a young kid growing up. I grew up believing almost everything was going to condemn me to hell, you know.... I also felt that if I was to have any kind of sexual encounter ... with a male ... I would be condemning that person to

hell as well. So, there was guilt compounded upon guilt . . . the scars of that are still with me.

(Lucies & Yick, 2007, p. 59)

Hate Crimes

Matthew Shepard was a gay student at the University of Wyoming. On the night of October 6, 1998, he was beaten, tortured, and left to die by two men who openly admitted that their violent actions were driven by anti-gay hatred. In fact, the attorney representing one of the perpetrators attempted to use *gay panic* as a legal defense, arguing that Shepard's alleged sexual advances drove him to temporary insanity. The judge rejected this defense, and both of the perpetrators were sentenced to two consecutive life terms after Shepard's parents publicly rejected the death penalty. His murder galvanized debate about hate crimes legislation in the United States. The Matthew Shepard and James Byrd Jr. Hate Crimes Prevention Act passed in 2009 despite opposition from religious conservatives such as Steven A. Schwalm of the Family Research Council, who said that hate crimes legislation "would criminalize pro-family beliefs" and "[send] a message that you can't disagree with the political message of homosexual activists" (Brooke, 1998). His talking points were typical of the debate surrounding hate crimes legislation.

According to a recent national study in the U.S., reports of hate-related homicides of LGBTQ and HIV-affected people are increasing, and survivors often report police indifference, hostility, hate language, and even violence (Waters, Jindasurat, & Wolfe, 2016). Gender minorities are at higher risk for homicide, and at least 21 transgender individuals were murdered in the U.S. in 2016. Most of these were trans women of color, and some of the murders involved explicit anti-transgender bias (Human Rights Campaign, 2016).

On June 12, 2016, a gay nightclub in Orlando, Florida became the site of the worst mass shooting by a single perpetrator in U.S. history, leaving 49 people dead and 53 injured. The victims were primarily GSM people of color, many of whom were just making the transition from adolescence to young adulthood. The shooting was interpreted as both an act of terrorism and a hate crime (Woolf, 2016).

Many people hold heterosexist attitudes without engaging in violence. These hate crimes provide striking examples of enacted heterosexism and remind us of the hatred that still exists despite social progress. In addition to the lives lost and injured, the Orlando massacre represented an attack on the nightclub as a safe space for those who have experienced rejection or hostility in other spaces (e.g., schools, churches). GSM youth often are aware of these stories but are unable to access support due to concealment of their identities and anticipated rejection from their families, churches, and communities. They are left to process their feelings in isolation or to find alternative support systems. Hate crimes—and the debates surrounding them—contribute to the loss of a sense of safety, belonging, and worthiness that many GSM youth experience.

Family Rejection

Family systems can either counter or augment the influence of societal discrimination on the lives of GSM youth. The evidence is undeniably clear: Family rejection is highly correlated with suicide ideation (D'Augelli, Hershberger, & Pilkington, 1998) and with depression, substance abuse, suicide attempt, and high-risk sexual behaviors (Ryan, Huebner, Diaz, & Sanchez, 2009). LGB adolescents experiencing psychological distress report family rejection as a leading cause (Diamond et al., 2011), and GSM youth experiencing homelessness most frequently cite family rejection as a contributing factor (Durso & Gates, 2012). Whatever the social and political realities of the world we live in, families seem to bear the greatest responsibility for the well-being of GSM youth.

Intersectionality

Many GSM youth are also members of other stigmatized minority groups. These youth are subjected to sexual stigma within heterosexist communities as well as stigma against other aspects of their identities within GSM communities. The term *intersectionality* comes from feminist theory and refers to the overlapping of multiple identities that are contrasted in terms of relative sociocultural power (Shields, 2008). Intersectionality is an additive predictor of psychological stress and health outcomes (Parent, DeBlaere, & Moradi, 2013), and GSM discourses in popular media and social networking often advance intersectional critiques on topics such as sexual racism (e.g., Rodriguez, 2016) and discrimination based on body size (e.g., Peitzman, 2013). These discourses demonstrate the additional challenges many GSM adolescents and young adults face in seeking belonging and support within GSM communities.

Psychological Distress and Resilience

The previous section examined various forms of enacted heterosexism that influence GSM youth. Enacted heterosexism is correlated with negative psychological, academic, and health outcomes and with risk-taking or self-harm behaviors. But what is the underlying psychological mechanism? How do GSM youth experience enacted heterosexism, and how do these experiences influence their development? Further, how do GSM youth demonstrate resilience in the face of these challenges? This section examines various theoretical perspectives on the psychological distress that results from social stigma, as well as GSM youth resilience and protective factors.

Conceptualizing Distress

Minority Stress Theory

Meyer (1995) proposed *minority stress theory* as a model to describe the distress that gay men experience as a result of social stigma. Contemporary scholarship has applied this model more broadly to all GSM (e.g., Skinta & Curtin, 2016). According to this theory, three psychological processes underlie the experience of minority stress: (a) *internalized oppression*,[2] which refers to the direction of negative societal attitudes toward oneself; (b) *perceived stigma*, which refers to one's vigilance and expectations of rejection, discrimination, and violence; and (c) deep feelings of rejection and fears of violence that may be disproportionate to actual prejudice events due to their association with broader cultural meanings. These three processes are empirically correlated to five domains of distress: demoralization, guilt, suicide ideation and behavior, AIDS-related traumatic stress response, and sex problems (Meyer, 2003).

Internalized Oppression

Weinberg (1972) introduced the term *internalized homophobia* to refer to the self-loathing of lesbians and gay men. Meyer and Dean (1998) broadened the definition to "the gay person's direction of negative social attitudes toward the self, leading to a devaluation of the self and resultant internal conflicts and poor self-regard" (p. 161). The construct *internalized oppression* refers more generally to members of any stigmatized and oppressed group who adopt the dominant group's ideology and accept a subordinate status. Both terms are used widely in scholarship on psychology and education as well as in popular discourse, and Meyer (1995) integrated them into the minority stress model. In order to understand and critique these constructs, one must understand that they developed from psychodynamic theory, which posited that homosexual children and adolescents internalize beliefs from society and that this internalized content

> becomes an aspect of the ego, functioning as both an unconscious introject, and as a conscious system of attitudes and accompanying affects. As a component of the ego, it influences identity formation, self-esteem, the elaboration of defenses, patterns of cognition, psychological integrity, and object relations. Homophobic incorporations also embellish superego functioning and, in this way, contribute to a propensity for guilt and intropunitiveness among homosexual males.
>
> (Malyon, 1982, p. 60)

Critiques of Internalized Oppression

Scholars tend to restate the presumed symptoms of internalized homophobia and internalized oppression without critiquing their psychodynamic roots or offering alternative theoretical explanations (Russell & Bohan, 2006). Some theorists have argued that the word *internalized* implies that the problem lies within the stigmatized individual rather than the attitudes and actions of society (e.g., Tappan, 2006). Russell and Bohan (2006) pointed out that "the usual distinction between homophobia-in-the-world and internalized homophobia as experienced and expressed by non-heterosexual individuals is a false one" (p. 343) and proposed that GSM individuals *ventriloquate* the *homonegating processes* pervasive in society. This theoretical lens emphasizes learning and behavior instead of psychodynamic concepts (e.g., internalization, ego, superego) that are not empirically based. Some evidence supports this position, suggesting that GSM youth's narratives about the expected trajectory of their lives sometimes are repetitions of narratives from their learning history rather than expressions of actual self-loathing (Russell, Bohan, & Lilly, 2000).

Shame

One word occurs universally throughout the literature on GSM: *shame*. Shame occurs at high rates in GSM individuals and is empirically correlated with psychological distress (Hequembourg & Dearing, 2013). In a study of young LGBT people's views and experiences of self-destructive behaviors, McDermott et al. (2008) argued that social stigma positions GSM youth as abnormal, dirty, and disgusting. The young people interviewed described shame as underlying self-harm behaviors. Evidence also suggests that shame plays an important role in substance use disorders and addictive behaviors among GSM (Matthews, Lorah, & Fenton, 2006).

Blum (2008) offered an experiential definition of shame that involves: (a) intense pain, discomfort, and anger; (b) a desire to hide; and (c) a feeling of being no good, inadequate, and unworthy. Educators and care providers should be aware of the role that shame might play in the lives of GSM youth. Since shame is strongly associated with a desire to conceal and hide, however, they might find it difficult to introduce or address directly in conversation.

GSM Youth and Resilience

Protective Factors

Decades of research demonstrates the prevalence and risk factors of negative outcomes for GSM youth, but it is also important to note the factors that promote psychological adjustment. A review of the small body of resilience literature identified several key protective factors in schools: sensitive HIV instruction, policies that explicitly prohibit bullying and discrimination, teacher confrontation of slurs and harassment, and the existence of a Gay–Straight Alliance, for example (Russell, 2005). Unsurprisingly, family acceptance is the most important protective factor. It is correlated with greater self-esteem, self-support, and general health status, and it protects against depression, substance abuse, and suicide ideation and attempts (Ryan, Russell, Huebner, Diaz, & Sanchez, 2010).

Resilience Strategies

In GSM discourses, *coming out* is a common term that refers to disclosing one's gender or sexual identity to others—especially family, friends, and coworkers. Coming out is a significant experience for many GSM youth. It often is associated with pride and courage, which are contrasted to the shame of hiding and concealment. One week after the Orlando massacre, *The New York Times* ran a story about gay adolescents and young adults who responded to the shooting by coming out to their families (Turkewitz, 2016). Coming out to one's family after a major hate crime is a remarkable example of the resilience of GSM youth.

McDermott et al. (2008) identified three narrative strategies that LGBT youth use to avoid shame: (a) routinization and minimization of prejudice events (e.g., portraying them as normal and not a big deal); (b) portraying oneself as self-reliant or as an adult; and (c) constructing a *proud* identity. These shame-avoidance strategies might be seen as contributing simultaneously to both resilience and risk. On the one hand, they represent the resilience of GSM youth reaching toward maturity and personal responsibility. On the other hand, GSM youth are more vulnerable to self-destructive behaviors when they handle social stigma individually, without expectation of support. Educators and care providers should exercise sensitivity and discernment when helping GSM youth explore the blurry line between self-reliance and self-isolation.

Wexler, DiFluvio, and Burke (2009) argued that affiliation with an oppressed group and active resistance of discrimination are key components of GSM youth resilience. Their view is that group affiliation provides GSM youth an opportunity to reconceptualize their personal difficulties as a politicized collective struggle, creating a context for ideological commitment and concrete action. This theory is consistent with the widely accepted view that community belonging and a commitment to social justice are integral parts of positive LGB identity formation and are empirically correlated with psychological well-being (Riggle, Mohr, Rostosky, Fingerhut, & Balsam, 2014). Choosing one's own spiritual pathway is also an important resilience strategy, especially for those who have experienced religious discrimination or trauma (Reygan, Curtin, & Moane, 2016).

Research on the experiences of trans and gender nonconforming youth has revealed two other resilience strategies that are especially important for gender minorities: (a) the ability to define and theorize one's own gender and (b) reframing mental health challenges (Singh, Meng, & Hansen, 2014). In practice, this means that educators and care providers should support gender minority youth to explore and express gender outside of the typical categories of the rigid binary system. It also means that they should help GSM youth reframe their emotional difficulties as a normal reaction to stigma and discrimination rather than as a personal failing or a disorder.

Helping and Affirming GSM Youth

The Disorder Model

The field of psychology historically has contributed to the stigma against GSM. Non-heterosexuality was considered a diagnosable disorder until the revised third edition of the *Diagnostic and Statistical Manual* (DSM-III-R; American Psychiatric Association, 1987), and numerous cases of involuntary hospitalization, lobotomy, and electroconvulsive therapy have been documented (Katz, 1992). The removal of sexual orientation from the revised third edition of the DSM (American Psychiatric Association, 1987) was mediated by a diagnosis of *ego-dystonic homosexuality* in the third edition (American Psychiatric Association, 1980). *Gender identity disorder* was first included in the third edition, and it was replaced by *gender dysphoria* in the fifth edition (American Psychiatric Association, 2013).[3]

The terms *ego-dystonic* and *dysphoria* represent a gradual paradigm shift in the field of psychology. They locate the disorder in the discomfort or dissatisfaction some GSM individuals feel about their gender and sexual identities rather than in the gender or sexual identity itself. According to minority stress theory, however, one might reasonably expect GSM youth to experience dissatisfaction and discomfort given the various forms of stigma they face in their families, schools, and communities. So what does it mean to diagnose someone for feeling uncomfortable or dissatisfied with a stigmatized gender or sexual identity in a hostile societal context? Should we not instead locate the disorder in the attitudes of society and work to change them? Some argue that the continued use of diagnostic categories allows gender minorities to access health and psychological services. Others argue that it increases and perpetuates stigma. Advocates for depathologizing gender variance point out that advances in civil rights followed the depathologizing of sexual orientation (Lev, 2013). By depathologizing gender variance, the field of psychology could unequivocally affirm gender identity as a natural extension of human diversity. This could mitigate the harmful effects of minority stress and pave the way for advances in human rights.

Although homosexuality is no longer considered a diagnosable disorder, various interventions have been developed to change one's sexual orientation. Some faith-based organizations still promote harmful and pseudoscientific sexual orientation change efforts through therapy (Williams, 2005), and mindfulness and acceptance techniques have been proposed to reduce same-sex attraction (Tan & Yarhouse, 2010). Following a special task force investigation of such sexual orientation change efforts, the American Psychological Association (Anton, 2010) advised parents and families to avoid any treatments that portray homosexuality as a disorder. At the time this chapter was written, a number of cities, provinces, and states throughout the U.S. and Canada have prohibited mental health providers from practicing sexual orientation change efforts with youth. Despite growing scientific and political consensus, U.S. Vice President Mike Pence has a long record of opposing GSM rights, and he has publicly advocated for directing federal resources to "those institutions which provide assistance to those seeking to change their sexual behavior" instead of to organizations that provide services to individuals living with HIV/AIDS (Stack, 2016). It is also worth noting that webpages dedicated to LGBT rights were removed from the White House and Labor Department websites on the day that Donald Trump was inaugurated (Itkowitz, 2017).

Practical Points

Treating GSM youth as disordered legitimizes stigma and contributes to the psychological distress and negative health and learning outcomes of many GSM youth. Educators, helping professionals, and caring members of the community can help to reduce stigma against GSM youth and to support their exploration and self-expression. It is important to remember that each individual is unique and that one should not make assumptions or apply a standardized model of care. Based on the theory and research presented in this chapter, here are 10 practical points for supporting GSM youth.[4]

1. Do not assume that gender or sexual identity is the cause of an individual's distress or even the most important issue an individual needs support with. At the same time, avoid implying that gender and sexual identity do not matter (e.g., "Your gender or sexuality make no difference to me" can be experienced as invalidating and discourage exploration).
2. Validate the experiences of GSM youth and support them to reconceptualize their difficulties in terms of social stigma instead of personal failings. This can be done without blaming the world for one's problems or making excuses for one's actions.
3. Let GSM youth open up in their own time. Create a safe and supportive environment, but do not force the issue.
4. Hold existing categories for gender and sexual orientation lightly. Encourage youth to think critically and creatively, and allow them to change their minds. Trust them and follow their lead without imposing rigid labels or ways of thinking.
5. Encourage GSM youth to connect with school and community organizations that provide social and advocacy opportunities with their peers.

6. Take bullying and harassment seriously, and intervene to stop them. The National Education Association has published a toolkit to help intervene effectively (NEA, n.d.).
7. Support the parents and siblings of GSM youth as well. When appropriate, initiate conversations about acceptance and connect them with professional, religious, and social resources in the community.
8. Do not be afraid to have honest conversations about safe sex and substance use.
9. Do more of your own homework. Continue to raise your awareness through reading, education, and community involvement.
10. Advocate for GSM youth. Support campaigns to prohibit sexual orientation change efforts and to promote civil rights. Speak up within your church, school, workplace, and other community organizations.

Discussion Questions

1. How would you describe the relationship between societal discrimination and psychological distress among GSM youth?
2. What is meant by "the blurry line between self-reliance and self-isolation"? How might some common resilience strategies of GSM youth paradoxically contribute to distress or increase the risk of self-destructive behaviors?
3. What opportunities do you have to advocate for GSM youth in your community, your profession, and in the political arena?

Notes

1. Most of the empirical evidence cited in this chapter comes from the United States. More research on GSM youth victimization and homelessness is needed, particularly in Canada.
2. Meyer (1995) used the term *internalized homophobia* because his model was developed for gay men specifically. Inclusive language is used in this context to apply to GSM more broadly.
3. Other diagnostic categories such as *transvestic fetishism* and *transvestic disorder* have been used to pathologize men. These diagnoses have been arbitrarily applied and are plagued with philosophical problems.
4. The author would like to thank his colleagues Kelly J. Hutton, MA, and Jonathan Brady, PhD, for their thoughtful contributions to this list.

References

Abramovich, I. A. (2012). No safe place to go: LGBTQ youth homelessness in Canada: Reviewing the literature. *Canadian Journal of Family and Youth, 4*(1), 29–51.

American Psychiatric Association. (1980). *Diagnostic and statistical manual of mental disorders* (3rd ed.). Washington, DC: American Psychiatric Association.

American Psychiatric Association. (1987). *Diagnostic and statistical manual of mental disorders* (3rd ed., rev.). Washington, DC: American Psychiatric Association.

American Psychiatric Association. (2013). *Diagnostic and statistical manual of mental disorders* (5th ed.). Washington, DC: American Psychiatric Association.

Anderson, J. (2014). Providing a safe learning environment for queer students in Canadian schools: A legal analysis of homophobic bullying. *Journal of LGBT Youth, 11*, 212–243. doi:10.1080/19361653.2013.879463

Anton, B. S. (2010). Proceedings of the American Psychological Association for the legislative year 2009: Minutes of the annual meeting of the Council of Representatives and minutes of the Board of Directors. *American Psychologist, 65*, 385–475. doi:10.1037/a0019553

Barker, E. D., Areseneault, L., Brengden, M., Fontaine, N., & Maughan, B. (2008). Joint development of bullying and victimization in adolescence: Relations to delinquency and self-harm. *Journal of American Child and Adolescent Psychiatry, 47*(9), 1030–1038. doi:10.1097/CHI/ObO13e31817eec98

Blum, A. (2008). Shame and guilt, misconceptions and controversies: A critical review of the literature. *Traumatology, 14*(3), 91–102.

Boesveld, S. (2011, October 17). "This hurts too much," gay teen says in last blog before suicide. *National Post.* Retrieved from http://www.nationalpost.com

Brooke, J. (1998, October 13). Gay man dies from attack, fanning outrage and debate. *New York Times.* Retrieved from http://www.nytimes.com

Cohn, A., & Canter, A. (2003). *Bullying: Facts for schools and parents.* Retrieved from www.naspcenter.org/factsheets/bullying_fs.html

Diamond, G. M., Shilo, G., Jurgensen, E., D'Augelli, A., Samarova, V., & White, K. (2011). How depressed and suicidal sexual minority adolescents understand the causes of their distress. *Journal of Gay & Lesbian Mental Health, 15*(2), 130–151. doi:10.1080/19359705.2010.532668

D'Augelli, A. R., Hershberger, S. L., & Pilkington, N. W. (1998). Lesbian, gay, and bisexual youth and their families: Disclosure of sexual orientation and its consequences. *Journal of Orthopsychiatry, 68*(3), 361–371. doi:10.1037/h0080345

D'Augelli, A. R., Pilkington, N. W., & Hershberger, S. L. (2002). Incidence and mental health impact of sexual orientation victimization of lesbian, gay, and bisexual youths in high school. *School Psychology Quarterly, 17*(2), 148–167. doi:10.1521/scpq.17.2.148.20854

Durso, L. E., & Gates, G. J. (2012). *Serving our youth: Findings from a national survey of service providers working with lesbian, gay, bisexual, and transgender youth who are homeless or at risk of becoming homeless.* Los Angeles, CA: The Williams Institute with True Colors Fund and The Palette Fund. Retrieved from http://williamsinstitute.law.ucla.edu/wp-content/uploads/Durso-Gates-LGBT-Homeless-Youth-Survey-July-2012.pdf

Fedewa, A. L., & Ahn, S. (2011). The effects of bullying and peer victimization on sexual-minority and heterosexual youths: A quantitative meta-analysis of the literature. *Journal of GLBT Family Studies, 7*, 398–418. doi:10.1080/15504 28X.2011.592968

Greene, B. (2000). Homophobia. In A. E. Kazdin (Ed.), *Encyclopedia of psychology, Vol. 4* (pp. 146–149). Washington, DC: American Psychological Association.

Grossman, A. H., & D'Augelli, A. R. (2007). Transgender youth and life-threatening behaviors. *Suicide and Life-Threatening Behaviors, 37*(5), 527–537. doi:10.1521/suli.2007.37.5.527

Herek, G. M. (1996). Heterosexism and homophobia. In R. P. Cabaj & T. S. Stein (Eds.), *Textbook of homosexuality and mental health* (pp. 101–113). Washington, DC: American Psychiatric Association Press.

Herek, G. M. (2000). Homosexuality. In A. E. Kazdin (Ed.), *Encyclopedia of psychology, Vol. 4* (pp. 149–153). Washington, DC: American Psychological Association.

Hequembourg, A. L., & Dearing, R. L. (2013). Exploring shame, guilt, and risky substance use among sexual minority men and women. *Journal of Homosexuality, 60*, 615–638.

Human Rights Campaign (2016). Violence against the transgender community in 2016. Retrieved from www.hrc.org/resources/violence-against-the-transgender-community-in-2016

Itkowitz, C. (2017, January 20). LGBT rights page disappears from White House website. *The Washington Post*. Retrieved from www.washingtonpost.com

Kann, L., Olsen, E. O., McManus, T., Harris, W. A., Shanklin, S. L., Flint, K. H., . . . Zaza, S. (2016). *Sexual identity, sex of sexual contacts, and health-related behaviors among students in grades 9-12—United States and selected sites, 2015*. Atlanta, GA: Centers for Disease Control and Prevention. Retrieved from www.cdc.gov/mmwr/volumes/65/ss/pdfs/ss6509.pdf

Katz, J. (1992). *Gay American history: Lesbians and gay men in the USA: A documentary history*. New York, NY: Meridian.

Keuroghlian, A. S., Shtasel, D., & Bassuk, E. L. (2014). Out on the street: A public health and policy agenda for lesbian, gay, bisexual, and transgender youth who are homeless. *American Journal of Orthopsychiatry, 84*(1), 66–72. doi:10.1037/h0098852

Kosciw, J. G., Greytak, E. A., Palmer, N. A., & Boesen, M. J. (2013). *The 2013 national school climate survey: The experiences of lesbian, gay, bisexual and transgender youth in our nation's schools*. New York, NY: Gay, Lesbian & Straight Education Network. Retrieved from www.glsen.org/sites/default/files/2013%20National%20School%20Climate%20Survey%20Full%20Report_0.pdf

Kubicek, K., McDavitt, B., Carpineto, J., Weiss, G., Iverson, E. F., & Kipke, M. D. (2009). "God made me gay for a reason": Young men who have sex with men's resiliency in resolving internalized homophobia from religious sources. *Journal of Adolescent Research, 24*(5), 601–633. doi:10.1177/0743558409341078

Lev, A. I. (2013). Gender dysphoria: Two steps forward, one step back. *Clinical Social Work Journal, 41*(3), 288–296. doi:10.1007/s10615-013-0447-0

Lucies, C., & Yick, A. G. (2007). Images of gay men's experiences with antigay abuse: Object relations theory reconceptualized. *The Journal of Theory Construction & Testing, 11*(2), 55–62.

Malyon, A. K. (1982). Psychotherapeutic implications of internalized homophobia in gay men. In J. C. Gonsiorek (Ed.), *Homosexuality and psychotherapy: A practitioner's handbook of affirmative models*. New York, NY: Haworth Press.

Matthews, C. R., Lorah, P., & Fenton, J. (2006). Treatment experiences of gays and lesbians in recovery from addiction: A qualitative inquiry. *Journal of Mental Health Counseling, 28,* 111–132.

McDermott, E., Roen, K., & Scourfield, J. (2008). Avoiding shame: Young LGBT people, homophobia and self-destructive behaviours. *Culture, Health & Sexuality, 10*(8), 815–829. doi:10.1080/13691050802380974

Meyer, I. H. (1995). Minority stress and mental health in gay men. *Journal of Health and Social Behavior, 36*(1), 38–56.

Meyer, I. H. (2003). Minority stress and mental health in gay men. In L. D. Garnets & D. C. Kimmel (Eds.), *Psychological perspectives on lesbian, gay, and bisexual experiences* (2nd ed., pp. 699–731). New York, NY: Columbia University Press.

Meyer, L. H., & Dean, L. (1998). Internalized homophobia, intimacy, and sexual behavior among gay and bisexual men. In G. M. Herek (Ed.), *Stigma and sexual orientation: Understanding prejudice against lesbians, gay men, and bisexuals* (pp. 160–186). Thousand Oaks, CA: Sage.

National Education Association. (n.d.). *How to intervene in a bullying incident.* Washington, DC: National Education Association. Retrieved from www.nea.org/assets/docs/BullyFree_How_to_Intervene_in_a.pdf

Parent, M. C., DeBlaere, C., & Moradi, B. (2013). Approaches to research on intersectionality: Perspectives on gender, LGBT, and racial/ethnic identities. *Sex Roles, 68*(11), 639–645. doi:10.1007/s11199-013-0283-2

Peitzman, L. (2013, October 10). It gets better, unless you're fat [Web log post]. Retrieved from www.buzzfeed.com/louispeitzman/it-gets-better-unless-youre-fat

Pharr, S. (1997). *Homophobia: A weapon of sexism.* Berkeley, CA: Chardon Press.

Reygan, F., Curtin, A., & Moane, G. (2016). Religion, spirituality, and gender and sexual minorities: What clinicians need to know. In M. Skinta & A. Curtin (Eds.), *Mindfulness and acceptance for gender and sexual minorities: A clinician's guide to fostering compassion, connection and equality using contextual strategies* (pp. 187–206). Oakland, CA: New Harbinger.

Riggle, E. D. B., Mohr, J. J., Rostosky, S. S., Fingerhut, A. W., & Balsam, K. F. (2014). A multifactor lesbian, gay, and bisexual positive identity measure (LGB-PIM). *Psychology of Sexual Orientation and Gender Diversity, 1*(4), 398–411. doi:10.1037/sgd0000057

Rodriguez, M. (2016, June 1). Here's one brutal truth every white gay man needs to hear. *Mic.* Retrieved from http://mic.com/

Russell, S. T. (2005). Beyond risk: Resilience in the lives of sexual minority youth. *Journal of Gay & Lesbian Issues in Education, 2*(3), 5–18. doi:10.1300/J367v02n03_02

Russell, G. M., & Bohan, J. S. (2006). The case of internalized homophobia: Theory and/as practice. *Theory & Psychology, 16*(3), 343–366. doi:10.1177/0959354306064283

Russell, G. M., Bohan, J. S., & Lilly, D. (2000). Queer youth: Old stories, new stories. In S. Jones (Ed.), *A sea of stories: The shaping power of narrative in gay and lesbian cultures* (pp. 69–92). New York, NY: Haworth.

Ryan, C., Huebner, D., Diaz, R. M., & Sanchez, J. (2009). Family rejection as a predictor of negative health outcomes in white and Latino lesbian, gay, and bisexual young adults. *Pediatrics, 123*(1), 346–352.

Ryan, C., Russell, S. T., Huebner, D., Diaz, R., & Sanchez, J. (2010). Family acceptance in adolescence and the health of LGBT young adults. *Journal of Child and Adolescent Psychiatric Nursing, 23*(4), 205–213. doi:10.1111/j.1744-6171.2010.00246.x

Schuck, K. D., & Liddle, B. J. (2001). Religious conflicts experienced by lesbian, gay, and bisexual individuals. *Journal of Gay & Lesbian Psychotherapy, 5*(2), 63–82. doi:10.1300/J236v05n02_07

Sears, J. (1997). Thinking critically/intervening effectively about homonegativity and heterosexism. In J. Sears & W. Williams (Eds), *Overcoming heterosexism and homophobia: Strategies that work* (pp. 11–48). New York, NY: Columbia University Press.

Shields, S. A. (2008). Gender: An intersectionality perspective. *Sex Roles, 59,* 301–311. doi:10.1007/s11199-008-9501-8

Singh, A. A., Meng, S. E., & Hansen, A. W. (2014). "I am my own gender": Resilience strategies of trans youth. *Journal of Counseling & Development, 92*(2), 208–218. doi:10.1002/j.1556-6676.2014.00150.x

Skinta, M., & Curtin, A. (Eds.) (2016). *Mindfulness and acceptance for gender and sexual minorities: A clinician's guide to fostering compassion, connection and equality using contextual strategies.* Oakland, CA: New Harbinger.

Stack, L. (2016, November 30). Mike Pence and "conversion therapy": A history. *New York Times.* Retrieved from www.nytimes.com

Tan, E. S. N., & Yarhouse, M. A. (2010). Facilitating congruence between religious belief and sexual identity with mindfulness. *Psychotherapy, 47,* 500–511. doi:10.1037/a0022081

Tappan, M. B. (2006). Reframing internalized oppression and internalized domination: From the psychological to the sociocultural. *Teachers College Record, 108*(10), 2115–2144.

Toomey, R. B., Ryan, C., Diaz, R. M., Card, N. A., & Russell, S. T. (2010). Gender-nonconforming lesbian, gay, bisexual, and transgender youth: School victimization and young adult psychosocial adjustment. *Developmental Psychology, 46*(6), 1580–1589. doi:10.1037/a0020705

Turkewitz, J. (2016, June 21). Orlando massacre inspires some to come out as gay. *New York Times.* Retrieved from www.nytimes.com

Waters, E., Jindasurat, C., & Wolfe, C. (2016). *Lesbian, gay, bisexual, transgender, queer, and HIV-affected hate violence in 2015: 2016 Release Edition.* New York, NY: National Coalition of Anti-Violence Programs. Retrieved from www.avp.org/storage/documents/ncavp_hvreport_2015_final.pdf

Weinberg, G. (1972). *Society and the healthy homosexual.* New York, NY: St. Martin's Press.

Wexler, L. M., DiFluvio, G., & Burke, T. K. (2009). Resilience and marginalized youth: Making a case for personal and collective meaning-making as part of resilience research in public health. *Social Science & Medicine, 69*(4), 565–570. doi:10.1016/j.socscimed.2009.06.022

Williams, A. (2005, July 17). Gay teenager stirs a storm. *New York Times.* Retrieved from www.nytimes.com

Woolf, C. (2016, June 13). What do we call the attack in Orlando? "Hate crime" or "terrorism"? *Public Radio International.* Retrieved from www.pri.org/

13 Grief, Adolescents, and Social Media

Carla Sofka

If you were asked to conjure up an image of a "typical" teenager, would the adolescent in your mind's eye be using some type of technology? The Pew Internet and American Life project reported that 88% of teens between the ages of 13 and 17 have access to a mobile phone, with a majority (73%) having smartphones (Lenhart, 2015). 92% percent of the teens in the study reported going online daily, with 24% saying they are online "almost constantly" (p. 2), aided by access to an average of three to four devices (e.g., a desktop or laptop computer, smartphone, basic phone, tablet, game console). A survey by Common Sense Media reported that teens spend an average of 1 hour and 11 minutes each day on social media, with vast differences in the use of "screen media" (watching TV, using social media, listening to music, playing video or mobile games, reading, browsing websites, or other online activities). 6% of teens do not use screen media at all, and 17% use it for 2 hours or less; 31% of teens spend 4 to 8 hours with screen media, and 26% use screen media for more than 8 hours a day (Rideout, 2015).

In a previous report from the Pew project, these "multichannel teens" with a high degree of mobile connectivity were described as "supercommunicators" (Lenhart, Madden, Macgill, & Smith, 2007). In a review of thanatology in the digital age, Smith and Cavuoti (2013) noted the important role of *hyperconnectivity*, defined by Biggs (2012) as "super-fast connectivity, always on, on the move . . . wherever we go—anywhere, anytime" (p. 47). The Common Sense Media report concluded that screen media has an enormous presence in the lives of young people and that this element of their lives is well worth our continued attention (Rideout, 2015).

Now imagine that a friend or family member of this typical teenager dies. Due to the significant role that digital/social media has in the life of an adolescent, there is a strong possibility that he or she may find out about a death in a manner other than face-to-face notification by a trusted family member, friend, or familiar adult. Since a significant number of teens use Facebook (71%), Instagram (52%), or Twitter (33%) (Lenhart, 2015), it is highly likely that these and other types of social media or communication technology will play a role in death notification and other aspects of an adolescent's bereavement experience.

In the mid-1990s, I began to monitor how *thanatechnology* (defined at that time as online resources, computer programs, and interactive videodiscs; Sofka, 1997) was impacting the ways that our society dealt with loss and grief. The continuous evolution of digital resources, communication technology, and the emergence of social media has vastly expanded this definition and created new opportunities and potential risks related to the expression of "virtual" or "digital" grief.

In December of 2012, I gained a new respect for the importance of understanding how social media is being used by adolescents while watching my 15-year-old daughter become involved in initiatives designed to provide support to the two survivors of a car crash who attended high schools in two neighboring communities and to the families of the two students who died in the crash (subsequently referred to as the "518 case" due to our area code; see the news report at http://www.timesunion.com/local/article/Police-focus-on-22-year-old-driver-in-fatal-crash-4084872.php). I also conducted an online survey that gathered data from social media users in the "518" about their experiences, and findings from that research are included in this chapter. A significant body of literature from a range of disciplinary perspectives has also been generated about the role that digital/social media plays in dealing with death, grief, and mortality (for recent compilations/reviews, see Bassett, 2015; Moreman & Lewis, 2014; Sofka, Noppe Cupit, & Gilbert, 2012; and Walter, Hourizi, Moncur, & Pitsillides, 2011).

Death Notification via Social Networking Sites, Social Media, and Text Messaging

According to the most recent report from the National Center for Health Statistics, the leading causes of death in 2012 among individuals between the ages of 13 and 19 included accidents (unintentional injuries), intentional self-harm (suicide), assault (homicide), and malignant neoplasms (Heron, 2015). During an analysis of 550 memorial pages on Facebook (FB), Kern, Forman, and Gil-Egui (2013) found that a majority of the pages were dedicated to people under 25 years of age. While teens may have advance notice of an impending death due to cancer or another life-threatening illness, the majority of deaths among peers at this age occur suddenly. Therefore, parents or adults in authoritative roles (e.g., school officials, teachers, coaches, etc.) may have no control over how or when a teen is notified.

After awaking one morning to learn that a classmate of her son had been killed in a car accident and speaking with her husband to prepare a strategy to break the news to their two teenagers, Goldschmidt (2013) described being surprised that her children had already heard about the accident moments after it happened via social media. "Bad news" can travel very quickly, evidenced by the fact that 61% of the teens in the "518" survey learned about the car crash within the first hour after it occurred at 10:17 PM on a Saturday night.

What types of communication technology or digital/social media are being used to deliver "bad news?" Within 5 years, Twitter usage rose from 8% of teenagers (Lenhart, Purcell, Smith, & Zickuhr, 2010) to 33% (Lenhart, 2015). Therefore, it was not surprising to learn that 31.7% of the "518" survey participants who were in high school at the time of the car crash in my community found out about the crash on Twitter (e.g., #rip-chrisanddeanna). Almost 12% learned about the crash via Facebook and a small percentage (3.3%) learned about the crash via Instagram.

According to a study done by Common Sense Media (Rideout, 2015), 84% of teens have access to a smartphone in their home, with 67% having their own smartphone (78% of teens in higher income homes have their own vs. 51% in lower income homes.) Texting behavior ranged from 10 or fewer in a day (28%) to 11–30 (33%) to 51 or more (21%) texts per day. A similar study by the Pew Research Center reported that a typical teen between the ages of 13–14 sends an average of 45 text messages a day, and 15–17-year-olds send an average of 74 per day (Lenhart, 2015). While the national surveys of texting behavior among teens have not documented the subject matter of these texts, text messaging was a factor in how news and information in the "518 case" was shared. Almost 17% of the teens learned about the crash via a text. The following description from one respondent eloquently captures how a combination of types of communication technology and social media was used to determine who was involved in the crash:

> I became aware that there was a deadly accident involving Shen students, began texting my friends to make sure they were okay. When Chris and Deanna didn't respond, I took to Twitter to find out they were at the Siena game, did the math to discover they would have been on their way home at approximately where the accident occurred. I then received a phone call from one of Chris's teammates, who was at the hospital, confirming his death.

Do teens have a preference for personally sharing bad news (e.g., face to face or via a phone conversation) or through the use of thanatechnology? Comments in the qualitative data from the "518 case" reflect a range of preferences, mirroring the fact that there are significant variations in individual reactions to loss:

> Preference for face to face: "I was glad that I received the news from someone in person. It decreased the shock of seeing the news over social media."
> Preference for technology mediated: "As someone who is not always completely comfortable showing strong emotions in front of people, I am okay with receiving the news over text."

In an article by Valhouli (2012), experts note that sharing bad news on Facebook can be good (e.g., it is the least draining or difficult way to get the word out; it gives people freedom to respond—or not—in whichever way they are most comfortable since knowing what to say to someone who has delivered bad news is a socially challenging situation) or bad (posting online may be perceived as trivializing the news; posting may represent trying to show bravado or pretending that someone is not devastated by the news—avoiding the feelings may interfere with grief).

Rideout (2012) reported that "despite their love of new technology and their seemingly constant text messaging, teens' favorite way to communicate with their friends is still to talk with them face to face" (p. 15). In a study of patterns of media use for social sharing among undergraduates, Choi and Toma (2014) found that intense negative events were more likely to be shared through face-to-face interactions by this slightly older group of respondents. Based on the limited data from teens about the impact of death notification via thanatechnology, it seems wise to consider strategies that facilitate the ability of parents and other caring adults to help teens (a) gain the social skills needed to participate in difficult conversations involving the delivery and receipt of "bad news," (b) understand the pros and cons of sharing "bad news" via social media, and (c) to communicate their preferences so that everyone can make informed decisions about how to proceed when faced with situations involving tragedy.

Online Communities of Bereavement: Emotional and Informational Support

Following one of the most public tragedies involving teens at Columbine High School in April of 1999, Linenthal (as quoted in Niebuhr & Wilgoren, 1999) noted that the creation of shrines following tragic deaths might indicate the desire to overcome feelings of powerlessness and to experience a sense of unity as a "community of bereavement." Since teenagers have grown up with technology, Atfield, Chalmers, and Lion (2006) recognized that adolescents may logically turn to cyberspace during times of grief, sometimes immediately after learning of a tragedy.

Participation on social networking sites (SNS) and social media appears to serve a variety of purposes for teens in the process of coping with loss, some of which appear to be dependent upon the relationship that the social media user had with the deceased. Research regarding the provision of social support during times of grief via social media among teens has produced some unexpected but heartwarming conclusions. Williams and Merten (2009) were surprised by postings from complete strangers, but were able to understand them based on research by Pfefferbaum and colleagues (2000); they reported that young people who did not personally know any of the affected individuals in a tragedy within a community still felt like part of the event.

According to a teen in the "518 case" who did not know the victims but participated in social media: "I connected very strongly with the story. The victims were my age and it was sort of a wake-up call that bad things can happen to you even if you're doing the right thing. I wanted to help in any way that I could." Another "518" teen stated: "I had a lot of mutual friends that knew the victims and I wanted to support them in their time of upset." Various social media platforms are frequently used to plan or share times and locations for memorial events or to coordinate efforts that demonstrate support, such as wearing the favorite colors of the deceased to school (see Wixon, 2014 and Goldschmidt, 2013, for examples).

DeGroot (2014) coined the term *emotional rubberneckers* to describe "online voyeurs who visit the FB memorials of strangers or distant acquaintances to read what others write and to post their own messages of grief" (p. 79). DeGroot (2014) noted that "although the term rubbernecking has a negative connotation, emotional rubberneckers are not always seen as negative elements" (p. 82) and appear to have similarities with the deceased in some manner (identifying with the deceased's age, cause of death, etc.). This author would like to propose the term *experiential empathy* to capture the social media user's motive for becoming involved due to his or her ability to relate to the other grievers based on a similar loss experience. For example, one "518" respondent who did not know anyone involved in the crash participated in social media because he related strongly to the current circumstances: "I was at a high school when my cousin passed away in an accident." Are there different "social norms" for grieving in cyberspace? There may be fewer "time limits" on grief expressed in virtual spaces; sadly, it may be more "socially acceptable" to grieve the death of a stranger online than it is to express one's deep and heartfelt grief for a loved one in the real world where many people are not comfortable providing social support to the bereaved.

Twitter is also frequently used by teens to publicly share their personal reactions to loss or to express support for peers who are grieving in a variety of ways. Within 72 hours, teens (including my daughter) from our local high school (a sports "rival" of the school that the victims attended) were sending messages of support from the "518" (using hashtags #518, #518Strong, or #518Family), such as "the best kind of rivalry is one where it goes away when something horrible becomes bigger than the rivalry ever could be." Friends of the survivors started Twitter campaigns designed to encourage the survivors' favorite athletes to call them in the hospital (#MissyCallBailey and #TebowCallMatt) that trended nationally (and both survivors received a call). The role of social media became newsworthy when a local columnist documented how reactions to this tragedy were being shared via digital technology (see Barlette, 2012). One of the crash survivors, a prolific tweeter, openly shared her grief journey on Twitter (see Wind, 2013; Barlette, 2013). Data from the "518" survey confirms that young adults in our community continue to tweet and post in honor of their friends ("Three years later and things never get easier, miss you both more every day. Keep watching over us") with themes and time frames that are further discussed in this chapter. For teens who prefer quick and easy technology, Twitter has become a popular option.

In addition to talking about their grief in online forums (see Sofka, 2014), teens can easily and anonymously access an overwhelming amount of information about health and mental health concerns (Schurgin O'Keefe, Clarke-Pearson, & the Council on Communications and Media, 2011) that would be relevant to coping with loss. While it is beyond the scope of this chapter to review all the types of online sites available for informational support (see Sofka, 2014, for a more detailed discussion), it is important to remind clinicians and parents to assist teens in gaining "information literacy" skills to evaluate the reliability of these sources (see Sofka, 2012).

Memorialization and Commemoration

Almost immediately after the death of a young adult, content on existing social networking sites containing expressions of grief and the preservation of the deceased teenager's digital legacy will begin. Sometimes accompanied by photos and/or videos (some of which may be created using digital media tools such as Storify), postings include the sharing of memories, thoughts, and feelings in reaction to the death and/or a description of the individual's connection or relationship with the deceased. In conjunction with the posting of video footage of her deceased friend, one teen in the "518 case" stated: "It's just so nice to hear his voice."

When asked about the origin of the Facebook memorial page in the "518 case" for one of the deceased teenagers, his mother noted that it was created by a friend of her son who eventually transferred administrative responsibilities to her. Since "death has always presented a delicate problem for Facebook and other social media sites" (Oremus, 2015, para. 1) for numerous reasons, a new option for proactively expressing one's wishes regarding the future of a personal Facebook page was rolled out in February of 2015. Facebook users can now designate a "legacy contact" who will be given privileges to manage the page following a death. The option to "memorialize" a page is still available in the event that a Facebook user dies without implementing this option.

Since unanticipated death is a reality for many families with teenagers, parents should familiarize themselves with these options and be prepared to have conversations with their children when they begin using social media. Helping professionals, particularly those who interact with teens experiencing a life-threatening illness, should be prepared to facilitate conversations about these options with families dealing with the untimely death of an adolescent (see Shavit, 2015, for user-friendly resources).

Continuing Bonds

According to Williams and Merten (2009), the most interesting finding from their study of online social networking among teens involved the posting of comments directly to the deceased (e.g., "We will miss you" or "I love you"). Communications frequently included reminiscing with the deceased about prior shared experiences, providing updates about current events, or sending messages on significant dates (e.g., birthdays, holidays, major life events where the deceased's presence is missed, the anniversary of the death). These communications demonstrate a "continuing bond" (Klass, Silverman, & Nickman, 1996) that allows teens to maintain a technology-mediated connection with their friend or loved one through the use of social media.

Social networking sites and social media also seem to provide teens with an opportunity to take care of "unfinished business" with the deceased or express regrets. Private messaging functions on social media provide teens with a non-public forum to say "I'm sorry" in cases where friends were unable to resolve a disagreement prior to the death. Following the sudden death of his friend, one teen in the "518 case" stated: "In some ways I felt like they were going to respond. Because at that point, it was all still a dream. It was almost like my way of saying goodbye." Williams and Merten (2009) also reported comments from peripheral friends (those on the outer circle of the social network of the deceased) that appear to reflect regret at not having known someone better (e.g., "I wish I would have takin [sic] you up on those 'wanna hang out?'s," p. 83).

Why do teens communicate with the deceased via social media? Within a meta-commentary to a deceased peer, a Facebook user provided a possible answer: "I want you to know that I still care about you. . . . I feel like writing on here is somehow going to enable my message to get to you better. . . . It feels more real. I can see it, I send it, I know that it's going someplace. And I feel like somewhere, you will read it" (Williams & Merten, 2009, p. 82). Gathering additional information about the reasons for and impact of these types of conversations on the bereavement process merits attention by clinicians and researchers who interact with grieving teens.

Digital Survivor Advocacy

According to the Trauma Foundation (2001), some people who survive the traumatic loss of a loved one channel their grief into preventive action. They become "survivor advocates" who work to save others from experiencing a similar loss and trauma through raising awareness and advocating for policy change. For guidance regarding how to facilitate this type of change through the use of social media, readers are encouraged to consult the work of Aaker, Smith, and Adler (2010), who developed a model for enacting change called the "Dragonfly Effect." Since the small actions of a dragonfly can create big movements, their model is designed to guide "people who, through the passionate pursuit of their goals, hope to make a positive impact disproportionate to their resources" (p. xiii).

In addition to expressing their grief, teenagers are also participating in digital survivor advocacy through the use of social media. Following the suicide of a high-school sophomore, Carboneau (2013) described how fellow students utilized Twitter and Facebook to express their grief. They also posted stories and photos to a Facebook page (The Makayla Fund) that continues to raise awareness of teen suicide and the impact of suicide on survivors, combat stigma, and solicit donations for the fund established in Makayla's name that awards athletic scholarships in her home community. Following the December 2012 car crash in my community, when the news media released information that the driver of the vehicle whose car struck the teenagers was allegedly intoxicated, the following request was tweeted: "Can we all make a pledge right now that WE WILL NOT DRINK AND DRIVE? RT [retweet] this if you're willing to MAKE and KEEP that promise." This message was retweeted by 247 people. Each year on the anniversary of the crash, similar messages reemerge as an ongoing way to remember the victims.

Teens may feel the need to "do something" following a loss, and digital technology makes it convenient and seemingly effortless to become involved. Research documenting the level of participation in survivor advocacy and social action by adolescents through the use of social media and the impact of doing so on the process of coping should be conducted (Sofka, 2017a).

Cyberbullying, Memorial Trolling, and Facebook Depression

While there are many positive consequences of digital device and social media use among teens, there are also risks to their emotional and physical safety. After surviving the "518 case" car crash that claimed the lives of her boyfriend and another friend, Bailey Wind (2013) eloquently documented her experiences with cyberbullying, some of which occurred as a result of negative reactions to her public expression of grief on social media. Bailey stated: "One tweeted that I didn't know that my fifteen minutes of fame was up. . . . Another boy said I had turned the attention I was receiving into a popularity stunt" (p. 171). (Note: The term *attention whore* was used in the conversations on Twitter.) Bailey educated readers that "I will continue to talk about Chris and post pictures of us, but I won't be doing it to get attention. I will do it for me and only me. You may not understand, but it makes me feel better" (p. 174).

While describing the harassment that Bailey experienced, the local social media reporter also noted that supportive comments defending her (e.g., "Please don't think what U R feeling is wrong or U need 2B strong all the time or U need to get over it right away—it's OK") outnumbered the offensive ones (see Barlette, 2013). Methods for studying this phenomenon are being developed (Underwood & Card, 2013) and merit ongoing attention.

There are also cases of cyberbullying that have resulted in *cyberbullicide,* defined by Hinduja and Patchin (2010) as suicide indirectly or directly influenced by experiences with online aggression. A recent case involved Rebecca Ann Sedwick; after being cyberbullied for over a year (e.g., receiving messages saying "Why are you still alive? "Can u die please?"), Rebecca changed her user name on Kik Messenger (a cellphone app) to "That Dead Girl" and delivered a message to two friends, saying goodbye forever before leaping to her death (Alvarez, 2013). It is fascinating to note that over 750 comments expressing a range of reactions to the case and diverse viewpoints about cyberbullying were posted online in response to Alvarez's article. Comment sections after media accounts of cyberbullying provide a helpful resource to understand public sentiment regarding these incidents. When it comes to being the victim of a cyberbully, words do hurt; for some, words can kill (Edgington, 2011).

A teen's emotional safety can also be impacted by an unsettling phenomenon that occurs in the context of "memorial trolling/RIP trolling": Abusive remarks and insensitive images are posted anonymously on SNS or shared through various types of social media. Even though the driver who caused the fatal crash in the "518 case" was speeding and texting at the time of the crash, teens described "inconsiderate people (who) took it upon themselves to use social media as a platform to accuse Chris (the driver of the vehicle who was killed) of driving drunk, saying it was 'his fault' or saying 'he should have been a better driver.'" When asked to describe the most important things that had been learned about social media use during times of tragedy, one teen in the "518" stated: "People will hate on you and what you have to say; there will be drama and fights on social media."

Interviews conducted by Phillips (2011) with memorial trolls revealed that fundamentally different beliefs about the appropriateness of publicly sharing one's grief, particularly by individuals who did not personally know the deceased, sometimes called "grief tourists," appear to be at the heart of this phenomenon. One teen in the "518" speculated that these comments may be a remnant of inappropriate behavior by teens who are not respectful of the situation. Almost 40% of teens in the "518" survey reported that they themselves or someone they knew had had a negative/unhelpful experience while using social media related to the crash. Some teens reported that they stopped using social media as a result of bad experiences; others noted that the benefits of social media use outweigh the risks.

Data regarding the incidence of cyberbullying and memorial trolling are limited, but the reality of these inappropriate behaviors is a documented risk of using digital/social media (Goodstein, 2007; Phillips, 2011). When creating a memorial site, it is important to carefully weigh the pros and cons of allowing anyone to post versus applying more restrictive privacy settings. Site administrators need to monitor these sites for egregious postings and handle any situations that arise quickly and appropriately. Raw emotions may also be shared in postings, and while they may not be intended to be offensive, it is possible that they may have a negative impact on some visitors to an SNS. Adolescents should be reminded to inform a trusted adult if they perceive or experience a threat to their safety as a result of online activities. A recent survey by the Pew Research Center documented digital monitoring efforts by parents and found that most parents speak frequently or occasionally with their teen about what constitutes appropriate or inappropriate behavior online (Anderson, 2016). Helping professionals can consider strategies to help parents have conversations with their teens about cybersafety and to provide both groups with digital literacy skills (see Sofka, 2017b).

In a report compiled for the American Academy of Pediatrics, the authors described a new phenomenon called "Facebook depression," defined as "depression that develops when preteens and teens spend a great deal of time on social media sites, such as Facebook, and then begin to exhibit classic symptoms of depression" (Schurgin O'Keeffe et al., 2011, p. 802). Following analysis of data that evaluated the relationship between SNS use and depression among older adolescent university students, Jelenchick, Eickhoff, and Moreno (2013) found no association and recommended ongoing work to inform practice guidelines. Exploring the existence of Facebook depression among bereaved teens would be a complicated proposition, but merits attention.

Counselors working with bereaved teens should routinely ask if they have had any negative social media experiences (see the appendix at the end of this chapter). Sample scripts for use in conversations about cyberbullying are available at www.cyberbullying.us/resources. While a comprehensive discussion of cybersafety is beyond the scope of this chapter, helping professionals and parents are encouraged to consult resources available to facilitate discussions with teens about how to stay safe online (e.g., www.internetsafety.com/internet-safety-resources.php or https://staysafeonline.org/stay-safe-online/resources/) or to assist with preventive efforts and appropriate responses when cyberbullying occurs (e.g., Kowalski, Limber, & Agatston, 2012; Patchin & Hinduja, 2012). Information about current policies and laws regarding cyberbullying can be found at www.stopbullying.gov.

Conclusion

Based on comments shared by the teens in the "518" survey and findings from the literature, digital/social media can not only be powerful resources to facilitate the process of coping with loss but also sources of potential risks and challenges. Box 13.1 summarizes the pros and cons of digital/social media use.

In her book about the social lives of networked teens, Boyd (2014) provided helping professionals, researchers, and parents with some useful advice: "Rather than resisting technology or fearing what might happen if youth embrace social media, adults should help youth develop the skills and perspective to productively navigate the complications brought about by living in networked publics. Collaboratively, adults and youth can help create a networked world that we all want to live in" (p. 213). The title of this book, *It's Complicated*, accurately reflects the challenging process that lies ahead as we continue to understand and document the use and impact of digital and social media on adolescents dealing with grief.

Box 13.1   Benefits and Risks/Challenges of Digital and Social Media Use

Benefits:

- Notification of a death: Factual information can be sent quickly to multiple recipients (can reduce the burden of making numerous phone calls or sending multiple messages) provided that the intended recipients see the information.
- Links to online information can be shared easily (e.g., online obituary, information about funeral services or memorial events, online guestbook, fundraising sites, coordinating a "casserole brigade" [at www.mealtrain.com]).
- Memorial (RIP) pages/blogging/microblogging:
  ◦ Provides a 24/7 outlet for the expression of thoughts and feelings through the sharing of photos and memories.
  ◦ Memorial pages creates a "social support internetwork"; visitors can express condolences and post messages of support.
  ◦ Postings can educate social media users about grief; comments can validate a person's experiences.

Risks/challenges:

- Notification of a death:
  ◦ Some people may prefer to receive "bad news" in a more personal way (face to face or a phone call) or under different circumstances (in a public vs. private place when receiving the news; being alone vs. with someone to provide support).
  ◦ Inaccurate information can be shared prematurely, particularly in the case of a sudden/accidental death.
  ◦ Once the information is shared publically, no one can control how and with whom the information is ultimately shared.
- Anyone can post anything online; digital/social media users must carefully evaluate the reliability of information.
- Memorial (RIP) pages/blogging/microblogging:
  ◦ Administrator(s) of sites need(s) to monitor postings, remove inappropriate comments, and/or block trolls.
  ◦ Users may experience distress in reaction to photos or content that is unanticipated, upsetting, or unwanted.
  ◦ Users may experience cyberbullying or criticism for publically sharing one's personal experiences.
  ◦ Public postings online may contribute to a loss of privacy in "real life."
  ◦ Users may experience a dilemma about the decision to stop blogging/posting (feeling responsible for "followers").

Discussion Questions

1. The availability of social media has created interesting debates about the private vs. public nature of grief. What factors might influence whether an individual is a public vs. private griever?
2. Identify a recent news story (from your community or the national media) that involved the death of a teenager. Explore how social media has been used in response to this death.
3. What areas of a person's life might be impacted by social media use? What might change (in a positive or negative way) as a result of social media use during times of grief? How might social media help or hinder a person's ability to cope with loss?

References

Aaker, J., Smith, A., & Adler, C. (2010). *The dragonfly effect: Quick, effective, and powerful ways to use social media to drive social change*. San Francisco, CA: Jossey-Bass.

Alvarez, L. (2013, September 13). *Girl's suicide points to rise in apps used by cyberbullies*. Retrieved from www.nytimes.com/2013/09/14/us/suicide-of-girl-after-bullying-raises-worries-on-web-sites.html

Anderson, M. (2016, January). *Parents, teens, and digital monitoring* (Report released by the Pew Research Center). Retrieved from www.pewinternet.org/2016/01/07/parents-teens-and-digital-monitoring/

Atfield, C., Chalmers, E., & Lion, P. (2006, November 21). Safety net for grief—anguished teens reach out across cyberspace. *The Courier Mail*, News, p. 9.

Barlette, K. G. (2012, December 7). *Grief in the Shen/Shaker accident spread over social media*. Retrieved from http://blog.timesunion.com/kristi/grief-in-the-shenshaker-accident-spread-over-social-media/52333/

Barlette, K. G. (2013, February 27). *Using Twitter to heal—and to inflict pain*. Retrieved from www.timesunion.com/local/article/Using-Twitter-to-heal-and-to-inflict-pain-4311314.php

Bassett, D. J. (2015). Who wants to live forever? Living, dying, and grieving in our digital society. *Social Sciences (Open Access)*, *4*(4), 1127–1139. doi:10.3390/socsci4041127

Biggs, P. (2012). Emerging issues for our hyperconnected world. In S. Dutta & B. Bilbao-Osorio (Eds.), *The global information technology report 2012: Living in a hyperconnected world* (pp. 47–56). Retrieved from www3.weforum.org/docs/GITR/2012/GITR_Chapter1.3_2012.pdf

Boyd, D. (2014). *It's complicated: The social lives of networked teens*. Retrieved from www.danah.org/books/ItsComplicated.pdf

Carboneau, A. (2013, July 15). In Brockton area and nationwide, grieving finds a place on social media. Retrieved from www.enterprisenews.com/article/20130715/NEWS/307159844/0/SEARCH

Choi, M., & Toma, C. L. (2014). Social sharing through interpersonal media: Patterns and effects on emotional well-being. *Computers in Human Behavior*, *36*, 530–541.

DeGroot, J. M. (2014). "For whom the bell tolls": Emotional rubbernecking in Facebook memorial groups. *Death Studies*, *38*(2), 79–84.

Edgington, S. M. (2011). *The parent's guide to texting, Facebook, and social media: Understanding the benefits and dangers of parenting in a digital world.* Dallas, TX: Brown Books.

Goldschmidt, K. (2013). Thanatechnology: Eternal digital life after death. *Journal of Pediatric Nursing, 28,* 302–304.

Goodstein, A. (2007). *Totally wired: What teens and tweens are really doing online.* New York, NY: St. Martin's Press.

Heron, M. (2015, August 31). *Deaths: Leading causes for 2012.* Retrieved from www.cdc.gov/nchs/data/nvsr/nvsr64/nvsr6410.pdf

Hinduja, S., & Patchin, J. W. (2010). Bullying, cyberbullying, and suicide. *Archives of Suicide Research, 14*(3), 206–221.

Jelenchick, L. A., Eickhoff, J. C., & Moreno, M. A. (2013). "Facebook depression?" Social networking site use and depression in older adolescents. *Journal of Adolescent Health, 52,* 128–130.

Kern, R., Forman, A. E., & Gil-Egui, G. (2013). R.I.P.: Remain in perpetuity. Facebook memorial pages. *Telematics and Informatics, 30,* 2–10. doi:10.1016/j.tele.2012.03.002

Klass, D., Silverman, P. R., & Nickman, S. L. (1996). *Continuing bonds: New understandings of grief.* Washington, DC: Taylor & Francis.

Kowalski, R. M., Limber, S. P., & Agatston, P. W. (2012). *Cyberbulling: Bullying in the digital age.* Oxford, UK: Wiley-Blackwell.

Lenhart, A. (2015). *Teens, social media, & technology overview 2015.* Pew Research Center. Retrieved from www.pewinternet.org/2015/04/09/teens-social-media-technology-2015/

Lenhart, A., Madden, M., Macgill, A. R., & Smith, A. (2007, December 19). Teens and Social Media. Report from the Pew Internet & American Life Project retrieved from http://www.pewinternet.org/2007/12/19/teens-and-social-media/.

Lenhart, A., Purcell, K., Smith, A., & Zickuhr, K. (2010, February 3). *Social media and mobile internet use among teens and young adults.* Retrieved from www.pewinternet.org/Reports/2010/Social-Media-and-Young-Adults.aspx

Moreman, C. M., & Lewis, A. D. (2014). *Digital death: Mortality and beyond in the online age.* Santa Barbara, CA: ABC-CLIO.

Niebuhr, G., & Wilgoren, J. (1999, April 28). *Terror in Littleton: Shrines.* Retrieved from www.nytimes.com/1999/04/28/us/terror-littleton-shrines-shock-violent-deaths-new-more-public-rites-mourning.html

Oremus, W. (2015, February 12). *Death on Facebook just got a little less awkward.* Retrieved from www.slate.com/blogs/future_tense/2015/02/12/facebook_legacy_contact_who_manages_account_when_you_die.html

Patchin, J. W., & Hinduja, S. (2012). *Cyberbullying: Prevention and response—Expert perspectives.* New York, NY: Routledge.

Pfefferbaum, B., Gurwitch, R. H., McDonald, N. B., Leftwich, M. J.T., Sconzo, G. M., Messenbaugh, A. K., & Schultz, R. A. (2000). Posttraumatic stress among young children after the death of a friend or acquaintance in a terrorist bombing. *Psychiatric Services, 51,* 386–388.

Phillips, W. (2011). LOLing at tragedy: Facebook trolls, memorial pages, and resistance to grief online. *First Mind, 16*(12). Retrieved from http://firstmonday.org/ojs/index.php/fm/ article/ view/ 3168/3115

Rideout, V. (2012). Social media, social life: How teens view their digital lives. Retrieved from https://www.commonsensemedia.org/research/social-media-life-how-teens-view-their-digital-lives

Rideout, V. (2015). *The common sense census: Media use by tweens and teens.* Retrieved from www.commonsensemedia.org/research/the-common-sense-census-media-use-by-tweens-and-teens

Schurgin O'Keeffe, G., Clarke-Pearson, K., & the Council on Communications and Media (2011). *The impact of social media on children, adolescents, and families.* Retrieved from http://pediatrics.aappublications.org/content/early/2011/03/28/peds.2011-0054

Shavit, V. (2015). *Digital dust blog / resources.* Retrieved from http://digital-era-death-eng.blogspot.com

Smith, A., & Cavuoti, C. (2013). Thanatology in the digital age. In D. K. Meagher and D. E. Balk (Eds.), *Handbook of thanatology* (2nd ed., pp. 429–439). New York, NY: Routledge.

Sofka, C. (2017a). Digital survivor advocacy: Fighting so you may never know tragedy. In S. E. Elswick (Ed.), *Data Collection: Methods, ethical issues, and future directions* (pp. 111–145). Hauppauge, NY: Nova Science Publishers.

Sofka, C. (2017b). Role of digital and social media in supporting bereaved students. In J. Brown & S. Jimerson (Eds.), *Supporting bereaved students at school* (pp. 96–111). Oxford, UK: Oxford University Press.

Sofka, C. (2014). Adolescents' use of technology and social media to cope with grief. In K. Doka & A. S. Tucci (Eds.), *Living with grief: Helping adolescents cope with loss* (pp. 247–255). Washington, DC: Hospice Foundation of America.

Sofka, C. J. (2012). Appendix A: Informational support online: Evaluating resources. In C. J. Sofka, I. Noppe Cupit, & K. R. Gilbert (Eds.), *Dying, death, and grief in an online universe: For counselors and educators* (pp. 247–255). New York, NY: Springer.

Sofka, C. J., Noppe Cupit, I., & Gilbert, K. R. (2012). *Dying, death, and grief in an online universe: For counselors and educators.* New York, NY: Springer.

Sofka, C. J. (1997). Social support "internetworks," caskets for sale, and more: Thanatology and the information superhighway. *Death Studies, 21*(6), 553–574.

Trauma Foundation. (2001). *Moving through grief to survivor advocacy.* Retrieved from www.traumaf.org/featured/7-01-survivor_advocacy.shtml

Underwood, M. K., & Card, N. A. (2013). Moving beyond tradition and convenience: Suggestions for useful methods for cyberbullying research. In S. Bauman, D. Cross, & J. Walker (Eds.), *Principles of cyberbullying research* (pp. 125–140). London, UK: Routledge & Psychology Press.

Valhouli, C. (2012, December 14). *On Facebook, bad with the good.* Retrieved from www.nytimes.com/2012/12/16/fashion/using-facebook-to-announce-bad-news.html

Walter, T., Hourizi, R., Moncur, W., & Pitsillides, S. (2011). Does the internet change how we die and mourn? Overview and analysis. *Omega: Journal of Death and Dying, 64,* 275–302.

Williams, A. L., & Merten, M. J. (2009). Adolescents' online social networking following the death of a peer. *Journal of Adolescent Research, 24*(1), 67–90.

Wind, B. (2013). *Save me a spot in heaven: A loving tribute to Christopher F. Stewart #69.* Troy, NY: Troy Book Makers.

Wixon, C. (2014, October 12). *Analysis: Social media becomes the new tool teens use to share grief.* Retrieved from www.tcpalm.com/news/education/analysis-social-media-becomes-the-new-tool-teens-use-to-share-grief-ep-667325740-33550 8151.html

Chapter Appendix

Assessing Use of Thanatechnology/ Social Media and Digital Social Support (Social Support "Internetworks")

Question #1: Have you ever used technology or social media in any way to deal with any aspect of coping with illness, dying/death, and/or grief? ____ No ____ Yes

If so, please list the types of technology/digital and social media resources that you have used in each categories:

    a.   Communication technology (texting/IM, Skype, Facetime, etc.): _____

    b.   Social networking sites (Facebook, etc.): _____ _____

    c.   Blogs or microblogs (Twitter, Tumblr, etc.): _____ _____

    d.   Online communities (support groups, interest groups, etc.): _____

    e.   Video-based sites (YouTube, etc.—Did you watch existing videos and/or create your own?): _____ _____

    f.   Music-related sites to access music or playlists: _____ _____

    g.   Online obituary/guestbook: _____ _____

    h.   Other: _____ _____

Question #2: Have you ever learned about a death or a tragedy via technology or social media? ____ No ____ Yes

If yes, please answer questions 2a–2b:

    2a. Please describe how and when you found out: _____ _____

2b. Please share your reaction(s) to the way in which you first received the news:_____

(Possible prompts: Was it helpful to receive the news in this way? Any advantages to receiving the news this way? Were there any disadvantages or any negative consequences as a result of receiving the news this way?)

Question #3: How frequently do you use social media and/or technology to deal with illness, dying/death, or grief? (If it would be helpful, use a Likert-type scale, with 1 = *never* and 5 = *all the time,* or ask how many times per day or how many hours per day are spent on social media.)

3a. What do you think influences your use of these resources? (Possible prompts: Access? Comfort with technology? Public or private griever? Familiarity with how these resources can be used to cope with loss? Are there dates/times of the year/events when you use these resources more?)

3b. How has the use of these resources been helpful? A mixed bag? Any negative experiences (e.g., cyberbullying/trolling) or negative consequences as a result of using social media?

Question #4: Has the use of digital technology or social media had an impact on your ability to have face-to-face conversations about sensitive topics? (When you use these resources, is it easier or harder to have face-to-face conversations with someone later?)

Question #5: Is there anything else that you'd like to teach me about how technology/social media has influenced the way you deal with loss?

14 Supporting Resilience in Grieving Kids in Today's World

Linda Goldman

> I've learned that people will forget what you said, people will forget what you did, but people will never forget how you made them feel.
>
> Maya Angelou (from Angelou & LaNae, 2012)

Maya Angelou's quote reflects an awareness of the intimate relationship caring adults can create with children experiencing grief, loss, and trauma. By establishing a loving, accepting environment, adults are capable of promoting resilient and self-assured children. The challenge for caring adults is facilitating the interplay between bereaved young people who are often carrying feelings of low self-esteem and emotional abandonment and developing strength-based techniques that support nurturance and inclusion, ultimately leading to resilience.

Although some children may appear unaffected by the outside world, more and more of our kids are showing signs of stress. Too many young people are coping with multiple challenging issues, seldom openly experienced or discussed in the past. These include death-related tragedies involving terrorism, war, suicide, homicide, natural disasters, global warming, and disease. They must also face social traumas, such as violence and abuse, bullying and victimization, poverty, being part of GSM (gender and sexual minorities; often referred to as LGBTQ), community deportation, imprisonment, immigration, sex trafficking, military death, and substance abuse. Some issues are new and frightening to this generation, a challenging by-product of modern times.

The media can also ignite consistent triggers that provoke fear, panic, stress, and extreme anxiety. A media barrage of real or exaggerated threats to the home, community, nation, and world heightens these feelings almost daily. Auditory and visual media input can retrigger past difficulties and instantaneously heighten present tragedies. Patchin and Hinduja (2010) explained:

> As online social networking has become an immersive and pervasive phenomenon, traditional considerations and expectations of personal privacy have been drastically altered. This paradigmatic change has led

to adolescents possibly making themselves vulnerable to embarrassment, censure, damage to one's name or reputation, or even victimization by others because of unwise postings or revelations online.

(p. 1818)

Yet, news, internet, and other social media can also act as a guide to kids already marginalized by first-hand experiences of grief, loss, and trauma. Through chat rooms, Facebook, Snapchat, YouTube, and Twitter, youngsters can navigate the world of communication, covering the spectrum of memorializing a loved one online, finding grief support groups, and participating in chat rooms that resonate with public and private challenging events.

Often children's instinctual reactions to terrifying events are tension and uncertainty about physical or psychological trauma or actual threats of impending loss by politicians, economic instability, or sudden illness and death. A groundswell of young people is often left in an unsuccessful attempt to deal with catastrophe, and they are becoming increasingly overwhelmed with their feelings and distracted by their thoughts. We must help young people transform fear, sadness, worry, and anger into stronger emotional, intellectual, and spiritual growth and development. We need a new paradigm to guide them through adversity and toward resilience.

One approach is to create an environment whereby youngsters can survive and indeed, thrive, by enlarging their capacity for empathy, understanding, and resilience after crisis. Our task as parents, educators, and health professionals is to provide an atmosphere that stands strong as an oasis of safety, comfort, and hope. This enables kids to grieve without judgement, ask questions, feel heard and cared for, and eventually to use individual strengths to transform challenging thoughts, feelings, and situations into self-affirming and hopeful attitudes. By highlighting children's ideas and actions that are encouraging and positive, we can dispel past myths that view bereaved children as "broken" and "needing to be fixed." We can strive to extinguish adult interpretations and projections that see children's reactions to difficult life issues as personality deficits or emotional disorders. Instead the focus can be shifted to supporting resilient strengths and working through complex situations with respect. Our ultimate responsibility is to enhance children's ability to cope with and overcome adversity, grief, and trauma during dramatically challenging times.

The Nature of Children's Grief and Trauma

Grief is not just about death. "It is a normal, internalized reaction to the loss of a person, thing or idea—our emotional response to loss" (Goldman, 2014, p. 26). Childhood losses range from the death of a family member or friend, to divorce, relocation, custody changes, abuse, bullying, or neglect. Moreover, children often carry secondary losses that arise following experiences with trauma and/or loss. These may include loss of their daily routine, loss of skills and abilities in school performance or activities, loss of the protection from the adult world, and loss of a perceived future.

Any of these challenging situations can traumatize children, as trauma can be conceptualized as an event or based on individual perception. Such experiences can result in feeling powerless, hopeless, and helpless. The safe, familiar world of childhood may suddenly change, if not personally, then vicariously through media coverage of traumatic public events. A week after the 9/11 terrorist attacks, Tari, a 5-year-old Muslim child, came to her kindergarten teacher and asked, "Are you still going to let me go to school here?" fearing she would be blamed for the events. Children hear political rhetoric threatening to deport parents or students that have lived life in America their entire lives. This can create disturbing and heightened fear and anxiety. In the current political climate, a comment such as this expressed individually, nationally, and internationally can have significant consequences for the well-being of young people. A racial slur, an anti-gay comment, a religious judgement, or a bullying bravado can have devastating effects for kids and families directly or indirectly challenged by their use—and hinder the very resilient attitude and outlook we are working so diligently to anchor in our young people.

Disease, violence, crime, suicide, and fatal accidents rob children of their parents, siblings, friends, relatives, and even pets. Young people also find themselves affected by a variety of difficult situations and/or losses, such as bullying, family separation, financial issues, parents working several jobs, foster care, deportation, or imprisonment; all of these are important examples of issues involving abandonment, neglect, or bereavement.

Additionally, diverse minorities are subjected to a bombardment of discrimination by laws, unacceptable violence, and dislocation from home and country. Gender issues and sexuality concerns leave pre-teens, teens, and young adults torn between speaking up about these issues and fearful that, if they do, they will be teased or ostracized by others. With limited coping mechanisms and perceived ambivalent support, many youngsters respond to their anger and pain by hurting themselves or others, or withdrawing from friends and family.

Common Signs of Grief, Trauma, and Resilience

Traumatized children often have difficulty putting their behaviors into any context of safety. Frightening, overwhelming feelings engulf them when they least expect them. Kids may withdraw and isolate themselves, some regress and appear anxious while others distance themselves from an incident, and can exhibit difficulty with eating or sleeping. It is essential for adults to recognize the signs of grief or trauma and to be mindful that both involve various types of loss. Knowing what bereaved children usually think and feel helps to normalize their experiences and reduce their anxieties and fears.

By *accepting* reactions as common signals for bereaved young children, we help them take an initial step towards strengthening resilience. Providing the grieving child with advocacy in school, open modeling of grief at home, and counseling and peer grief-support groups, we can create a safe haven for processing present grief and help prevent carrying any unresolved issues into adulthood. This lays the groundwork for stronger, more resilient young people.

Parents and educators can build on children's strengths during challenging times that support well-being and promote resilience. The following adaption from Truebridge (2014a, p. 79) suggests the indicators of resilience in youth presented in four categories: (a) *social competence* includes responsiveness, flexibility, empathy, caring, communication skills, and a sense of humor; (b) *emotional autonomy* manifests through positive identity, initiative, mastery, and self-awareness; (c) *cognition or problem solving* occurs with skills of planning, seeking alternatives, critical thinking, and resourcefulness; and (c) a *moral or spiritual component*, which consists of a child's sense of purpose and future. This final category includes connectedness, goal directness, imagination, aspirations, a special interest, persistence, optimism, faith, and a sense of meaning. Awareness, recognition, and nurturing of these personal resilience strengths are the foundation for supporting children through difficult times.

Building Resilience

Resilience is often referred to as the resources one uses to cope during difficult times and the ability to rebound from these hard situations. Truebridge, in serving *Creating Inclusion and Well-being in Marginalized Students* (Goldman, in press), defined resilience as "the self-righting and transcending capacity to spring back, rebound, and successfully adapt in the face of loss, trauma, adversity, and/or everyday stress." Truebridge offered a more in-depth definition of resilience in her book *Resilience Begins with Beliefs* (2014a) as "the dynamic and negotiated process within individuals (internal) and between individuals and their environments (external) for the resources and supports to adapt and define themselves as healthy amid adversity, threat, trauma and/or everyday stress" (p. 12). She explained the internal process involves tapping into one's strengths, and the external process involves support, services, and resources for young people.

Additionally, Bonnie Benard developed the resilience model to include three interrelated essential protective factors. These factors must exist together in any single environment—home, school, community, or peer group—to foster meeting children's needs. The protective factors are (Benard, 2004, p. 31; Truebridge, 2014b):

1. Developing caring relationships—the ability for adults or peers to show compassion, listening, believing, patience, and basic trust.
2. Maintaining high expectations—the ability for adults or peers to believe in a child's capacity for resilience, show firm guidance, use rituals, and provide a strengths-focused approach.

3. Providing meaningful opportunities for participation and contribution—the ability for adults or peers to provide safe places and inclusion, maintain a youth-centered orientation, and provide an environment for contribution and caring for others.

Truebridge (Goldman, in press) maintained that these protective factors "provide the developmental supports and opportunities that mitigate and buffer the negative effect that any loss, trauma, adversity, and/or stress may have on an individual." She also expressed the power of beliefs, stating:

> Changing the life trajectories of people from risk to resilience starts with changing belief and underscores the following beliefs: (1) Belief in our resilience (2) Belief that changing life trajectories from risk to resilience starts with changing beliefs (3) Belief in positive life outcomes.
>
> (Truebridge, 2014b)

Exploring Resilience Research

Masten is a formidable researcher on resilience. She defined resilience in her book *Ordinary Magic* (2015) as "the capacity of a dynamic system to adapt successfully to disturbances that threaten system function, viability, or development" (p. 10). Masten reported that "risk researchers were struck with the observable fact that numerous children in the risk groups were thriving in the face of formidable odds" (2015, p. 6). Researchers began asking a different set of questions:"1) Who stays well and recovers well? 2) How (is it done)?, and 3) What can we do to promote and protect health and positive development?" (p. 6). Various researchers have explored these questions by considering the impact of resilience on youth of many diverse cultures in the following studies from Alaska, South Africa, Native American youth, and Australia. Due to the cultural diversity in these studies, along with the breadth of this research, summaries will be presented of these research projects in order to appreciate the scope of current resilience literature.

Ramus, James, and Ford (2014) explored circumpolar indigenous pathways to adulthood (CIPA) in a long-term, community-based, and participatory research study designed to look at way of living, as well as traditional and contemporary youth experience. They then created a comparison study to examine youth stress and resilience. Such research was necessary due to the fact that suicide for males ages 15–35 is the highest in Alaska. Twelve youth were interviewed in the Yup'ik village who had been recruited through a community program over a 2-week period. These young people provided narratives that led to a grounded theory analysis, and their resilience allowed a systematic structure to develop amidst challenge, offering hope.

Ramus et al. (2014) defined resilience as "a dynamic process involving networks of people, events, and settings sharing relationships, linkages, inter-actions and transactions that distribute and transform resources across these networks" (p. 715). Research substantiated that within indigenous cultures, many social changes occurred swiftly and often imposed hardships. For example, outside environmental dangers created concerns ranging from an overturned kayak and blizzards to family and community challenges involving substance abuse and suicide. Joel was one young boy in the study who struggled with learning to catch a seal with family members—a traditional marker of manhood and social status. This challenge occurred alongside contemporary stressors such as completing school, staying out of trouble, and abstaining from marijuana and alcohol.

Heath, Donald, Theron, and Lyon (2014) offered a study that reviewed the impact of AIDS on children in Africa and the many concerns they have regarding care of ill and dying parents and siblings. Poverty added an overlay to the existing challenges of AIDS. The authors reviewed ideas about how children cope with grief and the customary non-inclusion of children after a death, with the suggestion to go on as "normal" and a hesitancy to address sensitive feelings. The authors pointed out this getting on with "normal life" soon after a mourning period may suggest a type of *hidden resilience*, whereby children silently adjust because they must. "The cultural script is one of getting on with life" (Heath et al., 2014, p. 315).

Researchers maintained that positive adjustment is bolstered by the sociocultural ecology in which a child develops. *Hidden resilience* may not be supported by mainstream understanding yet still creates a level of adaption. In South Africa, the expectation for a quick rebound may be unrealistic, yet the common expectation to get on with daily living can provide a buffer from emotional pain when living in poverty, simply because there is little time and energy to grieve. There is also an expectation for kids to get on, not be a burden, and make one's family proud and that this can somehow mask psychological distress. The authors found the use of song, group fire, sharing cultural rites of passage, and guiding children's thoughts as they grow and develop were effective in bringing sensitive and often-hidden feelings of grief and loss to the surface in a safe way (Heath et al., 2014).

The Suitcase Project (Clachery, 2008) included 11 refugee children who narrated stories of loss, which were recorded verbatim. The project demonstrated that it was helpful to encourage children to express loss through creativity. Memory boxes, dream work, and creative expression were incorporated, allowing refugee children an opportunity to express feelings through stories. "Clachery explained the therapeutic value of encouraging children to work through their traumatic grief by creating symbolic artwork (painting and drawing pictures on the outside and inside of small suitcases) representative of life experiences" (Heath et al., 2014, p. 325).

In their research on fostering resilience among Native American youth, Garrett et al. (2014) offered a solid understanding of strengths and protective factors discussed within a Native context; indigenous ways of knowing, cultural identity, tribal wisdom, and family identity are interwoven and contextual factors were explored including history and healing of the intergenerational trauma, along with effects of acculturation and social and economic influence on Native communities. The purpose of this research was to present implications and therapeutic responses for healing historical trauma and oppression, while embracing both practical considerations as well as working from a social justice perspective.

Garrett et al. (2014) highlighted the 2011 census, stating that, of the 5.2 million Native young people living the United States, 33.9% of them are under age 18. Native American youth may be at greater risk than their peers due to a world that is drastically different than traditional indigenous ways. "Researchers continue to identify links between historical trauma and feelings of anxiety, depression, anger, and avoidance among Native Americans" (Garrett et al., 2014, p. 471; Sarche & Whitesell, 2012). To counter these outcomes, Native communities are creating wellness centers based on promoting youth resilience. "At the heart of these efforts is the ongoing cultural belief in the sacredness of children as a focal point for the health and well-being of the entire community" (Garrett et al., 2014, p. 472).

Promoting resilience includes teaching language, strong kinship ties, ceremonies and rituals, and belonging and identify. Too often, Indigenous children and teens are underrepresented in history, with a focus on obstacles rather than strengths. This traditional way of focusing on strengths actually promotes resilience, including cultural resilience, achieved by protecting and nurturing children offered through a new term, IWOK, or Indigenous Ways of Knowing. Conclusions drawn by Garrett et al. (2014) offered ways to promote wellness that included working in tribal-specific ways, promoting cultural identity, reducing generational splits, and working from non-interference. Spiritual ways, communication, and humor, are also highlighted as paths to resilience within indigenous communities.

Collishaw, Gardner, Aber, and Cluver (2016) presented research on predictors of mental health resilience in children parentally bereaved by AIDS in Africa. The authors explain that "15 million children in sub-Saharan Africa have lost one or both parents to the AIDS epidemic" (p. 719) resulting in stigma, poverty, violence, and educational disruption. These children are at risk of mental health issues, and parental bereavement is a predictor of subsequent health issues because these children are a vulnerable group. An urgent priority for the authors was "attending to the physical health needs of children in AIDS-affected families . . . (as it) may also offer benefits for children's mental health" (p. 729).

Although there is little evidence to address resilience with these young people, there is a better-than-expected adaptation given exposure to risk. Collishaw et al.'s (2016) study emphasized the "importance of addressing community level risks (such as stigma, bullying and violence), enhancing high quality relationships with peers, and ensuring food security" (p. 729). These authors maintained that predictors of resilience would include psychological factors, such as optimism and physical health, quality of relationship between child and caregiver, and consequences of parental bereavement, such as an increase in poverty or broader community influence. Community influences included economic conditions, culture and prevailing attitudes and beliefs, and community-level supports.

Collishaw et al.'s (2016) "ecological model of resilience in AIDS-orphaned children included considering risk and protective influences jointly across multiple ecological levels including the child, their family and the community" (p. 720). This ecological model "predicts that there would be cumulative influences, with resilience most likely among children with multiple strengths across different ecological levels" (p. 721). Findings by Collishaw et al. (2016) concluded that mental health concerns are not inevitable. One fourth of AIDS-orphaned children did not experience negative mental health concerns over a 4-year period. Lastly, food security and low exposure to stigma were among the strongest positive aspects of mental health. The authors maintained that improvements in the lives of children in one area can deeply impact another. "Interventions to reduce community stigma may help reduce the likelihood of bullying; addressing children's food insecurity is likely to benefit their physical health" (p. 729).

Azri, Cartmel, and Larmar (2014) presented research in Australia in their review of the Healthy Mindset for Superkids Program. Azri et al. (2014) published with Jessica Kingsley (Azri, 2013), a preventative universal program, *Healthy Mindsets for Superkids (HMSK): A Preventative Programme for Children Ages 7–14 years old.* The HMSK program is comprised of 10 modules that included self-esteem, communication skills, positive thinking, anxiety and stress management, anger management, peer pressure, healthy relationship, and healthy bodies. The author had positive findings and positive feedback, suggesting the creation of a strengths-based program for children is needed rather than programs that focus on pathology. The researcher's review instilled the idea that resilience needs to be consistently taught over time and barriers to supporting kids must be considered.

In this study, resilience was defined as "one's ability to overcome negative events" (Azri et al., 2014, p. 122) and may depend on various factors such as personality, interactions with family and friends, environment, resources, and skill, and resilience can be positive and adaptive over time. The authors underscored three protective factors: personality traits, supportive family, and positive community input. In Australia, the government focus is to provide service for the minority of kids who are viewed as at risk, thus this program seeks to address the existing gap in service and offers important life skills for all children. Skills presented within this service are intended to build resilience by promoting confidence and well-being, which is a benefit for all children, not just those who are identified as needing support.

Each research study presented shares a path to resilience within a range of diverse cultures, which promotes the use of creative expression, the need to protect and nurture children, the utility of dismissing myths such as *getting on*, and the benefit of promoting well-being through cultural identity, family, and spiritual ways. Professionals and parents who care for, and about, children can strive to instill qualities of adaptability, acceptance, patience, and fortitude through childhood and adolescence. Our goal is to identify children's strengths that promote resilience and to support and nurture their implementation. The following are significant factors to discover and encourage in children:

- Choice
- Optimism
- Courage
- Realistic goals
- Humor
- Self-confidence
- Appreciation of self
- Acceptance and comfort
- Productive action
- Creativity
- Spirituality
- Service (adapted from Goldman, 2006).

Strategies That Support Resilience

One difficult question to ask ourselves is "How can we prepare our children to live in a world that is sometimes not understandable to adults themselves?" Young people are living with intimate exposure to war, terrorism, random violence, bullying and abuse, and death and disease through first-hand experience or constant media exposure.

Children must be allowed to grieve their losses, reduce their fears, and feel a sense of safety and protection. It benefits kids to incorporate the understanding that horrific events have occurred throughout history, our country, and indeed our world which has survived and will continue to do so through strength, faith, and human resiliency. Andrew's following poem expresses his strength, faith, and courage, manifesting in a resilient attitude.

> When terrorists provoke fear they win.
> Their victims aren't the deceased.
> Their victims are those who change their lives due to
> the fear stemming from the terrorist.
> To be scared is to lose.
> To lose is to die.
> Andrew, Age 17, (Goldman, 2006, p. 244)

Children can be encouraged to express their feelings and thoughts through drawing, play, writing, music, memory work, and problem solving. Sophie, age 7, was a second-grader experiencing terror after a sniper terrorized her community. Her school was in lockdown, with no outdoor play and no visitors to the building. The children and their families were living in fear, and Sophie's classroom reflected a safe space for expression of feelings.

Figure 14.1 Scary TV

Source: (Goldman, 2006, p. 178) Reprinted with permission

The children were asked to draw or write their feelings about the sniper and his violent actions. Sophie drew a picture about how she felt after hearing about a murder close to her home. Her artwork showed her perception of her parent's reaction to this violence and also showed a television in the background playing scary images. Allowing Sophie to express her feelings during this trauma in a safe way helps release her from the fear of experiencing another violent event that could be in her neighborhood. Permitting children to play a role in developing coping skills empowers them throughout their lives.

Including the following skills when working with bereaved children can provide understanding and create a safe environment at home, at school, and in the community:

- Teach children that having many different kinds of feelings is normal, especially after a personal, community, or national traumatic event. All feelings are okay.
- Allow them to express their feelings in safe ways. First-grader Marie shared emotions after a sniper had murdered people in her neighborhood. Her teacher encouraged her students to draw or write how they were feeling that morning. Marie was very sad.
- Encourage kids to remember events and loved ones in a variety of creative ways.

- Let them know that it is normal to have fears and express them in safe ways.
- Invite them to write letters to public figures, compose poetry or plays, or advocate for beliefs.

Letter writing and advocacy are concrete ways children can enhance resilience. Sofi Cruz was 5 years old when Pope Francis came to America in 2015. She amazingly wove through the enormous crowds of people to hand deliver an important message to the Pope, and she even got a hug from him. Her letter pleaded for help with immigrant rights in America. Sofi's parents were among 4 million undocumented immigrants waiting for final immigration action. She explained, "All immigrants, just like my dad, need this country. They deserve to live with dignity. . . . Don't forget the children, or anyone that suffers because they don't have their parents" (Sakuma, 2015).

Megan wrote to President Bush after 9/11 offering him advice. Her letter illustrates her strengths of connecting with others and displaying productive action that supports resilience (see Figure 14.3).

Various activities can be implemented with young people to help alleviate their worries and fears. Children can prepare lists of their top five worries and be encouraged to discuss these worries with a responsible person they trust. They can also construct safety and fear boxes where they can physically place items or pictures of things that make them feel safe or frighten them. In this way, they begin to take troubling emotions and place them outside themselves. Children can also help others by participating in various fundraising activities, or express national pride by wearing or displaying flags or ribbons. Memorials can be produced for any loss, be it a deceased pet, a loved one, or a community or national tragedy. Active commemoration as part of a community grief team allows children to be included in funerals, memorial services, family religious traditions, or a group prayer for peace and unity.

The necessity of such activities in helping children adapt and heal can be seen in the work of Stiles et al. (2015), who noted a recent increase in racial violence in urban communities. Their paper presented a Missouri-based graduate program's response to the shooting and death of Michael Brown in 2014 in Ferguson, Missouri. The authors stated that almost no attention was given to how youth might be affected by the shooting of a peer about their age. This shooting ignited protests for many months. Stiles et al. (2015) concluded that most of the 54 schools studied did not provide psychologically beneficial responses to the Ferguson crisis. Those schools who recognized and supported students during this trauma helped by using the crisis as an opportunity for "learning, healing, and community building" (2015, p. 21). The recommendations by Stiles et al. (2015) included school-wide approaches that encouraged students to engage in open discussions and share individual responses to the crisis.

"Draw a picture of how ... now. If you want to write about your picture on th..."

"I fell said ritg how."

Figure 14.2 After a Sniper

Source: (Goldman, 2006, p.103) Reprinted with permission

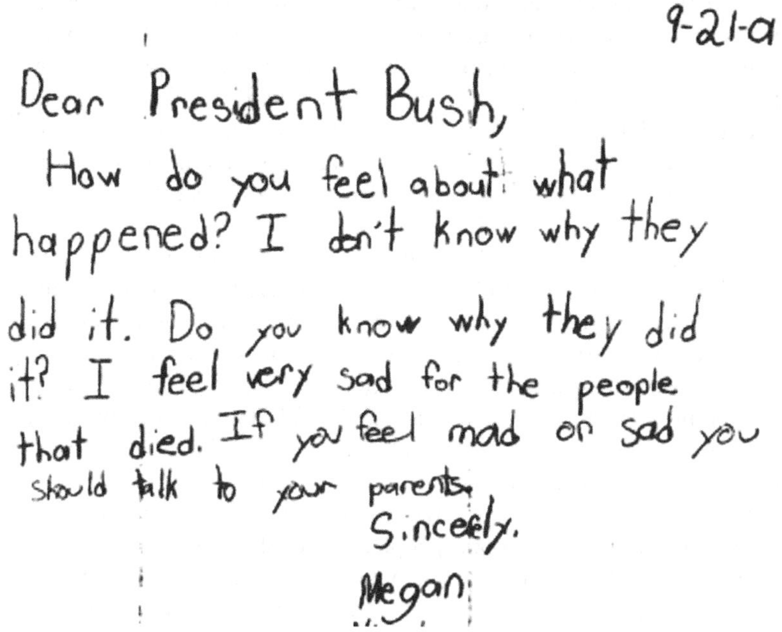

9-21-a

Dear President Bush,
How do you feel about what
happened? I don't know why they
did it. Do you know why they did
it? I feel very sad for the people
that died. If you feel mad or sad you
should talk to your parents.
                              Sincerly,
                                 Megan

Figure 14.3 Letter to President Bush

Source: (Goldman, 2006, p. 136) Reprinted with permission

The Need for Supportive Adults

Why is resilience important to talk about? How can one use it to help children once it is explained? A major aspect of resilience may be the feeling that "I'm not totally alone against the world"—that somehow, somewhere, "I'm part of something bigger than me." Regardless of which lens it is viewed through—spiritual, religious, social, community, or family—resilience provides and encourages altruistic urges to help others.

Siegel (2001) proposed the idea that emotionally attuned communication that resonates with nonverbal signals allows children to be heard and feel understood. When in the presence of an attuned adult, the child's mind reflects coherence between the self and the other. Siegel (2001) explained:

> This defining focus of the self as a "self-with-attuned-other" is, I believe, the developmental origins of our natural capacity for caring about and feeling connected to others in the world. The heart of the emotional transactions with the growing child can be described as being the sharing and amplification of positive emotional states, and the sharing and reduction of negative states. These repeated and reliable emotional transactions allow a child to feel connected in the world.
>
> (p. 85)

Many children do not like to feel different, so they choose not to discuss the losses they have experienced, but that does not mean that they are not feeling pain, grief, anger, and despair. Each child's grief is unique and may last for weeks, months, or years. Kids need to know that they do not have to "get over their grief" or "move on" and that adults are safe havens for expression of their feelings and thoughts, without judgement. Remember, *what we can mention, we can manage.* Using age-appropriate dialogue for discussion of complex life events helps bring deep issues into the open.

It is helpful for children when adults clarify any misinformation that young people have acquired. Children may misinterpret the facts after a difficult experience, and adult clarification of misinformation is important. For example, one 6-year-old explained that every time she watched the replay of the planes crashing into the towers after 9/11, she thought the event was happening over and over again. It is often useful to limit television watching, monitor programs being viewed, and highlight teachable moments that may arise for discussion and clarification of disconcerting occurrences.

School involvement is essential in the process of developing adaptive coping mechanisms for young people. School shootings, suicides, terrorist threats, natural disasters, disease, and bullying create an environment in which educational populations are thrust into danger at unsuspecting times. As prepared as many systems have become, the unexpected events that can unfold in today's schools leave kids, teachers, and parents feeling shocked or vulnerable. Strong guidelines, planned crisis procedures, and education about grief and trauma are necessary in order to establish a plan of action during challenging times.

The advantages of this type of approach are illustrated in the story of Zoe, a student who lived in Washington. After the 2011 terrorist attack in Washington DC, many students knew friends or relatives affected by the event, as many parents worked in or near the Pentagon. Most of the children and their families in Zoe's school were affected by 9/11 in some way. Educators in Zoe's school felt a responsibility to monitor how children were coping after the traumatic event and identify at-risk behaviors, inform parents, and screen troubled children vigilantly to ensure their needs were addressed. Teachers, principals, and all staff were encouraged to see their role as nurturers and providers of safety, presenters of accurate information, helpers to release thoughts and fears, identifiers of troubled students, and emergency planners for the future. Teachers reminded students that they are survivors dealing with challenging experiences. Educators have the ability to shape traumatic events into teaching experiences that will aid our young people in moving forward, with feelings of safety, protection, and hope. A memory board was posted in the hall that allowed students to share feelings, ideas, and essays about the experience. Additionally, the student body voted on projects that would be helpful and held a school-sponsored dance as well as a poster contest.

Julie's best friend Zoe was killed by a terrorist attack. Zoe and her family were on the plane that crashed into the fields of Pennsylvania. Julie chose to

Figure 14.4. The Winning Poster

Source: (Goldman, 2006, p. 201) Reprinted with permission

be involved and proactive, a sign of a resilient child. She became the judge of a poster contest at the school dance marathon. The dance was a fundraiser to buy warm gloves and coats for the firefighters and police officers that helped in Washington, DC at the Pentagon attack. Julie announced the following winning poster that asked the question, "What can we do to make this world a better place?"

Community-based outreach programs also have a responsibility to help children who have experienced personal or public trauma. They can offer safe havens that allow traumatized children to express, reflect upon, process, and overcome the challenges they face. Support groups, one-on-one and group counseling, camps, mentoring programs, and after-school activities all serve to build resilience, healing, and hope.

Young people need to feel empowered by their own inner strength and guidance and know that they have internal resources and external adult supports to help them through experiences of grief or trauma. Building resilience gives children the freedom to grow and develop into productive adults, regardless of past traumas or losses.

Relationships such as those of family, friends, psychotherapy, and the collaborative environment of nurturing communities might facilitate the development of flexible self-regulation and a more integrated way of life for all ages. If we can find a way to facilitate neural integration within the minds of individuals across the lifespan, we may be able to promote a more compassionate world of human connections.

(Siegel, 2001, p. 90)

Conclusion

What began as a quest to understand the extraordinary has revealed the power of the ordinary. Resilience does not come from rare and special qualities, but from the everyday magic of the ordinary, normative human resources in the minds, brains, and bodies of children, in their families and relationships, and in their communities.

(Masten, 2001, p. 235)

We must develop increasingly comprehensive training programs to prepare educators, therapists, and other caring professionals working with bereaved youth. New paradigms, informed by the multifaceted nature of children's grief and trauma as well as by holistic healing processes, are to be developed with age-appropriate vocabulary, grief and trauma resolution techniques, resources specific to each complex loss, and critical understandings of the nature of childhood grief. Building our children's capacities to positively endure, adapt, and overcome life's adversities with optimism is our ultimate goal. Our role as parents and professionals is to protect and prepare our children to accept present and future circumstances, and develop flexibility in adapting to an ever-changing global perspective.

We are *powerless* to control the losses and catastrophic events our children may need to face. But, by honoring their inner wisdom, providing mentorship, and creating safe havens for expression, we can *empower* them to become more caring and more capable human beings.

(Goldman, 2005, p. 72)

In this complex and ever-changing world, it is important that we join together as a global community with a shared vision of our work with children's grief, trauma, and resilience as one that recognizes the preciousness of life, the endurance of love, and the essential quality of a listening heart.

Discussion Questions

1. In what ways do you cultivate resilience in your own life?
2. Choose three activities that you could implement with a bereaved child that would promote the development of resilience.
3. Based on what you have read in this chapter, create your own definition of resilience.

References

Angelou, M., & LaNae, T. (July 4, 2012). A conversation with Dr. Maya Angelou: *Beautifully Said*. Retrieved from www.beautifullysmagazine.com

Azri, S. (2013). *Healthy mindsets for superkids: A resilience program for children Ages 7–14*. New York, NY: Jessica Kingsley.

Azri, S., Cartmel, J., & Larmar, S. (2014). A review of the healthy mindsets for superkids program. *Australian Journal of Guidance and Counselling, 121*(24), 121–131.

Benard, B. (2004). *Resiliency: What we have learned*. San Francisco, CA: WestEd.

Brooks, R., & Goldstein, S. (2003). *Nurturing resilience in our children: Answers to the most important parenting questions*. Chicago, IL: Contemporary Books.

Clacherty, G. (2008). *The suitcase stories: Refugee children reclaim their identities*. Cape Town, South Africa: Double Story Books.

Collishaw, S., Gardner, F., Aber, L., & Cluver, L. (2016). Predictors of mental health resilience in children who have been parentally bereaved by AIDS in urban South Africa. *Journal of Abnormal Child Psychology, 44*, 719–730.

Garrett, M., Parrish, M., Williams, C., Grayshiled, L., Portman, T., Rivera, E., & Maynard, E. (2014). Invited commentary: Fostering resilience among Native American youth through therapeutic intervention. *Journal of Youth Adolescence, 43*, 470–490.

Goldman, L. (2005). *Children also grieve: Talking to children about death and healing*. London, UK: Jessica Kingsley.

Goldman, L. (2006). *Raising our children to be resilient: A guide to helping children cope with trauma in today's world*. New York, NY: Taylor & Francis.

Goldman, L. (2014). *Life and loss: A guide to help grieving children* (3rd ed.). New York, NY: Taylor & Francis.

Goldman, L. (Ed) (in press). *Creating inclusion and well-being for marginalized students*. London, UK: Jessica Kingsley.

Heath, M., Donald, D., Theron, L., & Lyon, R. (2014). AIDS in South Africa: Therapeutic interventions to strengthen resilience among orphans and vulnerable children. *School Psychology International, 35*(3), 309–337.

Masten, A. (2001). Ordinary magic: Resilience processes in development, *American Psychologist, 56*, 1–12.

Masten, A. (2015). *Ordinary magic: Resilience in development*. New York, NY: The Guilford Press.

Patchin, J., & Hinduja, S. (2010). Changes in adolescent online social networking behaviors from 2006 to 2009. *Computers in Human Behavior, 26*, 1818–1821. Retrieved from www.elsevier.com/locate/comphumbeh

Ramus, S., James, A., & Ford, T. (2014). Where I have to learn the ways how to live: Youth resilience in a Yup'ik village in Alaska. *Transcultural Psychiatry, 51*(5), 713–734.

Sarche, M. C., & Whitesell, N. R. (2012). Child development research in North American Native communities—looking back and moving forward: Introduction. *Child Development Perspectives, 6*, 42–48.

Sakuma, A. (2015). *A 5-year old's message to Pope Francis*. Retrieved from www.msnbc.com/msnbc/child-immigration-note-pope-francis

Siegel, D. (2001). Toward an interpersonal neurobiology of the developing mind: Attachment relationships, "mindsight," and neural integration. *Infant Mental Health*

Journal, 22(1–2), 67–94. Retrieved from https://pdfs.semanticscholar.org/07cd/e956bb02668cdedd260417a398f8f72e4c43.pdf

Stiles, D., Moyer, J., Brewer, W., Klaus, L., Falconer, J., & Moss, L. (2015). Practising psychology in challenging times: Schools and the Ferguson crises. *Educational & Child Psychology, 2*(4), 21–38.

Truebridge, S. (2014a). *Resilience begins with beliefs: Building on student strengths for success in school.* New York, NY: Teachers College Press.

Truebridge, S. (2014b). *Resilience: It's a process—Not a program.* [PowerPoint slides].

15 Ethical Practice and Maintaining Well-Being

Adam Koenig and Carrie Arnold

Successful employment in a helping profession requires a multidimensional approach for practitioners to be competent, find meaning in their work, and have longevity in the field. Being psychologically present and empathically engaged with youth who are grieving or in despair requires self-awareness, theoretical knowledge, and clinical skill. The helping professional's use of "self" needs to be embedded within a thoughtful framework that is guided by professional ethics and boundaries and a culturally conscientious practice (see Garcia, Cartwright, Winston, & Borzuchowska's [2003] transcultural integrative model of ethical decision making).

Working with children and adolescents involves further consideration related to consent, confidentiality, the duty to inform, and the role of caregivers within the educational or therapeutic setting. Bereaved children and youth may also experience suicidal ideation or behavior, which requires sound judgement and appropriate knowledge of the ethical and legal guidelines needed to ensure safety and appropriate support. Thus, this chapter includes a brief overview of general ethical guidelines followed by a summary of the ethical considerations that typically arise when working with bereaved children and teens. An overview of occupational stressors is included, along with encouragement for professionals to maintain their well-being as an integral part of sound ethical practice.

Ethical Standards of Practice

Ethical principles and standards are determined by the specific roles and responsibilities of each occupation and are designed to provide a knowledge base, describe activities sanctioned by the respective profession, and offer a clear picture of the boundaries of the professional activity (Sommers-Flanagan & Sommers-Flanagan, 2004). Common themes within codes of ethics include promoting consumer welfare, practicing within the scope of one's competence, maintaining confidentiality, avoiding exploitation, and upholding the integrity of the profession (Corey, Corey, & Callanan, 2011).

While ethical guidelines provide values and a helpful framework, they must be accompanied by common sense, sound judgement, and professional competence with respect to working with children and adolescents (Servaty-Seib & Tedrick, 2010). Various codes of ethics (e.g., American Psychological Association, 2014; Canadian Counselling and Psychotherapy Association, 2007) clearly state the limitations of these guidelines in that they do not contain all the answers, nor are they singularly sufficient in addressing all ethical dilemmas. It is the responsibility of each individual to be informed of the ethical codes of conduct of their respective profession and to actively integrate them into their work. Various organizations oversee the provision of ethical guidelines and codes of conduct. In Canada, the Canadian Counselling and Psychotherapy Association (CCPA) is one such organization. In the United States, many helping professionals seek guidance from the American Counseling Association (ACA) or the National Board of Professional Counselors. Examples of ethical standards are provided by the CCPA (2007) and the ACA (2014), where both espouse six ethical principles, five of which are common to both:

Beneficence—promoting the well-being of clients
Nonmaleficence—avoiding harm to clients
Justice—treating all clients fairly and equally
Fidelity—making realistic commitments and maintaining responsibility in
    the relationship
Autonomy—respecting and promoting the client's right to self-determination

The sixth principle for the CCPA is *societal interest*, which refers to respecting the need to be responsible to society; while the final principle for the ACA is *veracity*, which refers to being truthful in the profession along with the obligation to engage in honest interactions with clients. These ethical principles are embedded within professional relationships that are characterized by confidentiality, respect, and trust. Self-awareness, competence, and ongoing self-reflection are also necessary elements of being a conscientious and ethical practitioner.

Numerous organizations, such as the ACA (2014) or the CCPA (2007), have established decision-making models that guide clinicians facing a range of ethical dilemmas (see Corey, Corey, & Callanan, 2011, for a review). The choice of decision-making model is determined by the complexity of the situation, the unique context, and the nature of the relationship with the client. In ethical decision-making, the outcome is important. However, the process is also an essential element; therefore, the process needs to be thoroughly documented in case files. Additionally, consultation with a supervisor, colleague, or an ethical governing body can be advantageous when addressing more complex ethical dilemmas. Familiarity with the decision-making models in one's professional organization can provide a solid foundation from which to address ethical situations that may arise with young clients or their families, such as the use of touch, client gift giving, or more complex situations that involve the duty to inform, contact with family members, complimentary health-care alternatives, or the legal system.

While ethical principles and standards of practice are outlined for different health-care professions, organizations do not typically provide a specific set of guidelines or standards for working with children and adolescents (Servaty-Seib & Tedrick, 2010). For example, the CCPA (2007) Code of Ethics provides a brief paragraph referring to obtaining consent when working with children or those with diminished capacity. The CCPA (2015) Standards of Practice offers general guidance with respect to children, parents, and confidentiality, yet does not offer further direction for working with young clients. Given the general lack of child-specific standards of practice, it is essential that a helping professional be adept at combining relevant developmental information with the necessary ethical guidelines that pertain to their work with youth.

Ethical Considerations Related to Children and Adolescents

Canadian provinces and territories and each of the American states have specific guidelines and regulations with respect to working with minors, informed consent, and assent. Minors may be youth under the age of 16 or 18 years of age, thus helping professionals must be informed regarding the guidelines in their own jurisdiction. The capacity to provide consent is based not only on age but also on one's ability to "voluntarily, knowingly, and intelligently" (CCPA, 2015, p. 15) provide consent to treatment without pressure or coercion. Corey, Corey, and Callanan (2011) outlined several considerations for practitioners, addressing such issues as minors accessing treatment without parental consent and the age at which this is appropriate (i.e., a 15-year-old calling on his or her own). Limits to confidentiality and the parameters of informed consent also need to be considered. General guidelines are provided within ethical codes of conduct, yet the practitioner often finds him- or herself needing to assess each unique situation. For example, a 15-year-old with income from a part-time job and a highly conflictual relationship with his or her caregiver could potentially be seen for counseling without parental consent. Conversely, a practitioner likely needs to contact caregivers for a 15-year-old who seeks treatment for suicidal ideation, even if he or she does not wish for caregivers to be involved. These kinds of situations highlight the integration of ethical principles, standards of practice, and competence in working with vulnerable youth.

Younger children (e.g., ages 6–12) do not have the cognitive capacity to understand the implications of informed consent, and caregivers have greater decision-making ability in the treatment. Practitioners can obtain informed consent from the caregivers and ask permission, or assent, from the child. *Assent* is a lesser form of consent, which involves the child being given information in developmentally appropriate ways and actively integrates their own decisions into the treatment process (Corey, Corey, & Callanan, 2011; Servaty-Seib & Tedrick, 2010). The helping professional may also find him- or herself in the role of advocate, facilitating conversations with caregivers or educators about the needs of a bereaved child (Servaty-Seib & Tedrick, 2010).

With respect to confidentiality, practitioners have an ethical responsibility to ensure that they take reasonable precaution to safeguard client information and uphold rights to privacy and confidentiality that occurs both in person and via technological communication (e.g., text, email, teleconference; ACA, 2014; CCPA, 2007). Limits to confidentiality include:

1. Imminent danger to self or an identifiable third party,
2. Reasonable suspicion of child abuse or neglect,
3. When disclosure is ordered by a court,
4. When a client requests disclosure,
5. When a client files a complaint, issues of professional liability, or a lawsuit (CCPA, 2015).

During the first session, it is necessary for the practitioner to inform the caregivers and the child or teen of these limits. Some youth may request absolute confidentiality, yet it is unrealistic and unethical for a practitioner to agree to this. In our experience, trust, collaboration, and respect become part of the therapeutic process when young people are educated in age-appropriate ways, actively invited into the process, and respectfully informed about the roles of the counselor, caregiver, and themselves. Additionally, Hendrix (1991) provided four approaches to confidentiality, including complete confidentiality, limited confidentiality, informed forced confidentiality, and no guarantee of confidentiality. The practitioner can determine which model is most advantageous with a particular client and family. Strauss (personal communication, May 31, 2013) advocated for flexibility of confidentiality whereby she informs parents and youth that she will do her utmost to ensure privacy and respect yet uses reasonable judgement with regard to what caregivers ought to know. She actively involves her young clients in the decision-making process and aims to facilitate collaboration from caregivers in the young person's healing.

When balancing consent, confidentiality, and the needs of the child and caregiver, ethical principles need to be actively integrated into the process. At the outset of therapy, consent, confidentiality, and the limits to confidentiality are explained to both caregiver and child. In circumstances where confidentiality cannot be maintained (e.g., suicidal ideation), the helping professional is upholding *fidelity* and *veracity* by recognizing the realistic commitments and responsibilities of her or his role in an honest and authentic way. Obtaining consent or assent from a child or teen recognizes *nonmaleficence*. Involving the child in age-appropriate ways acknowledges his or her *autonomy* and the ability to be and active participant. When caregivers need to be informed about aspects of the therapeutic process, the helping professional can decide to share only information that will further the healing process, recognizing the role of *beneficence*. Lastly, while each child or teen will have her or his unique experience of grief and loss, the helping professional is required to provide skilled and competent care for all clients (i.e., and not better care for clients viewed as easier to work with), honoring both *justice* and *societal interest*.

Maintaining Well-Being

Within any helping profession where interpersonal interactions occur, natural work-related consequences can develop as a result of these interactions. Add in the emotionally laden elements of death and grief, and the effect on practitioners can become even more evident (Breen, O'Connor, Hewitt, & Lobb, 2014). From the type of death to the secondary losses and potentially tumultuous relationship between the bereaved and the deceased, the experience can be overwhelming, even traumatic, in a variety of ways for both the client and practitioner. That said, it is *essential* for those working with bereaved children and adolescents to not only understand the purpose of maintaining one's well-being but also to implement such practices on a continual and consistent basis. Additionally, it is necessary to be aware of the natural work-related consequences and know how to mitigate their effects; this is especially true when working with bereaved children whose grief is compounded with trauma (Maschi & Brown, 2010).

Various professional organizations within the human services area emphasize the importance of conducting self-care and/or self-reflective practices on a regular basis in order to decrease the risks of work-related consequences as well as uphold the ethical standards of one's profession (see ACA, 2014; CCPA, 2015; Canadian Nurses Association, 2008; and National Association of Social Workers, 2013). Consequences typically discussed within the literature and seen within all types of helping practitioners are burnout, compassion fatigue (CF), and vicarious trauma (VT).

Burnout

Typically viewed as a natural work-related consequence that occurs over time versus an acute consequence (Pryce, Shackleford, & Pryce, 2007), Freudenberger was the first to coin the term *burnout* and described it as "a progression of unsuccessful attempts by an individual to cope with a variety of conditions that are perceived to be threatening" (Gold & Roth, 1993, p. 30). The term became popularized by Maslach and Jackson in the 1980s thanks to the development of the Maslach Burnout Inventory (MBI; Maslach & Jackson, 1981) and is defined as "a syndrome of emotional exhaustion, depersonalization, and reduced personal accomplishment" (Maslach, Jackson, & Leiter, 1996, p. 4). As such, emotional exhaustion is characterized by a decrease in energy and overall depletion which negatively affects a practitioner's ability to be responsive to the needs of their clients; depersonalization occurs when a practitioner treats others as impersonal objects, creating distance between themselves and those they care for; and lack of personal accomplishment is when practitioners feel that they are unable to relate to the population they work with and thus feel ineffective.

Working with children and teens can have considerable effects on professionals, both personally and within the roles and responsibilities of their chosen profession. Barford and Whelton (2010) described the increased susceptibility of child- and youth-care workers to experience burnout due to working with high-risk children. Additionally, Maslach, Jackson, and Schwab (1996) created the MBI-Educators Survey due to the negative impact educators were experiencing in their work with their students; as such, working in the human service area, and with children, comes with potential consequences. Thus, it is necessary for helping professionals to be informed of the potential occupational risks as well as the importance of attending to one's own health and well-being.

The Effects of Burnout

Smullens (2015) noted how burnout can affect four different, yet interconnected, areas in one's life: professional, personal, social, and physical. Smullens described how some practitioners used phrases such as "I don't even want to go to work," "This is killing me," "I'm miserable," and "My clients are not making progress," (2015, p. 28) which were attributed to burnout affecting them professionally. A loss of compassion and enthusiasm for clients, as well as struggling to maintain boundaries with clients, was also noted in counselors struggling with professional burnout (Thompson, Frick, & Trice-Black, 2011). In research conducted with social workers in child welfare settings, disengagement from the work was seen as a consequence of burnout (Travis, Lizano, & Mor Barak, 2016).

Symptoms of personal burnout were primarily viewed as a decline in mood with common phrases such as "I am going to fail this client," and "How can I help anyone else when I can't even help myself" (Smullens, 2015, p. 31). Moreover, burnout has also been shown to be a predictor of reduced psychological well-being (de Beer, Pienaar, & Rothmann, 2016). According to Smullens (2015), symptoms of social burnout were characterized by acting out in various relationships (e.g., anger, irritation), withdrawing, always feeling the need to be the caregiver, and being unable to fulfill other roles in one's life (e.g., parent, partner, etc.). Finally, physical burnout is when the body displays physical symptoms related to the strain of burnout (Smullens, 2015). Research by Kim, Ji, and Kao (2011) examined the effects of burnout on a sample of social workers and found that burnout was positively correlated with, and in fact led to, greater health issues such as respiratory infections, gastrointestinal problems, and headaches. All these factors can then negatively impact the care the professional provides to bereaved children and their families.

Other Elements Related to Burnout

Other elements shown to be correlated to burnout include age, gender, and what Maslach and Leiter (as cited in Ray, Wong, White, & Heaslip, 2013) identified as six factors predictive of burnout: workload demands, control in decision-making, rewards or being recognized for one's work, social community within the workplace, fairness or open culture within the workplace, and degree of alignment between values of the workplace and worker. With regard to age, evidence suggested that those who are younger/newer to the profession tend to be at greater risk of developing burnout compared to seasoned professionals (Galek, Flannelly, Greene, & Kudler, 2011; Hamama, 2012; Kim, Ji, & Kao, 2011). Other research with child welfare workers has also demonstrated the greater risk younger professionals have in developing burnout when working with children/youth (Sprang, Craig, & Clark, 2011; Van Hook & Rothenburg, 2009).

With respect to gender, research has been mixed. In a meta-analysis, Purvanova and Muros (2010) found women tended to experience emotional exhaustion slightly more than men, whereas men tended to experience more depersonalization than women. Finally, regarding the six factors predictive of burnout, results compiled by Ray and colleagues (2013) indicated significant negative associations with the burnout subscales of emotional exhaustion and depersonalization with all six factors, while a significant positive association was found between the six factors and personal accomplishment.

Compassion Fatigue

Compassion fatigue (CF; also referred to as *secondary traumatic stress*) is considered to be almost identical to posttraumatic stress disorder (PTSD). In PTSD one is directly affected by a traumatic stressor and exhibits various symptoms, whereas in CF an individual is emotionally affected by a trauma experienced by someone the individual has helped or cared for (i.e., typically clients or close relationships; Figley, 2002). Those with CF exhibit similar symptoms to those affected by PTSD, such as reexperiencing the traumatic event through thoughts, dreams, perceptions, or images (e.g., when the client/family member told them about the event); numbing or avoiding reminders of the trauma (e.g., avoiding the client or places described in the traumatic event); and increased arousal (e.g., difficulty sleeping, concentrating, outburst of anger; Figley, 2002). As with PTSD, CF can develop after a single traumatic exposure (Figley, 1999).

The Effects of Compassion Fatigue

Research conducted by Bride, Jones, and Macmaster (2007) determined a positive correlation between child protective service workers with higher levels of CF and variables such as workers having their own previous trauma history and large caseloads. Additionally, McKim and Smith-Adcock (2014) found that counselors working with clients who had experienced trauma tended to have high levels of CF when various factors, such as becoming overinvolved with clients and a lack of control/autonomy in the workplace, were present. Conclusively, Bride and Kintzle (2011) found those with high levels of CF tended to be less satisfied in their job and less committed to their work. Signifying the impact of human service work done with children, Sprang, Craig, and Clark (2011) found that child welfare workers experienced a statistically significant higher amount of CF compared to other types of health personnel in their study (i.e., inpatient/outpatient workers, psychiatrists, school social workers/psychologists). In all, practitioners need to be aware of signs that they may be affected by CF and how their own experiences may make them more vulnerable to CF and less available to support bereaved youth.

Vicarious Trauma

Another term commonly discussed within the literature is vicarious trauma (VT). Coined by McCann and Pearlman (1990) through their work with trauma therapists, *vicarious trauma* is defined by Pearlman and Mac Ian (1995) as a transformation within a practitioner who works with traumatized individuals and empathetically engages with these individuals over their trauma narratives. As a result of this engagement and bearing witness to graphic trauma narratives, the practitioner's experience of the world, themselves, and others are affected over time and different relationships—meaning VT is a cumulative process. Practitioners working with individuals who are traumatized may experience intrusive imagery related to the trauma they have heard as well as changes to the way they organize their thoughts, feelings, and behaviors (i.e., cognitive schemas).

The Effects of Vicarious Trauma

In a meta-synthesis of works published on VT, Cohen and Collens (2013) identified various themes. The researchers noted how the literature reflected various negative emotional and somatic reactions to client stories such as feeling powerless, frustrated, nauseous, or experiencing difficulties conducting therapy and experiencing distress. Cohen and Collens (2013) also noted changes to participants' cognitive schemas in that some schemas tended to turn negative, where those involved in trauma work came to view the world as unsafe and had a pessimistic view of reality. At the same time, positive schematic changes were also noted, such as appreciating life more and becoming more compassionate. Much of the schematic changes led to existential questioning and overall changes to the practitioner's worldview, values, self, and day-to-day life.

Self-Care and Maintaining Well-Being

In order to attain and maintain an ethical practice when working with children and teens, a practitioner's personal and professional well-being is a significant component. Crucial to well-being is the practitioner's ability to conduct self-care on a regular basis in order to mitigate the natural work related consequences of burnout, CF, and VT. Wang, Strosky and Fletes (2014) emphasized the importance of engaging in practices that help with mitigating the natural work-related consequences; as such, self-care is a concept often emphasized within the literature as a way to help prevent or mitigate such consequences. Other practitioners actively state that it is an ethical requirement (Harris & Winokuer, 2016).

Although no consensus exists about a "true" definition of self-care (Lee & Miller, 2013), it is often seen as proactive and intentional (Thompson et al., 2011). *Self-care* is an action designed to increase one's well-being and meet the needs of the various dimensions of the self, which often includes one's emotional, psychological, physical, social, and spiritual selves (Moore, Bledsoe, Perry, & Robinson, 2011). Urdang (2010) stressed that a critical component of self-care is having an awareness of self. When one is aware of one's feelings, relationships, and attitudes, and possesses an ability to be self-analytical, a practitioner is then better able to mitigate the negative aspects of one's work.

In their work, Cohen and Collens (2013) emphasized the need for both practitioners and organizations to understand and recognize the effect working with those impacted by trauma and loss has on supportive professionals. What follows are various ways practitioners and organizations can help mitigate the negative effects of the natural work related consequences.

Practitioners

Psychological/Emotional/Spiritual

In order to take care of one's own emotional and psychological well-being, Lee and Miller (2013) suggested practitioners should have the goal of practicing and maintaining a positive and compassionate perspective of one's self. Practitioners could do so by engaging in various self-care activities, such as practicing stress-management techniques, problem solving, and mindfulness. Mindfulness has demonstrated its effectiveness in social workers-in-training where participants experienced a significant increase in their counseling self-efficacy compared to a control group (Gockel, Burton, James, & Bryer, 2013). Other research has suggested mindfulness (a) helps increase awareness and acceptance of the self and others; (b) can decrease judgemental and defensive reactions; and (c) fosters patience, empathy, and attentiveness (Campbell & Christopher, 2012; Christopher et al., 2011).

Creative practices in self-care can also be engaged in to increase self-awareness. Drawing, journaling, and scrapbook journaling can be approaches practitioners conduct to explore emotions and overall well-being (Bradley,

Whisenhunt, Adamson, & Kress, 2013). Furthermore, individual personality factors such as optimism and spirituality can help practitioners with the negative impact of their work (Cohen & Collens, 2013). Some qualitative research even found the self-care utility of various religious practices, such as prayer and attending services (Moore et al., 2011).

Social

The importance of having social support was demonstrated by Galek et al. (2011) in their study of professional chaplains. It was found that those who felt they gained support from their family and friends had lower levels of burnout. Additionally, friend and family support was negatively associated with CF. In another study by Thompson and colleagues (2011), counselors-in-training even identified the importance and utility of connecting with supportive significant others, friends, and family as way to conduct self-care.

Physical

Norcross and Guy (2007) emphasized the importance of physical self-care to mediate occupational-related stress. The authors highlighted simple yet effective tactics, such as getting 8 hours of sleep a night, addressing body tension and fatigue through massage, exercising on a regular basis, engaging in contact with significant people in one's life, maintaining a healthy diet, and drinking enough fluids. *Canada's Food Guide* provides guidelines on the recommended daily intake of various foods based on one's age and gender (see Health Canada, 2011), while the National Academy of Sciences (2004) recommends drinking approximately 3.7 L of water a day for men and 2.7 L for women. Another way to increase physical self-care can be through mindfulness, as participants who conducted mindfulness over a long period of time noted increased energy, flexibility, and the effective use of breath awareness to decrease distress (Christopher et al., 2011).

Organizational

Maltzman (2011) highlighted the importance of developing an organizational culture supportive of self-care. If a self-care culture is not established, the organizational culture may unintentionally encourage self-deprivation and/ or overworking; staff may hide feelings, such as sadness, horror, or anxiety after hearing traumatic narratives due to stigma; or staff may feel support can only be gained from within an organization versus external relationships (i.e., family, friends, significant others, etc.). In their research with counselors, Bradley et al. (2013) suggested that this population of practitioners should not lose sight of the "small steps" of progress clients have made in therapy. Although client goals may not have been reached, therapeutic gains of any kind should be celebrated and acknowledged. Acknowledging progress for what it is could help decrease feelings of being ineffective in one's role.

As Bride and Kintzle's (2011) research suggested, occupational commitment was mediated by job satisfaction in those suffering from high levels of CF, the researchers underscored the importance of administration increasing their efforts to promote job satisfaction. That said, seen as potentially instrumental in mitigating negative work-related effects, strong organizational support should be part of a practitioner's professional experience where personal self-care practices are encouraged and supported by the practitioner's organization (Cohen & Collens, 2013). Organizational support could be offered to practitioners through professional development, which includes opportunities for self-reflection, as this has been shown to be beneficial for various educational professionals when working with children and youth (Koenig, Rodger, & Specht, 2017).

Professional

Engaging in self-care within one's profession, Smullens (2015) emphasized the importance of having support from one's organization, supervisor, and coworkers. Concerning organizational practices, van Heugten (2011) emphasized that managers should consult front-line staff about changes that are being put in place. When changes were implemented without adequate consultation between upper management and front-line service workers, participants noted the changes often hindered service delivery and created more distress among workers.

Supportive supervision through individual or group consultations and/or mentorship should also be a part of any social worker's or practitioner's clinical routine (van Heugten, 2011). Merriman (2015) emphasized supervisors should be facilitating dialogue about such topics as CF and do their best to destigmatize conversations on such topics. Supervision should also be offered from a strengths-based perspective (van Heugten, 2011), as evidence has suggested the importance of having supportive supervision and coworkers to help mitigate the effects of burnout due to their negative correlation (Galek et al., 2011; Hamama, 2012). The same has been demonstrated with compassion fatigue and peer support (Bride, Jones, & Macmaster, 2007).

Education

Education is another important element in self-care. In order to help reduce distress, terms such as *burnout*, *CF*, and *VT* should be taught within education programs and a precedent should be put in place where the natural consequences related to human service work should be openly discussed (Pryce et al., 2007; Newell & MacNeil, 2010; van Heugten, 2011). The more open conversations are about the consequences, the less stigmatized the topics will be within the profession. Moreover, Maltzman (2011) emphasized staff education should be continual where psycho-education on self-care, and the natural work-related consequences, could be implemented by organizations.

During the education, staff should be encouraged to consider self-care as an essential and necessary aspect of their work. Maltzman suggested separating supervisors and staff, as staff may feel more comfortable engaging in conversations when management is not present. Self-reflective skills should also be developed among practitioners within their educational training (Urdang, 2010) and mindfulness training integrated into any curriculum (Campbell & Christopher, 2012).

Discussion Questions

1. Discuss some of the unique ethical situations that might arise when working with bereaved children and adolescents.
2. Identify and discuss what you do for self-care. What might you add to your self-care plan?
3. Discuss what you can do to promote self-care amongst your peers and colleagues.

References

American Counseling Association. (2014). *ACA code of ethics*. Retrieved from www. counseling.org/resources/aca-code-of-ethics.pdf

Barford, S. W., & Whelton, W. J. (2010). Understanding burnout in child and youth care workers. *Child Youth Care Forum, 39*, 271–287. doi:10.1007/s10566-010-9104-8

Bradley, N., Whisenhunt, J., Adamson, N., & Kress, V. E. (2013). Creative approaches for promoting counselor self-care. *Journal of Creativity in Mental Health, 8,* 456–469. doi:10.1080/15401383.2013.844656

Breen, L. J., O'Connor, M., Hewitt, L. Y., & Lobb, E. A. (2014). The "specter" of cancer: Exploring secondary trauma for health professionals providing cancer support and counselling. *Psychological Services, 14*(11), 60–67. doi:10.1037/a0034451

Bride, B. E., Jones, J. L., & Macmaster, S. A. (2007). Correlates of secondary traumatic stress in child protective services workers. *Journal of Evidence-Based Social Work, 4*(3–4), 69–80. doi:10.1300/J394v04n03_05

Bride, B. E., & Kintzle, S. (2011). Secondary traumatic stress, job satisfaction, and occupational commitment in substance abuse counselors. *Traumatology, 17*(1), 22–28. doi:10.1177/1534765610395617

Campbell, J. C., & Christopher, J. C. (2012). Teaching mindfulness to create effective counselors. *Journal of Mental Health Counseling, 34*(3), 213–226. Retrieved from https://amhca.site-ym.com/store/ViewProduct.aspx?id=4043223

Canadian Counselling and Psychotherapy Association. (2007). *Code of ethics*. Retrieved from www.ccpa-accp.ca/wp-content/uploads/2014/10/CodeofEthics_en.pdf

Canadian Counselling and Psychotherapy Association. (2015). *Standards of practice* (5th ed.). Retrieved from www.ccpa-accp.ca/wp-content/uploads/2015/07/Standards OfPractice_en_June2015.pdf

Canadian Nurses Association. (2008). *Code of ethics for registered nurses*. Retrieved from www.cna-aiic.ca/~/media/cna/page-content/pdf-fr/code-of-ethics-for-registered-nurses.pdf?la=en

Christopher, J. C., Chrisman, J. A., Trotter-Mathison, M. J., Schure, M. B., Dahlen, P., & Christopher, S. B. (2011). Perceptions of the long-term influence of mindfulness training on counselors and psychotherapists: A qualitative inquiry. *Journal of Humanistic Psychology, 51*(3), 318–349. doi:10.1177/0022167810381471

Cohen, K., & Collens, P. (2013). The impact of trauma work on trauma workers: A metasynthesis on vicarious trauma and vicarious posttraumatic growth. *Psychological Trauma: Theory, Research, Practice and Policy, 5*(6), 570–580. Retrieved from http://dx.doi.org/10.1037/a0030388

Corey, G., Corey, M. S., & Callanan, P. (2011). *Issues and ethics in the helping professions* (8th ed.). Belmont, CA: Brooks/Cole.

de Beer, L. T., Pienaar, J., & Rothmann Jr., S. (2016). Work overload, burnout, and psychological ill-health symptoms: A three-wave mediation model of the employee health impairment process. *Anxiety, Stress, & Coping, 29*(4), 387–399. doi:10.1080/10615806.2015.1061123

Figley, C. R. (1999). Compassion fatigue: Toward a new understanding of the costs of caring. In B. H. Stamm (Ed.), *Secondary traumatic stress: Self-care issues for clinicians, researchers, and educators* (pp. 3–28). Baltimore, MD: Sidran Press.

Figley, C. R. (2002). Introduction. In C. R. Figley (Ed.), *Treating compassion fatigue.* New York, NY: Brunner-Routledge.

Galek, K., Flannelly, K. J., Greene, P. B., & Kudler, T. (2011). Burnout, secondary traumatic stress, and social support. *Pastoral Psychology, 60,* 633–649. doi:10.1007/s11089-011-0346-7

Garcia, J. G., Cartwright, B., Winston, S. M., & Borzuchowska, B. (2003). A transcultural integrative model for ethical decision making in counselling. *Journal of Counseling and Development, 81*(3), 268–277.

Gockel, A., Burton, D., James, S., & Bryer, E. (2013). Introducing mindfulness as self-care and clinical training strategy for beginning social work students. *Mindfulness, 4,* 343–353. doi:10.1007/s12671-012-0134-1

Gold, Y., & Roth, R. A. (1993). *Teachers managing stress and preventing burnout: The professional health development.* London, UK: Burgess Science Press.

Hamama, L. (2012). Burnout in social workers treating children as related to demographic characteristics, work environment, and social support. *Social Work Research, 36*(2), 113–125. doi:10.1093/swr/svs003

Harris, D. L., & Winokuer, H. R. (2016). *Principles and practices of grief counseling* (2nd ed.). New York, NY: Springer.

Health Canada. (2011). *Eating well with Canada's food guide.* Retrieved from www.hc-sc.gc.ca/fn-an/alt_formats/hpfb-dgpsa/pdf/food-guide-aliment/view_eatwell_vue_bienmang-eng.pdf

Hendrix, D. H. (1991). Ethics and intrafamilial confidentiality in counseling with children. *Journal of Mental Health Counseling, 13,* 323–333.

Kim, H., Ji, J., & Kao, D. (2011). Burnout and physical health among social workers: A three-year longitudinal study. *Social Work, 56*(3), 258–268.

Koenig, A., Rodger, S., & Specht, J. (2017). Educator burnout and compassion fatigue: A pilot study. *Canadian Journal of School Psychology.* Advance online publication. doi:10.1177/0829573516685017

Lee, J. J., & Miller, S. E. (2013). A self-care framework for social workers: Building a strong foundation for practice. *Families in Society: The Journal of Contemporary Social Services, 9*(2), 96–103. doi:10.1606/1044-3894.428

Maltzman, S. (2011). An organizational self-care model: Practical suggestions for development and implementation. *The Counseling Psychologist, 39*(2), 303–319. doi:10.1177/0011000010381790

Maschi, T., & Brown, D. (2010). Professional self-care and prevention of secondary trauma. In N. B. Webb (Ed.), *Helping bereaved children: A handbook for practitioners* (3rd ed., pp. 345–373). New York, NY: The Guilford Press.

Maslach, C., & Jackson, S. E. (1981). The measurement of experienced burnout. *Journal of Occupational Behavior, 2,* 1–15. Retrieved from www.jstor.org/journals/01422774.html

Maslach, C., Jackson, S. E., & Leiter M. P. (1996). *Maslach Burnout Inventory manual* (3rd ed.). Mountain View, CA: CPP.

Maslach, C., Jackson, S. E., & Schwab, R. L. (1996). *Maslach Burnout Inventory—Educators Survey* (MBI-ES). In C. Maslach, S. E. Jackson, & M. P. Leiter, *MBI manual* (3rd ed.). Mountain View, CA: CPP.

McCann, L., & Pearlman, L. A. (1990). Vicarious traumatization: A framework for understanding the psychological effects of working with victims. *Journal of Traumatic Stress, 3*(1), 131–149. doi:10.1002/jts.2490030110

McKim, L. L., & Smith-Adcock, S. (2014). Trauma counsellors' quality of life. *International Journal of the Advancement of Counselling, 36,* 58–69. doi:10.1007/s10447-013-9190-z

Merriman, J. (2015). Enhancing counselor supervision through compassion fatigue education. *Journal of Counseling & Development, 93,* 370–378. doi:10.1002/jcad.12035

Moore, S. E., Bledsoe, L. K., Perry, A. R., & Robinson, M. A. (2011). Social work students and self-care: A model assignment for teaching. *Journal of Social Work Education, 47*(3), 545–553. doi:10.5175/JSWE.2011.201000004

National Academy of Sciences. (2004). *Dietary reference intakes: Water, potassium, sodium, chloride, and sulfate.* Retrieved from http://nationalacademies.org/hmd/reports/2004/dietary-reference-intakes-water-potassium-sodium-chloride-and-sulfate.aspx

National Association of Social Workers. (2013). *NASW standards for social work case management.* Retrieved from www.socialworkers.org/practice/naswstandards/casemanagementstandards2013.pdf

Newell, J. M., & MacNeil, G. A. (2010). Professional burnout, vicarious trauma, secondary traumatic stress, and compassion fatigue: A review of theoretical terms, risk factors, and preventive methods for clinicians and researchers. *Best Practices in Mental Health, 6*(2), 58–68. Retrieved from http://lyceumbooks.com/Mental HJournal.htm

Norcross, J. C., & Guy Jr., J. D. (2007). *Leaving it at the office: A guide to psychotherapist self-care.* New York, NY: The Guilford Press.

Pearlman, L. A., & Mac Ian, P. S. (1995). Vicarious traumatization: An empirical study of the effects of trauma work on trauma therapists. *Professional Psychology: Research and Practice, 26*(6), 558–565.

Pryce, J. G., Shackleford, K. K., & Pryce, D. H. (2007). *Secondary traumatic stress and the child welfare profession.* Chicago, IL: Lyceum Books.

Purvanova, R. K., & Muros, J. P. (2010). Gender differences in burnout: A meta-analysis. *Journal of Vocational Behavior, 77,* 168–185. doi:10.1016/j.jvb.2010.04.006

Ray, S. L., Wong, C., White, D., & Heaslip, K. (2013). Compassion satisfaction, compassion fatigue, work life conditions, and burnout among frontline mental health care professionals. *Traumatology, 19*(4), 255–267. doi:10.1177/1534765612471144

Servaty-Seib, H. L., & Tedrick, S. J. (2010). Ethical issues in counseling bereaved and seriously ill children. In C. A. Corr & D. E. Balk (Eds.), *Children's encounters with death, bereavement, and coping*. New York, NY: Springer.

Smullens, S. (2015). *Burnout and self-care in social work: A guidebook for students and those in mental health and related professions*. Washington, DC: NASW.

Sommers-Flanagan, J., & Sommers-Flanagan, R. (2004). *Counseling and psychotherapy theories in context and practice: Skills, strategies, and techniques*. Hoboken, NY: John Wiley & Sons.

Sprang, G., Craig, C., & Clark, J. (2011). Secondary traumatic stress and burnout in child welfare workers: A comparative analysis of occupational distress across professional groups. *Child Welfare, 90*(6), 149–168. Retrieved from www.ncbi.nlm. nih.gov/pubmed/22533047

Thompson, E. H., Frick, M. H., & Trice-Black, S. (2011). Counselor-in-training perceptions of supervision practices related to self-care and burnout. *The Professional Counselor: Research and Practice, 1*(3), 152–162. Retrieved from http://tpcjournal.nbcc.org/wp-content/uploads/thompson-triceblack-frick_DIGEST.pdf

Travis, D. J., Lizano, E. L., & Mor Barak, M. E. (2016). 'I'm so stressed!': A longitudinal model of stress, burnout and engagement among social workers in child welfare settings. *British Journal of Social Work, 46,* 1076–1095. doi:10.1093/bjsw/bct205

Urdang, E. (2010). Awareness of self-A critical tool. *Social Work Education, 29*(5), 523–538. doi:10.1080/02615470903164950

van Heugten, K. (2011). *Social work under pressure: How to overcome stress, fatigue and burnout in the workplace*. Philadelphia, PA: Jessica Kingsley.

Van Hook, M. P., & Rothenberg, M. (2009). Quality of life and compassion satisfaction/fatigue and burnout in child welfare workers: A study of the child welfare workers in community based care organizations in central Florida. *Social Work & Christianity, 36*(1), 36–54. Retrieved from http://search.proquest.com/openview/d92db15ada44851e4c3315e9f8e317bd/1?pq-origsite=gscholar&cbl=40430

Wang, D. G., Strosky, D., & Fletes, A. (2014). Secondary and vicarious trauma: Implications for faith and clinical practice. *Journal of Psychology and Christianity, 33*(3), 281–286. Retrieved from http://go.galegroup.com/ps/anonymous?id=GALE|A385805846&sid=googleScholar&v=2.1&it=r&linkaccess=fulltext&issn=07334273&p=AONE&sw=w&authCount=1&isAnonymousEntry=true

Appendix: *Just Keep Breathing!* Mindful Breath Awareness

A Brief Manual for Kids of All Ages

Brad Hunter

A few questions might arise around mindfulness with children and also mindfulness in the context of grief. At some levels, children may already be more "mindful" than most adults, in that there are brief moments when they can completely attend to the tiniest detail of something, to the exclusion of everything else. On the other hand, the ability to maintain this relaxed, focused attention cannot usually be sustained for any length of time. Cultivating activities and practices that can relax children can lead to emotional intelligence and incline young hearts and minds in the direction of clarity, contentment, and compassion; this is something desirable for individuals and for society as a whole.

Children can already be so "in the moment" that we can observe them completely absorbed in their grief for a period and then, shortly afterwards, happily at play. To us this might appear to be a kind of immature dysfunction, when in fact it is a great skill that many of us have lost. In the midst of grief, mindfulness can be a vehicle to safety that compassionately transports children and adults alike through the difficult grief journey and beyond.

Blowing Up a Balloon of Happiness

Feel your body sitting in the room you are in right now. Feel the air coming into the body through your nose and mouth. Feel where the body meets the floor or whatever you are sitting on. Feel how your clothes feel on the skin. Feel the air around the body. Now, imagine that all the air and space in the room is one huge balloon of happiness. Every time you breathe in and out, you fill the body more and more with happy and peaceful feelings. Sometimes it can be helpful to silently say a word when you are breathing in, too— words like *peace, happy,* or *calm.* Feel the body surrounded by calm, quiet, and peaceful happiness. Feel yourself held in this big balloon of safety and happiness and just keep breathing it in as much as you want.

Things happen in our lives that can make us feel sad or angry or frightened. It is natural to feel these feelings and there is nothing wrong with that, but we do not want to hurt others or ourselves because of our feelings. Spending some time feeling the body and breathing in happiness and calm can help us to safely feel the harder feelings and let them go. Many times we keep our sad, angry, or frightening feelings going just by thinking sad, angry, or frightening thoughts—and we just make ourselves feel worse! Paying attention to the body and breathing in a sense of peace and happiness can help us to settle down and sort through difficult and confusing thoughts and feelings.

When you are outside in the open air, you can imagine your balloon of happiness to be as big as you want! You can breathe in all the fresh air from the whole sky above you and around you! And you can try to imagine breathing out the happiness to share with other children and adults—even sharing with the dogs and squirrels, the birds, the trees, the grass, and the flowers!

Stop, Look, and Listen

Before we start walking across a street, we are taught to stop, not to run into the traffic; to look, to make sure there is no danger; and to listen, for whatever might be coming. Sometimes our thoughts and feelings are like a busy highway or a traffic jam; everything can whizz by so fast that we cannot see clearly, or things can feel jammed up and frustrating, like nothing is going anywhere. Whatever we are doing, whatever thoughts and feelings are running around in the mind and the body, we can take a few moments to stop (be still), look (see and feel what is going on inside us), and listen (hear the silent thoughts and the very soft voices that feelings have).

We do not have to be afraid of any of the thoughts and feelings that are running along the roadways inside us. When we are standing safely in a wide, happy field, we can watch a big, scary truck roaring by and disappear. We are still safe and happy, and the truck is long gone. Our happiness balloon and peaceful breath are always BIGGER than anything coming up the road. When sadness comes, we can just be sad and still be calm underneath. There is a kind of happiness in letting ourselves be sad sometimes.

And after we feel our sadness there can be a great relief and peace. If we feel angry, we can let ourselves feel our tummy, our muscles, our cheeks, and our eyes and just let the scary truckloads of anger drive off. If we don't hurt others or ourselves with angry words or actions, there can even be a calm and happiness in feeling anger, too. Sometimes anger feels more like a hurt, and we need to cry. Remember that crying and laughing are both different ways that the body breathes and speaks whatever we are thinking and feeling at that time.

Scary Feelings

When we think we are in danger, it is natural for us to be afraid. But sometimes we can get scared even when there is no danger. We can be afraid of what *might* happen. We can even make ourselves afraid by JUST THINKING about being afraid. Sometimes we can spend a lot of time being scared of being scared!

If there is really something dangerous right around us, being afraid might tell us to run, to hide, or to yell. But if there is nothing right here that is making us afraid, then we cannot run or hide or yell. But we can always breathe in the air around us. We can feel the support of the earth or the floor under our feet. We can feel the fluttery feelings in our belly and our chest and let the breath flow through and eventually calm those scary thoughts and feelings. We can feel the sun warming our body on a bright day. We can watch the clouds constantly changing shape in the sky and remind ourselves that feelings and thoughts are just like the clouds—they come and go, appear, disappear, and reappear again. We can feel the air and the clothing on our skin and remember that the only thing making us afraid right now is our own thoughts and feelings.

Air, Air, Everywhere!

All living things breathe in the air in some way—even animals and tiny insects that live underground. The whole earth is surrounded by air and even the trees and flowers and grasses breathe! Many living things breathe through noses and mouths, while many other living things breathe through their skin, leaves, bark, roots, and stems. Even fish breathe under water through their gills!

Breathing is not only important to all life, it can be fun too. And learning to pay attention to our breath can help us during those times when we might feel sad, uncomfortable, angry, confused, or frightened. Let's experiment with our breathing to see how important the breath is and how it can affect everything we do and feel!

Index

Page numbers in italics refer to figures. Page numbers in bold refer to tables.